STRIKE!

Politics ● Philosophy ● Art ● Subversion ● Sedition

CW00673482

STRIKE! magazine is a registered workers co-operative and operates according to the following ideals:

STRIKE! exists as a radical publisher, primarily in print publications.
STRIKE! will never contain content that promotes fascism, racism, sexism, homophobia, transphobia, the police, or affiliate itself with organisations that do.
STRIKE! will never sell any advertising.
STRIKE! is anti-capitalist, anti-profit and run on anarchist principles.

ISSUE ___ 1

THE DEBT COLLECTOR

THE MYSTERIOUS
MAN IN THE
RED COAT....

Fuckonomics
Breakthrough Economics

In keeping with the theme of this issue, one feature of today's world that most people agree is totally screwed is the global economy. We are constantly buffeted by financial storms, which seem as beyond our control as a meteor shower from outer space. Money has departed from its original function as a means of exchange to take on a crazed, computer-driven life of its own, surging through financial networks at the speed of light, building up huge walls of fictitious debt— which then suddenly collapse, creating mayhem in the lives of millions. We have reverted to the state of primitives, in awe of external forces, desperately searching for some way to find stability and predict the future.

Ironically, though, it is our very attempts to predict and control the economy that have turned it into the unrestrained beast it has become. Our sophisticated mathematical models have become part of the problem, not the solution. As I told an audience at the Breakthrough Capitalism Forum in London earlier this summer: in order to break through to a new kind of system, we need to rethink the way we do economics.

Order and Symmetry

Economics can be viewed as a mathematical model of the world. Such models are interesting because they encode a kind of story about reality. The models, and especially the assumptions on which they are based, tell a lot about the way we see the world and the way we see ourselves. A good example of this was one of the older mathematical models, the Greek model of the cosmos. This model was based on two main assumptions. The first was that everything moved in circles, which were considered the most perfect and symmetrical of forms. The other was that everything moved around the Earth. In Aristotle's scheme, the planets and stars were thought to be encased in crystalline spheres which moved at different speeds around us.

Of course, as we now know, both of these assumptions were wrong. But that didn't seem to matter, for the model persisted for well over a thousand years, until it was finally overturned in the Renaissance. How did it manage to last for such a long time?

One reason relates to the fact that, as Aristotle put it, man is a political animal. The Greeks believed that there was a strong parallel between what was going on in the cosmos and what was going on in human life. As with the model of the cosmos, Greek society was structured as a series of concentric rings, with slaves at the base, followed in ascending order by ex-slaves, foreigners, artisans, and finally the land-owning, non-working upper class. These men alone could be citizens, and oversaw everything from above, like the stars in the firmament (women did not take part in political life and took their social class from their male partner).

A model of the universe that suggested that each object, and each class, has its natural place in the cosmic scheme therefore supported the status quo, and would certainly have appealed to the male leisure class that ruled ancient Athens.

Perhaps a more important reason for the success of the Greek model of the cosmos, though, was that it could make accurate predictions of things like solar eclipses. In a time when human affairs were believed to be influenced by the movements of the celestial bodies, this was an impressive demonstration of the power of mathematics.

Breaking the Spheres

As mentioned, the model lasted for well over a thousand years. In 1543, though, Copernicus argued that the Earth went around the Sun, rather than vice versa. In 1572, the Danish astronomer Tycho Brahe observed a comet that passed between the planets, so if Aristotle's crystalline spheres had actually existed, it would have broken through them. Finally, in 1687, Isaac Newton combined Kepler's theory of planetary motion with Galileo's study of the motion of falling objects to derive his three laws of motion and the law of gravity. The Greek circles were replaced with dynamical equations.

Newton believed that matter was made up of 'solid, massy, hard, impenetrable, movable particles' governed by physical laws i.e. atoms. His work laid out a template that scientists have continued to follow until the present day. To understand and predict a system, you break it down into its constituent parts, find the mathematical equations that govern their behaviour, and solve.

This approach has been very successful in areas such as chemistry and physics. Newton was less confident that it would apply to other fields. After losing most of his fortune in the collapse of the South Sea bubble, he warned that, 'I can calculate the motions of heavenly bodies, but not the madness of people.' In the nineteenth century, though, economists decided to forge ahead anyway. The result, known as neoclassical economics, was directly inspired by Newton's 'rational mechanics'. As a mathematical model, it may have had as great an effect on society as the Greek model did in centuries past.

Efficient Markets

In order to mathematicise the economy, economists of course had to make a lot of assumptions. No one thinks these assumptions are completely true, but, as we will see, they have been amazingly influential.

The theory assumed that individuals and firms, who were the atoms of the economy, acted independently and rationally to maximize their own utility. This led to the famous caricature of rational economic man. The 'invisible hand' (usually attributed to Adam Smith, though the idea predates him) then drives the economy to a stable equilibrium. The result of all this was supposed to be maximal societal happiness.

As with the Greek models of the cosmos, the aim of the models was to make accurate predictions; however, in this case the models did not work quite as well. Predictions of things like gross domestic product are famously unreliable, and are not much better than random guessing even today.

In the 1960s the 'efficient market hypothesis' was floated as an explanation for the inaccuracy of economic forecasts. This was a physics-inspired theory which assumed that markets magically attain a stable and optimal equilibrium, and any changes are random perturbations that inherently cannot be predicted. However, it should be possible to calculate risk based on statistical methods such as the normal distribution (bell curve), or variants thereof.

This theory was used to create risk management techniques with names like the Black-Scholes formula and Value at Risk—all of which completely failed during the recent financial crisis, and indeed helped cause it by creating a feeling of false confidence. So why is it that economic storms still come as a surprise? Let's look at some of the assumptions in a bit more detail.

The Divine Love of the Universe

The theory assumes that the 'invisible hand' drives the economy to a stable equilibrium. But if you look at something like the price of gold, it is very unstable. The reason is that we buy an asset like gold because we hope it will go up in value. Therefore when it is going up in value, we get excited and buy more. This positive feedback drives the price up further. The same thing happens in reverse on the way down, resulting in an unpredictable series of booms followed by busts. The same effect is seen in other things like oil, housing, currencies, and so on.

Now, this kind of unpredictability is superficially consistent with efficiency. However, the theory also assumes that price variations are small, random and independent, and therefore normally distributed. But as we know markets are susceptible to sudden, catastrophic crashes. Their statistics are not 'normal', but are similar to those of earthquakes. Most price changes are small (just as the Earth is constantly experiencing small tremors) but there is the ever-present possibility of extreme events.

Another key assumption is that people act independently and make rational decisions to optimize their own utility (the proof of market equilibrium actually assumed infinite computational capacity, and the ability to plan into the future). But emotions such as trust and fear play a vital role in markets.

Finally, the original idea of neoclassical theory was to optimise happiness, and achieve what Francis Edgeworth called in 1881 'the maximum energy of pleasure, the Divine love of the universe'. But while the economy has grown enormously in recent decades, reported happiness levels have remained static or even declined slightly.

One reason for this is the saturation effect: once you have a certain amount of money it doesn't help that much to make more. But perhaps another reason is that we have internalised these values of rationality, independence, and utility optimisation; psychologists (or most human beings) can tell you that the things that make you happy have more to do with connectivity, communication with other people, and community. This theory of ours could be making us unhappy.

A New Economics

To summarise: our orthodox theory is based on ideas of stability and elegance that go back to the ancient Greeks. It is Aristotlean, but not in a good way.

We model people as if they were rational and can look into the future. We model the economy as if it obeyed the harmony of the spheres. Like the Greeks, we are imposing our ideas of rationality, order and logic onto the universe. But there is one important difference: the Greek model could make fairly accurate predictions. Our models don't have that degree of empirical validity.

As I argue in my book *Economyths: How the Science of Complex Systems is Transforming Economic Thought*, there is an alternative. A new theory is being forged, which is part of a larger shift in science from seeing the world as a Newtonian machine to seeing it as a living system.

Complex organic systems, from a living cell to the economy, to the Earth's atmosphere, are characterised by emergent properties that emerge from local effects and cannot be reduced to simple equations. They operate at a state that is far from equilibrium, far from stable. They exhibit power-law statistics, like earthquakes, as opposed to 'normal' statistics. They are based on network dynamics, as opposed to atomistic dynamics. Opposing positive and negative feedback loops create internal dynamic tension. Together, these factors result in an inherent uncertainty. This, rather than anything to do with efficiency, is the real reason we can't predict the future.

So why has the neoclassical model persisted for so long? In this case the answer has nothing to do with prediction. That leaves politics and the status quo. The idea that the system is stable, rational, optimal and efficient is clearly one that is favoured by the tiny elite—the sub-one percent—which derives the most benefit from the current arrangement.

Once again, it is time to break through to a new way of seeing, smash the metaphorical crystalline spheres, and build a new model of the world. Otherwise, we really are fucked.

HATE the
Daily Mail

Pick up a
STRIKE!

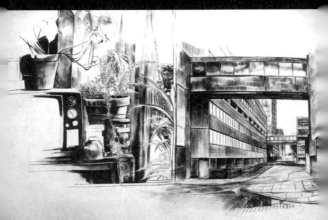

Dissent
Do Not Say No

The most important political breakthrough of the past five centuries will come when some desperate half mad truth seeker learns to justify his instinct to anarchy. It has to come, because it's the only possible reconciliation between a man's best instincts and his worst realities.

Hunter S. Thompson

Scurry from your house to the shops and scurry back again! Do not congregate anywhere other than your designated drinking den (now closed). For God's sake don't have the audacity to be any of the following things, or dare to participate in any sort of group while being it: young, black, Asian, Muslim, poor, unemployed, not in school or protesting. Do not on pain of immediate stop and search wear hoodies, smoke weed, wear a mask, chuck a banner-stick or occupy a building. Do not take photographs, stroke the policeman's horse or chant slogans. Do not write 'Tory scum' on the wall of their HQ. Do not go into the road, bang pans, smash windows or nick a policeman's hat for fun. Do not riot. Do not post jokes on Facebook or Twitter about blowing things up, your desire for things to kick off in your hometown, or how you think the royal wedding is a bit naff and the Olympics a colossal waste of time and money, with a hint of fascism thrown in. Do not go anywhere near any of the following events if even the smallest desire to protest or critique flickers in your shrivelled black heart: boat races (all sporting events, for that matter), jubilees, and anything that involves Union Jacks or the St George's Cross, particularly if carried by one or other of our many charming neo-fascist groups, 'cos we will beat you up if you interfere with their right to protest, which is sacrosanct. When people thousands of miles away protest, cheer them on and talk about 'democracy'; if they try it here, bash 'em over the head and then charge them with violent disorder: we've got enough freedom here already, with our regal biscuits and regulation bunting. Who are these irritating bastards who want more than that, more than this...?

And God forbid you join a group concerned with climate change, the arms trade or anything that might disrupt business as usual... but never fear, we've got you covered: our undercover agents are on hand to form relationships with you, to have children with you, and (unless you find our passports with our real name in 'em) what you and our kids don't know won't hurt you! Until it does, of course... in the meantime we'll put missiles on your roofs, the army on the street and warships on the Thames. We won't be happy, though, until we get water cannons, rubber bullets and firearms, like our American brothers. Ah, happy memories when we think of Bush coming to town in 2003, with marksmen where they belong: on the top of buildings, all ready to aim and fire at the rabble below! We had a right laugh at the student demo, bashing their skulls in, running our horses through the crowd and keeping 'em there for hours in the freezing cold while sending them to the other side to exits that didn't exist, over and over again! And the little bastards didn't win, that'll learn 'em. Except, they say, it won't, 'cos no one is going to borrow tens of thousands for a degree towards a job that doesn't exist. Still, these futureless brats will get restless, and what with there being no EMA for college, no libraries, no youth centres and no jobs, there'll be all the more work for us and our brothers and sisters in G4S! The private police have it lucky: all those people who grumble when we say racist things, or beat someone to death in the station, won't know who to complain to when these firms come in, will they now?!

Capitalist Realism

Is There Still No Alternative?

Capitalism rests on the astounding assumption that the most wickedest of men will do the most wickedest of deeds for the greatest good.

John Maynard Keynes

In late 2009, my book *Capitalist Realism* was published. I now joke that, as I was completing the book in the wake of the financial crisis of 2008, it felt as if capitalism might be finished before the book was. As we all now know, capitalism didn't collapse—but it would be a mistake to think that there is any possibility of a return to business as usual.

Capitalist realism can be seen as a belief: that there's no alternative to capitalism, that, as Fredric Jameson put it, it's easier to imagine the end of the world than the end of capitalism. Other systems might be preferable to capitalism, but capitalism is the only one that is realistic. Or it can be seen as an attitude of resignation and fatalism in the face of this—a sense that all we can do is accommodate ourselves to the dominance of capitalism, and limit our hopes to containing its worst excesses. Fundamentally, it's a pathology of the left, nowhere better exemplified than in the case of New Labour. Ultimately, what capitalist realism amounts to is the elimination of left-wing politics and the naturalisation of neoliberalism.

After the wave of militancy that spread across the world in 2011, the BBC's Economics Editor Paul Mason went so far as to declare the end of capitalist realism. The (non)events of 2012 show that judgment to be a little hasty. 2012 has been a year of restoration and reaction.

Slavoj Zizek's latest book, *The Year of Dreaming Dangerously*, begins with the Persian concept of *war nam nihadan*: 'to murder someone, bury his body then grow flowers over the body to conceal it.' Zizek argues that, in relation to 2011's efflorescence of militancy (Occupy Wall Street, the Arab Spring, the English riots etc) dominant ideology achieved a *war nam nihadan*. 'The media killed the radical emancipatory dimension of the events... and then threw flowers over the buried corpse.' This year, capitalist realism has reasserted itself. Instead of capitalist realism ending in 2008 (or 2011), it could be argued that the austerity measures that have been implemented have constituted an intensification of capitalist realism. Those measures couldn't have been introduced unless there was still a widespread sense that there is no alternative to neoliberal capitalism. The various struggles that have blown up since the financial crisis show a growing discontent with the panic-neoliberalism that has been put in place since 2008, but they have yet to propose any concrete alternative to the dominant economic model.

Capitalist realism is about a corrosion of social imagination, and in some ways, that remains the problem: after thirty years of neoliberal domination, we are only just beginning to be able to imagine alternatives to capitalism. Why is this still the case?

Partly, it is because the decomposition of solidarity on which the victory of neoliberalism depended has not yet been reversed. The various anti-capitalist movements (up to and including Occupy) have not yet constituted a counter-force capable of challenging the super-hegemony of capital. We've become used to a world in which workers fear capital, never the reverse. Capitalist realism was never about direct ideological persuasion; it's not that the population of the UK were ever convinced of the merits of neoliberal ideas. But what people have been convinced of is the idea that neoliberalism is the dominant force in the world, and that, consequently, there is little point resisting it. (I'm not suggesting that most people recognise neoliberalism by name, but they do recognise the policies and the ideological narrative which neoliberalism has so successfully disseminated.) This perception has arisen because capital has subdued the forces acting against it—most obviously, it has crushed unions, or forced them into being consumer or service institutions within capitalism. The situation has changed since the heyday of social democracy, and one of the principal ways in which it has changed is the globalization of capital. Indeed, this is one way that unions were outmanoeuvred: if your members won't work for these rates, we'll go to a place where workers will.

The decadence of parliamentary politics in the UK, with three parties all unabashedly representing the interests of capital, is one consequence of the decomposition of workers' solidarity. The fundamental mistake of New Labour, as the exemplary party of capitalist realism, was that it conceived of its project solely as a matter of adapting to the 'reality' that capitalism had already constructed. The dreary result of all its manoeuvrings was the melancholy prospect of 'power' without hegemony. Under Ed Miliband, it is clear that Labour has not yet learned the lesson that the point is not to occupy an already-existing centre ground, but to struggle to redefine what the centre ground is. The Thatcherite right had the confidence to plan just such a vertiginous shift of the centre ground in the 1980s, and Labour has been on the back foot ever since. As Stuart Hall so presciently noted in *The Hard Road To Renewal*, first published in 1988, it was the Thatcherites who dared to think and speak in revolutionary terms. Hall wrote of James Callaghan's shock at the thought that Thatcher, 'means to tear society up by the roots'. Such a 'radical attack on the status quo', Hall wrote, was unthinkable for those steeped in the compromises of social democracy. But Hall's trenchant observations on the inherent conservatism of the Labour Party of his own day apply with a painful piquancy to the current Labour Party, with its desperate claims to be the party of 'one nation', and its impotent, reactionary flirtations with family, flag and faith. Hall wrote,

The truth is that traditionalist ideas, the ideas of social and moral respectability, have penetrated so deep inside socialist consciousness that it is quite common to find people committed to a radical social programme underpinned by wholly traditional feelings and sentiments.

What remains, now that the socialist consciousness has succumbed to capitalist realism and the radical programme has given way to pragmatic adaptation to a world governed by neoliberalism, is the moralizing gestures and traditionalism alone.

Alain Badiou has argued that, with the collapse of the leftist experiments of the twentieth century, we are effectively plunged back into a situation similar to that in the nineteenth century, before the labour movements came together. I think that is correct, and we need to develop the same boldness of thinking, ambition and courage that the founders of the labour movement possessed. But rising to that challenge means that we shouldn't remain attached to the ideas and methods that those groups developed for different times. Instead of depressively reclining at the end of history, looking back longingly at all the failed revolts and revolutions of the past, we need to re-situate ourselves in history and claim the future back for the left. What is certain is that the right now has no monopoly on the future: manifestly, it has run out of ideas.

May '68 has left a legacy of anti-institutionalism in the left theoretical currents it has influenced—a legacy that is congruent with many of the assumptions of neoliberalism. But, as the right well understands, politics is not about feel-good parties in the street; it's about controlling and developing institutions. The question is: if the old leftist institutions have declined because they were too associated with Fordism, what institutions will work in the current conditions? My comrade Alex Williams has argued that leftist solidarity needs to assume a 'post-Fordist plasticity.' If capital has a certain plasticity, an ability to make alliances between heterogeneous groups, then anti-capital must be similarly plastic. Plasticity here doesn't mean 'adapting to the demands of capitalism', i.e. attaining the 'flexibility' demanded of workers in practically all job descriptions; it should mean thinking ahead of capitalism, being quicker than it.

Capital isn't literally global, but it is sufficiently global to be able to pit workers from different sides of the planet against each other. Anti-capital, similarly, needs to be globalized enough that workers' interests can be co-coordinated. At the same time, we need to agitate for much more autonomy and control for workers over their immediate work processes—perhaps on the model of worker-run factories in Latin America. Localism can't tackle global capitalism, and in any case, it is regressive.

As Fredric Jameson has argued, capitalism is the most collective society that has ever existed on earth, in the sense that even the most banal object is the product of a massive web of interdependence. At the moment, this global network is stupid and venal; but rather than abandoning it in favour of some return to agrarianism that will only be possible on the basis of a catastrophe, we need to make the planetary network an intelligent system that can act in the interests of the majority, instead of the tiny minority that profit under the current system. That's not impossible. In fact, we've got an unprecedented opportunity to make it happen.

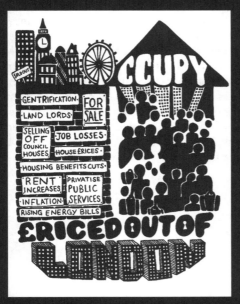

Climate, Land and Homes
You Are Fucked

Climate

Back in the heady days of Climate Camp 2007, when it seemed like a radical Green moment might be just around the corner, I remember a flyer that exclaimed 'You Are Not Fucked.' The aim was to release people from the paralysing fear of global climate meltdown: to reassure them that their efforts would not be in vain, if we all acted together. Five years on, that vision seems further away than ever: an ongoing economic crisis has pushed climate change off the agenda, the environment has gone out of fashion, and many of the green pundits seem to have given up hope. Perhaps it is finally time to say it: 'You *Are* Fucked.'

Sadly, our political and economic systems are inherently incapable of addressing the issue of climate change. We are facing a cascade of interlinked crises—ecological, economic and democratic—each of which feeds the other in a gluttonous orgy of consumerism and credit. At the root of all this lies a system of wealth distribution little changed since feudal times; it is the enormous inequality in land ownership and the precedence accorded to private property over basic human needs that explains the complete inertia of our governments in the face of these crises.

Land

In the UK, 0.3% of people own 67% of all the land in the country. It's no wonder that the other 99.7% of us struggle to eke out a reasonable existence on the remainder. Not only is the ownership of land centralised in the hands of a tiny group of aristocrats, little changed over hundreds of years, but large swathes of land are desperately under-used and ill-managed. Without land we cannot support ourselves. We literally cannot live: we have no food, no shelter, and no way to provide for ourselves. We are condemned to an indentured life, selling our existence to rent a little space to breathe. The spectre of the Bill hangs heavy over everyone—even the wealthier among us find they are just able to pay larger Bills.

Local food is very fashionable among the middle-class exponents of a green 'transition'—it is advocated as a panacea to many of our social and environmental problems. But we cannot grow food without land. It is not possible, nor is it reasonable, to meet the oppression of inequality solely with 'positive' programs behind which everyone can unite. The creation of new worlds is inherently linked to confrontation with the current one.

It is not a coincidence that access to land is a core issue in the crisis we face: the removal of access was a central element in the onward march of capitalism that has brought us into the unsustainable present. As land was gradually claimed and enclosed from the commons, those who were left without had to find other means to earn money; to buy food and to rent back the space to live in from the landowners who had taken it all. In some parts of the world this process is happening right now, igniting resistance from indigenous groups such as the Movimento dos Trabalhadores Rurais Sem Terra (MST) in Brazil, the Landless Workers' Movement.

Homes

As the economic crisis tightens its stranglehold, the preference of the government for the protection of private property over human dignity has become more blatant than ever. The Coalition have been digging the moat around the citadel of good fortune as fast as they have been pulling up the ladder of opportunity. The realisation that our planet, and therefore our economy, cannot support indefinite growth has highlighted the uncomfortable truth that we cannot all be rich. Either the wealthy need to share what they've got, or the poor need to live with a lot less than they've been promised. The capitalist dream has run up against the hard walls of reality, and the government will do everything they can to ensure it's not their mates who lose out.

The recent criminalisation of squatting is one part of the moat, and the massive cuts to housing benefits and homelessness provision are the rapidly receding ladder to self-advancement. Criminalising those who make a home in unused buildings is a particularly nasty manifestation of the cheapness of human dignity and its irrelevance to those in power. A young man is now languishing in Wormwood Scrubs simply for using an empty Housing Association building as a home without permission, and others are likely to follow him. The rapidity with which the law was rushed through, bypassing even the flimsy democratic procedures that we do have, illustrates the ideological determination of our leaders to ensure that nothing threatens the accumulation of wealth by the super-rich.

A little recap on the statistics: there are an estimated 600,000 homeless people in the UK. There are an estimated 930,000 empty properties. There are as many as 5million households languishing on council waiting lists. Street homelessness has risen by 23%, and research suggests that average life-expectancy on the street is just 47. Meanwhile, the government has axed housing benefits for under 25s, cut funding for homelessness groups by 30% and capped housing benefits in such a way that swathes of London are set to be cleansed of poor families—at the same time as the deposit needed to buy a home in London has hit £100,000. The situation is getting worse, and is exacerbated by government policies which protect those at the top. The Squash campaign has estimated that the costs of the new squatting laws may be as much as £790million over the next 5 years— money that could have been spent on housing provision instead of the persecution of the homeless.

The supposed support that is offered by the State to those in dire need is no more than salt in the wound, deliberately degrading those who seek help. A man I met recently told me of his experiences with No Second Night Out, the flagship homelessness initiative of London's Mayor. Following his council's withdrawal of his housing support under the current cuts, he was housed by NSNO. He was sent to the other side of London and placed in a large hall with lots of other men. He told me that the lights are kept on all night, and that you have to vacate by 8.30am every day. There is nowhere to keep your possessions, and if you miss shower-time at 7.30am then you cannot shower. He left the accommodation because it was too expensive for him to travel across London to where his support networks and his lawyer are, but also because the provision was fatally undermining his sense of self-worth. He was forced to return to the streets. The idea that this is an adequate response to our housing crisis is an embarrassment.

Action

It is almost a truism to describe UK politics as 'elitist'. That is what the representative system is designed to be, and to have political power is to be a member of the elite. But in the context of comprehending why we are so royally fucked, it is worth reminding ourselves of this basic fact: our government is unable to address the crises that we face, because to do so it would have to undertake a massive redistribution of land, and therefore wealth. This would undermine its own existence—it is, therefore, institutionally incapable of doing so.

As long as private property rights continue to trump all other needs, there is no way out of either the housing crisis or the climate crisis. One solution lies in communities coming together to reclaim control of land they need to grow on and live on. Internationally, many groups are struggling on this issue. Reclaim The Fields, for example, is a Europe-wide network of community food growers who are very concerned about access to land. Grow Heathrow, the squatted market garden where I live, is part of this network. In May last year I joined an RtF event in France, where about 200 people took over and cleared an abandoned field that lies in the path of another proposed airport near Nantes. The project is going from strength to strength, but continues to battle eviction threats alongside the numerous other communities who have established themselves on the land nearby. Grow Heathrow is also fighting an ongoing legal battle, in which the question of the importance of housing need and community interest versus the rights of private property owners to neglect and abandon their property is paramount.

We will almost certainly lose. The legal system, like the parliamentary system, is designed to ensure that we do. But as the economy, the climate, and the democratic procedures themselves come crashing down around the ears of the ruling classes, we hope that all these struggles will help people find new ways of relating to each other and the world around us. So that maybe, one day, things won't be quite so fucked.

THE WORLD IS FUCKED AND HAS BEEN SINCE AT LEAST 1972

International summits on the environment began in Stockholm in 1972. With each new summit comes news of unprecedented global fuck-ups.

"If current patterns of production and consumption of natural resources prevail and cannot be reversed and 'decoupled', then governments will preside over unprecedented levels of damage and degradation"
ACHIM STEINER. UNEP EXECUTIVE DIRECTOR

"While the conventional, political dangers appear to be receding, we have all recently become aware of another insidious danger... as menacing in its way as those more accustomed perils with which international diplomacy has concerned itself for centuries. It is the prospect of irretrievable damage to the atmosphere, to the oceans, to earth itself."
MARGARET THATCHER. 1989

"Unless we free ourselves from a dependence on these fossil fuels and chart a new course on energy in this country, we are condemning future generations to global catastrophe."
BARACK OBAMA. 2008

"If we don't act now, some of us will die."
KARL HOOD. FOREIGN MINISTER OF GRENADA. 2009

② SOLUTION SEA

World leaders can see that we're in a c
but their extraordinary powers of vision
The solutions to climate change are all tr
fiendishly difficult wordsearch which hea
have yet to crack. Can you help them? Go

```
F D W B H A Q Z R U G K B N R W S O
L M I U P Y R B E T R C S O E F P D
B A N D O M E S T I C F L I G H T S
K L D H J W N M R C V G S X A I R G
G E Q A S T E C O L P U I Y S T E R
S Q P F D S W A F C C K M N O G E Z
R E E Z X L A W I B H S A J A S S W
P V T A F E B I T O D R V D W R S P
B U B A N G L E R Z T D F U A K S T
O D I E T P E M U N R D O L C T P B
R M K J O P S T O P S H O P P I N G
L Q E Z G P Y B E V S S F T U D P O
U W S B J F R Q U S P E I G W A X P
A M R W P A V K L O W R T C H L U A
D E M O C R A C Y H P W R F J N M B
T Y S W Q I P G K D B D N L M P A Z
V N O F O S S I L S U B S I D I E S
```

① CLI CHA
WHY B

⑥ TAKE THE LEA

Billy Wimsatt says: *We need good people being CE*
politicians, and doctors. We gotta get power. We gotta
leadership won't lead without us. It's up to us to ta
start making changes where we can - in our com
our own lives and in positions
of power.

PUSH

CORPORATIONS OUT OF POLITICS

... MAKE YOURSELF AT HOME WIT

"Never doubt that a small group of citizens can change the world."
MARGARET MEAD

"The only recognizable feature of hope is action."
GRACE PALEY

"The greatest danger to our future is apathy."
JANE GOODALL

ACT

"The only thing necessary for the triumph of evil is for good men to do nothing."
EDMUND BURKE

BROUGHT TO YOU BY CLIMATE RUSH
DIRECT ACTION INSPIRED BY THE SUFFRAGETTES
WWW.CLIMATERUSH.CO.UK

GOVERNMENTS ARE BETTER AT EXCUSES

> I'm secretly scared of the dark side of the corporations..

> ...but I feel so safe and warm in their arms! They give me free pens and cuddles and cookies and love.

> I'm just trying to live in the moment, man.

> Yeah, future generations can't vote for us in the next election can they?

> Energy efficiency is all well and good but it's just that I've only budgeted for tax avoidance and fossil fuel subsidies.

> ...with the pocket money *I* have left I want to cover myself in oil and make a lot of cash that way.

③

④ **[BUT THE WORLD IS FULL OF MOONLIGHTERS]**

These majestic moonlighters include...

Judy Bonds was a hillbilly former pizza-hut waitress turned Mountain Watch activist and renewable energy advocate. After she found her grandson playing in a stream full of dead fish she became determined to fight coal mining in her local community. Judy fought for green jobs, clean water and the protection of future generations until she died of cancer in 2011.

> "We are here to steward this land. I know what I'm doing is right. I'm not stoppping."

JUDY BONDS

⑤

> "We want to see many Africans planting trees. There is absolutely no excuse to stop desertification because this is doable and cheap"

WANGARI MAATHAI

Wangari Maathai founded the Green Belt Movement in 1977 after hearing of women who were finding it more difficult to secure water, firewood and food. The Green Belt Movement employs rural women in tree planting, trains them in employable skills and fights land-grabbing - the Green Belt Movement has led to an estimated 45 million trees being planted in Kenya.

Majora Carter is from the South Bronx. Living in an area of high unemployment, she noticed that her neighbourhood was a pollution dumping-ground. She founded one of the first green jobs training academies in the US, which improves the neighbourhood's quality of life, both economically and environmentally.

> "If you feel helpless, the best thing you can do is help somebody else."

MAJORA CARTER.

Why War?

Towards a World Without It

The same week in November that David Cameron embarked on a campaign to sell British fighter jets to some of the most gruesome regimes in the Middle East was the week when fervour about the red poppy reached its crescendo.

The poppy is the symbol of remembrance, adopted after the hideous slaughter of the First World War. Remembrance Day has been widened to include remembering the dead in all wars, although in Britain these are still marked on what used to be Armistice Day, 11am on 11 November which signalled the end of the war in 1918.

It is officially a near-universally celebrated day, or at least that is what our rulers would like it to be. Everyone appearing on national television wears a poppy for weeks beforehand (with one or two honourable exceptions, such as Paul Mason on *Newsnight*). Even journalists reporting from the US election campaign were wearing red poppies, which must have been flown in from Britain. On 11 November, every national Sunday paper had a red poppy on the front. There is widespread coverage of all the wreath-laying events.

Unfortunately the prime movers behind the campaign use it more for promoting war than for ensuring peace. This year, London railway stations at times looked more like a military tattoo than a transport hub as pipers, bands and uniformed soldiers sold poppies to 'support our troops'. London Overground trains were painted with poppies and underground stations carried large ads.

Those who opposed the cult of the poppy are subject to harsh sanctions: a man in Kent was arrested for putting an image of a burning poppy on Facebook; another in Bristol for skateboarding in fancy dress.

So much for wars being fought in the name of democracy.

What is rarely acknowledged is that the vast majority of war dead in the past 100 years have been civilians. They are almost totally ignored in the remembrance events. While central London is full of statues and memorials to the military, there are few to civilian dead. It is only in relatively recent years that there have been memorials to women workers who died in the Second World War, or fire-fighters who gave their lives.

It is hard to escape the conclusion that politicians, press and right wing media use remembrance as a means to justify present wars. When I was growing up in the 1950s and 60s, there was no great fuss about the day. People wore poppies or not, depending on how they felt. Most people didn't observe a minute's silence. My parents and most of my friends' parents had lived through war, the men had fought in wars, and most of them did not want to glorify it.

Today, Britain has been at war in Afghanistan, Iraq, Libya and threatening future wars in Syria and Iran for more than 11 years. The war in Afghanistan began in October 2001 and is still going on. That is longer than the First World War, longer than the Second World War—in fact longer than the two put together. It is a war which is limping on, bloody and destructive. It is near-universally acknowledged, even by the military, that this war has been lost. There is to be no victory for western troops, only ignominious withdrawal at some stage, or a continued war of attrition that is taking thousands of lives each year.

The war is deeply unpopular, with recent polls showing as many as 4 out of 5 respondents seeing no point to it and consistent majorities wanting the troops out. The anti-war movement has helped to create widespread anti-war opinion in Britain. To counter this, the politicians and generals who are deliberately prolonging this war to save their own faces are trying to whip up support for the troops and to separate this from the question of unpopular wars.

During the summer, the troops were hailed as the saviours of the Olympics in another example of public money being spent to stand in for failed private security. They and their families were given free tickets for the games. David Cameron is now promising that troops and their families will receive preferential treatment for low-cost housing over and above groups like the unemployed.

The cult of the military extends to uncritical questioning on radio and television, the hushed tones of reports from embedded journalists, the promotion of the military wives' choir, and the propensity of the royal family to dress up in military uniform at the slightest excuse.

To challenge any of this is to be met with incredulity at best and hostility at worst. Yet challenged it has to be. No one wants British troops to be put in danger, but while they are fighting in unjustifiable wars that is precisely what will happen to them.

Wars also brutalise. There are a number cases of atrocities by British and US troops in Iraq, Afghanistan and elsewhere. Four US soldiers raped an Iraqi teenager and killed her and her family. A US soldier is now in trial charged with the deaths of 18 Afghans, mainly women and children, when he went on a murderous assault in villages near his base, returning covered with blood.

Baha Mousa was killed in Iraq by British soldiers. The long colonial history of Britain is peppered with atrocities such as those now coming out about the war in Kenya in the 1950s.

The support for war in capitalist society should not surprise anyone. It came into the world as a militarised system. It grew through plunder and conflict. Every nation-state has its armies and the most powerful states are the most highly militarised. The US ranks number one in every aspect of military spending and equipment, larger than many other countries combined.

It is at the centre of a system of imperialism, which began with the old European colonial empires and has become an economic and military system which extends its strategic control and influence throughout the world. Imperialism is intertwined with capitalism. It has produced the worst wars in history the First and Second World Wars and war has been ever present in some part of the world ever since.

For decades after 1945, peace between the major powers was maintained by a 'balance of terror' between the two heavily nuclear-armed superpowers, the US and the USSR. This situation ended in the late 1980s with the collapse of the Eastern Bloc and the emergence of the US as the sole superpower. At the same time it coincided with the drive to 'free markets', privatisation and deregulation which characterised neoliberalism. The end of the Cold War meant more hot wars, starting with the first Gulf War, followed by the Balkan wars and the War on Terror since 2001.

The economic crisis which has become acute in the west since 2008 has led to greater tensions between nations, with a declining US economic power threatened by rivals, especially China. This leads it to use it military weight more not less.

The Middle East has become a tinderbox, as the present conflict in Gaza shows. Any extension of the conflict there, or in Iran or Syria, is likely to spread throughout the whole heavily armed region causing terrible human and environmental devastation. Those who suffer are not the politicians and generals, but ordinary people whether in uniform or not.

Since the suffering of the First World War, there have always been people who campaigned for peace and who understood the horrors of warfare on an industrial scale. The anti war movement since the war on terror has been the biggest anti war movement ever and its legacy continues as we fight against current wars.

But if we remember how the First World War began, in jingoism and excitement, we should remember how it ended. The slaughter of the war led to opposition to governments across Europe. The weak link of the old empires, Russia, was plunged in revolution in 1917. A year later, German workers and soldiers ended their role in the war through revolution. Throughout the world, ordinary people wanted not just an end to war but to the capitalism which had produced it.

So wars can produce their opposite: from horror and misery we can create peace and hope for the future. That involves campaigning against war itself and linking those campaigns to those against inequality, austerity and injustice. They are not different fights but the same one.

That is something we should never forget. We can create a world without war, but only by ending the system which feeds it.

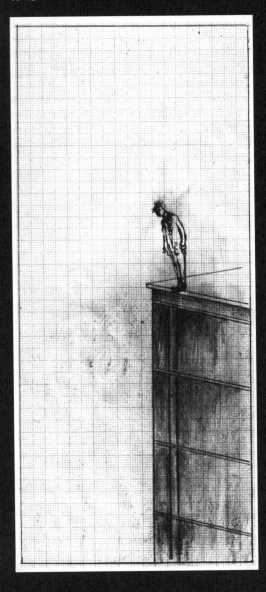

If Only I Was Fucked and Left Alone

An Ode To Escape

1.

Blue. Why does the sky have to be so blue? Today of all days? Standing up here, with only a mere knot of seconds left to my name. I look up again and it blinds me. My Hugo Boss suit whimpers under its brilliance. I clutch my leather briefcase to remind me of the decision made only moments earlier as I stared at another corporate lunch. Overpriced, lifeless prawns. 'Oh, I didn't know you were a cannibal,' my team leader said in a desperate attempt to cheer me up. I was looking around. A sea of dead faces in sad dark suits, all secretly dreading the moment it's time to leave the rooftop restaurant and return to hell. I recalled this scene as I moved an inch closer to the precipice. I looked down to consider the street below. I've always been afraid of heights, since I was a child, but that was somehow irrelevant now. The littered, Holborn cobblestones below look beautiful from here. But I was not anticipating that mocking blue sky. Fuck you. It should be grey, dead, like all of the other days, a low vaulted screen of mud that mirrors my movement backwards and forwards from the office.

Shouldn't I consider myself lucky? On the tube the other day I read a story about the Rat Catcher of Mumbai. They said it was the worst job in the world. What do I have to complain about? I'm overpaid. Eat in expensive restaurants. Have a beautiful girlfriend. I wish that made me feel better, but it doesn't. Inside my suit is someone I don't recognize or even like. A disgusting blip that makes money, sucks up to the boss, and is chained to a laptop that drains my time without end. I've got to get out. Whoever invented email ought to be shot. I hate sex. I despise holidays. They simply remind me that my life has been over for a long time. I want to leave, but can't. There seems to be no outside or exterior point. I want to be the Rat Catcher of Mumbai. Anything but this interminable nothingness that has stolen my body. I wake up in the middle of the night worrying about my boss, a report I fudged a figure on, mistakes that might come to light the next morning. I try to comfort myself: in a year's time I'll look back on all these small worries and wonder what the fuss was all about. Life will go on. But it is all put on repeat, and at 3am there is no way out. This work poisons everything, your past and future. Such a little thing, but it grows and gathers around me like a living coffin. I want to trade places with the Rat Catcher, but I wont. I can't even quit this stupid job. In the street below bustles an endless throng of coffins wandering back to the office. Maybe I will hit one of them with my coffin? Deep blue above.

2.

I don't seem able to tell exactly when I become this broken caricature of a person, completely taken over by my job. It kind of just happened, although I made it happen of course. By the way, I don't have much of a clue what work actually is: that notion assumes I know of a world beyond it, a counterpoint. It's said that a person is an enigma. Without wanting to sound self-important, I think that applies to me too. But that's only because the pointless habit of working is an enigma. It seems to be this autonomous thing, existing exclusively for it own sake, no longer linked to survival or whatever. At least the Rat Catcher makes a difference. As for me, overpaid and sad, I seem to be trapped inside a made-up job doing made-up things. And it's this immaterial aspect that makes it so hard to find a way out, since a job is no longer something I just do among other things. I am my job. It's in my DNA and gait, always with me, even when asleep. But no one will remember me or my made-up job in hundred year's time. And I know I ought to be thankful for that.

For some reason the blue sky above reminds me of my parents. They seemed to inhabit two distinct lives, two worlds. They had their working life, and then a private one. Like me, they would come home from the office, usually in a foul mood, but they would then turn into someone else, something more... akin to life? I'm not romanticizing the past. Really, they hated their jobs. They loathed how work made them put on fake smiles, greet people they wanted to kill and always suck up to the self-congratulatory boss. They were fucked—badly fucked—but only when at the office. After they left the building they could resurface again, dust off their job and start to live.

Things are different now, at least for me. Despite secretly fucking around with that report, my office managers actually seem to like me. And I hate them for it. They tell me, 'just be yourself.' Apparently, this is the new management approach. The boss loves it when I'm acting weird. He says that's really good, because it means I show my real self. It's all about authenticity. This place I'm working for... I don't want to say too much about it, but they have this farcical idea that we are youthful, edgy and counter-cultural artist-types. I hate art. They talk about Sartre and Marx, and then make these ludicrous connections to flat workplace hierarchies and 'task-autonomy'. As if we were cultural critics!

Why is death so often depicted by the colour blue in classical art? Why not black or grey?

I watched this documentary some time back. It perfectly summed up how my job makes use of me. It was about a brothel, somewhere in Nevada, USA. I'm not saying that these women loved what they were doing, but they seemed somehow resigned to lending their bodies to some unrefined truck driver who'd come in for a quick fuck. What really freaked them out was to spend a night with this creepy guy called Humping Hank. The name was ironic, because he didn't fuck them. That was the whole point. He bought the G-F-E, or girlfriend experience. Humping Hank only wanted long, long nights together. They'd watch TV, eat popcorn, laugh, kiss and hug.

That's how my company squeezes the life out of me. I think about it as this embodiment of Humping Hank. I'm not fucked and then left alone. Instead I'm hugged and nurtured. I'm asked to be myself and authentic. And as a result, I'm never left alone. Turning-off is no longer an option. Escape is impossible. Especially when things go wrong, like that report. My stupid little job follows me around like that monster chasing Dr. Frankenstein. And the monster's curse never stops whispering in my ear: I shall be with you on your wedding night!

That's when I tell myself: if only I was just fucked and left alone.

3.

A small, imperceptible step. Then the silent flight. Down the eight stories and onto Holborn. My team leader will say that it came out of the blue. He simply got up from his king-prawns and jumped. I will disrupt the traffic for a couple of hours. Commuters will be angry. Tomorrow they might feel a twinge of guilt as they browse through the newspaper to find a dry report, reading: 'Another city worker falls to his death from rooftop restaurant'. I like the anonymous sound. They are correct not to attach any glamour to it.

Yet it's hard to motivate myself to actually do it, not because I have a meaningful life to return to, or any happy moments looming in the near future. It's just hard to see the point of it, when I'm already infinitely closer to death than life. 'I am as sick of death as I am of life'. The philosopher E.M. Cioran wrote these words, and I find myself slowly repeating them. Death and life are indistinguishable. Or maybe it's the idea of death, my constant obsession with stepping off that rooftop, that makes me get through another dreadful day. I find myself using death as an excuse not to live. Isn't it ironic? By imagining a final terminus I rivet myself to a life of perpetual non-living, one that has neither beginning nor end. I thought it was supposed to be the other way round, that death would teach us how to live?

Out of the blue, something strange seems to emerge from this state of hyper-hopelessness. I wouldn't rehearse the cliché that I've seen the light at the end of the tunnel. I don't especially like tunnels, and I prefer life when it's dark. What I'm trying to say is that I feel weirdly relieved, as if a horrible weight has been lifted off my shoulders. The moment I abandon the thought of my own imminent death and instead accept that I am entirely subsumed by the imposing logic of work—I know, this doesn't sound very promising—it's precisely at that moment I begin to see a way out. This insignificant thing called a job now looks rather pathetic compared to dying. So I made a mistake, a few bad decisions.

Fuck it. Fuck this game of self-entrapment. I don't want to go out in a blaze. I don't need the ending from Fight Club, with its violent self-beatings and a good redundancy package. I don't need any accompanying soundtrack or fireworks. Nothing. I just need to get the fuck out. I need to leave these ruins behind. To cut myself loose. I will hand in my resignation letter, tell them to fuck off, and then I'll move on. I don't know where. All I know is that I will keep moving, and stay out of sight. I will fuck off, and finally be left alone.

The Devil is Dope

WHAT COMES BEFORE PART B? PART-AAAY!

'Why don't you just be like us?'
'Like how?'
'Like happy.'
Everyone in London is on drugs. Not just the cool kids. And
not just the weirdos. Even the plebs are doing it; the would-be
straights and the goody-goodies.
Worse than that, everyone's got a drug problem. No longer the
Golden Boys: paunches and hangovers, never mind the hang ups.
'Don't I know you from the Portobello Road?' someone asks some-
one else in Barden's buttfucked Boudoir.
'Yar. I'm moving to New York.'
In the PB Road days, at least the cocaine was good. Today, there
have been so many busts and 10-year sentences handed out,
that even the half decent stuff that gets through is cut to shit.
What's the point of binging on organic smoothies if you'll happily
sniff rat poison?

Two days after his brother committed suicide, she found herself
alone with him in the kitchen.
'Gems,' he said.
'Iphgenia,'
It's a reflex.
'Cocaine killed my brother.'
These are quite weird words to say.
To be honest, it was probably the Valium that sent him crazy in
the end. Plus, he'd been sober for a few weeks. It was an accumu-
lation, of decades spent at the peripheries of the Kate Moss crew.
They'd put on a good show at the funeral, carefully opting for the
non-waterproof mascara.

'Yeah. I know. I'm sorry.'
She remembered the time they'd stayed at his house. They'd gone to bed, he'd stayed up all night. She woke to the sound of sobbing from down the hall. He'd crawled into the linen cupboard and wouldn't come out. That was years back.
'I don't wanna do coke anymore.'
'Okay.'
'Okay.'

Bemoaning, in a conversation with JRTC, that her life (oh woe) had no meaning; a writer in an age where no one read, trading in ideas at a time when people were actually offended by them.
'I'm gonna be broke and fucked for the rest of my life, and prob'ly go nuts, and I can only fuck people who hate me and I fucking hate the lot of the stupid cunts, but I don't wanna end up with the freaks, but everyone, everything just ahhhh! Endless, nameless, shitty nothing.'
'Well you go raving every weekend.'
'That's not a thing!'
'Yes it is. Living for the weekend. It's a thing.'
'You know what mate? Fuck you.'

What started as a 10-pack of fags between eight—
Two pull pass yeah, two pull pass—has became a competition to see who can get most out of it the fastest, and for the longest. Tongue-lolling, puke-gurgling, pharmaceutical designer crap. I'm just not into that shit. I like getting away with it. Sitting through a mothers & babies screening of The Exorcist tripping my tits off; wandering through the crowds at South Bank, having been up for three days, and joining the submarine's marching band; getting on the tube so stoned that it seems to make more sense to go the whole way round the circle line rather than have to go through Sloane Square. Throwing full grams of cocaine into the Thames outside the houses of Parliament, hurling money and keys in after them.
Babble on Babylon! Slew dem cunts!'
Falling asleep on a rudeboy's shoulder on the bus home.

And what? And what? My sister would puke on you.

Sorry. Sorry.

Somewhere along the line, for most people, getting high became getting fucked. And they don't go out and cause trouble, they hole up in kitchens that look the same as their parent's kitchens; big pans hanging from the ceiling and something tiled, but mostly wood. Metaphysical education.

There are some people whose addiction is simply to oblivion. They are more charming because in their case the substance becomes less important. Cokeheads cling to their grams—using them as ways to keep and/or divide company. K-heads lose it; pawing through the multiple pockets of puffa jackets to find an oversized gram that has inevitably spilled out into their pockets, but there's loads left. Oblivion addicts, who have a humility and simply accept what is on offer to them, go from at first being impossible to spot, to then being impossible to miss. 12 Valiums and a Special Brew just to get through the Eastenders Omnibus.

Heroin is great. Because, you can lie around and feel like shit all day long, but when you've got to get something done, you have a little smoke and hey!

The stronger in body but weaker in mind become small-time conspiracy theorists, culturing a paranoia based on shaky foundations: There's only so many times you can stand about in your kitchen talking about David Icke and the fucking pyramids.

It is a case of circles and psychos. At all moments, you are untouchable, but Popularity comes in waves. At one of popularity's peaks, you can get away with anything. Smash someone's glasses, spit in the landlord's face, spray up people's Prius' with the words, HUNTERESS THOMPSON WILL FUCK YOU UP.

Don't you get it—people only behave like that in the movies.

Poison dwarf. The movies are based on real life!

Inevitably, this behaviour will outcast you. Getting 'left out' is a weird one. You understand that it is not really a thing, but it is. And you know not to care, but you do. You begin to think things like 'we all die alone!' but really, you know it's all your fault. You start to change the way you look at it: Very few people have the willpower to sit alone and exist, but knowing this is the noblest state of affairs (and the only way to get anything done), you force the hand of Fate and get yourself banished, then remember: I am not interested in cocaine cliques and bitchy photography. I never want to get a cab home in my life! Mi nuh like. I feel sorry for the Dalstonites, cos they'll never know how shit it is to be a kid; to catch trains to the end of the line and back again, smokin puffs of joints in garden sheds and setting fire to policeman's duvets and council estate bins with a gang of tearaway eight-year olds cheering you on.

You can't just push in like that!
You what?
You're not going in front of me. That's for sure.
Nor me.
Nor me.
Nigger please.
A real fucking fighter aren't you?
It has been known.
You should show some respect.
We're old!
She'll never love!
Up for 3 days. Turn to the old woman.
I can see your scalp.
Pahahahahaha.

Drugs show you what epiphanies feel like. It is, however, perfectly possible to reach dizzying heights of consciousness alone and totally sober. You can think things that are so cool that they can make you cum, dance, fall over. But thoughts on drugs can prove problematic. Inertia? Something similar happens when you are hungry in an unfamiliar city.
Shall we go in there?
Er.. dunno. Er.
Walk on.
There?
Approach the door.
Looks weird.

Veer away.
In there?
And you can walk until you are starving, like some retard child who thinks that he can survive on Haribo alone. This never happens when you are alone.

You always assume everyone else is stupid and not sensitive to these things. But they see it too.
JRTC again.
Well if they realise them, why don't they do something about them?
They're smart enough to realise that there's nothing they can do.
O—dead smart.
I've gotta go.

That Motion and Matter are inseparable &c; the key benefit of being blackballed from old drinking circles (asides from preservation of health) is that being on the outside makes it easier to watch the rest. It looks like people settling for these normal boring lives and they no doubt pity you but, another fucking wedding? I just sit back and just watch and just get nauseous and walk around with an empty bottle of Remi Martin startin shit like some 26-year old skinny Cartman.
GODDAMIT.

From a decade and a half of razzing it, everyone's got a style: Some leave before the party's over, nipping out with who they consider to be 'the good people' and exiting to a house or a hotel, then picking off the dregs by phone. Others hold out to the bitter end, stumbling over chairs and lurching at big cow-looking girls in the hopes of landing a lift home. There are tears, rucks, a spattering of taxis shared in two directions, text wars and lost phones, head kicking-ins, kidnappings and lynch mobs, whatever! What a bunch of tossers. The party's over! Everyone's old! Even the teenagers—dry as fuck! Those who cling on to the bitter end are trying to keep a party alive that ran out of tunes years ago, staggering and haggard, half-fucking blind.

The minibus is packed more tightly than ever.
Taxi for one?

Consider what cocaine is: the ultimate indulgence for people
that have everything. Sold from 3rd World countries to 1st world
countries, tax-free. Then you think of what cocaine does to
those that take it: fucks their heads. With that set of facts in your
fucked little mind (you can prove anything with facts), it can be
argued that the drug trade is a direct attack by people who have
nothing on people who have everything. Not through govern-
ment-sanctioned international diplomacy, but more real ways—
financially and psychologically.

There is no longer any balance between good and evil. All that
can happen these days is that something becomes so evil that
it gobbles itself up. But you can make, market and distribute
anything as if it is illegal, it doesn't have to be drugs. If someone
with great enough vision had the inclination, there is a model
already set up that they could employ to go about really fucking
some shit up.

Welcome to Part B

HERE COMES THE BOOM OF THE END OF
YOUR CIVILISATION AND DON'T YOU
LOOK PRETTY IN YOUR COOL NEW JEANS.
HERE COMES WHAT WE GET FOR
A HUNDRED YEARS OF PRIVILEGE
SQUANDERED AND NOTHING DONE TO
EDUCATE OUR CHILDREN OR SAVE OUR
PLANET. HERE COMES THE CABRIOLET
EDITION OF CAPITALISM AND THE END OF
AN EMPIRE YOU WERE TOO CONCEITED
TO EVEN PROTECT. HERE COMES THE
RISING TIDE. HERE COMES THE MIDDLE
EAST. HERE COMES THE WEATHER. HERE
COMES EVERYBODY

Abel and Cain

150 Years After Baudelaire

1.

Race of Abel, dine at The Ritz;
capitalism is such bliss.

Race of Cain, Big Mac and frites;
capitalism takes the

Race of Abel, your gram of coke
powders the nose of seraphim.

Race of Cain, inject or smoke
your £5 wrap of heroin.

Race of Abel, your haute couture
is so chic, so pleasant.

Race of Cain, your cheap sportswear
brands you 'urban peasant'.

Race of Abel, you're from good stock;
success begets success.

Race of Cain, you 'breed like dogs
—gratis—on the NHS.'

Race of Abel, your fat cat premium
is a tad invidious.

Race of Cain, your £5 minimum
is insulting and injurious.

Race of Abel, money fucks
in its penthouse suite.

Race of Cain, in towerblocks,
poverty sucks its teeth.

2.
Race of Abel, fill up your arks.
The flood is coming. Flee!

Race of Cain, your Christ, your Marx
haven't set you free.

Race of Abel, there is one bother:
money can't bribe death.

Race of Cain, kill Big Brother
and distribute his wealth.

An Iraqi Child

An Iraqi child
Is drawing bombers, like those
Which nearly killed him.

The bombs left his face
Swollen with fierce injuries—
Marks of angry pain.

He draws the bombers,
Though his arm and some fingers
Were amputated.

Now they're bandaged up,
With three crayons firmly taped
To the ends of his stumps.

He draws bleak, black lines
Chronicling his history.
Who did this to me?

They had many planes.
They'd brought bombs to fit into each
Of their cruel planes.

Why didn't they think
Of the people below?
Who drove all these planes?

One was called George Bush;
And one was called Tony Blair
With his friend, Campbell.

They'd made good friends
With lots of oil companies.
They wanted your oil.

To get into power
They'd made friends with newspapers
Who all said, 'Yes, bomb Iraq'.

Rupert Murdoch, boss
Of News International,
Told a hundred and twenty

Of his newspapers
To write a leader
Urging readers' to support war.

No one was immune:
Even *The Guardian*
(Financed by *AutoTrader*),

Was saying 'Bomb!'
Claiming that Gulf Wars
Were 'humanitarian' wars.

The simple cause,
Wrote The Guardian
In a pre-Iraq-war leader,

At the end, is just.
And with the magic word,
'Humanitarian', cunning PR

Could make the liberal media
Mouth-pieces for war propaganda.
There was a lifestyle

To be supported by Iraq's cheap oil
So opinion formers in wine-bars and clubs
And in Parliamentary tea-rooms
And in TV studios' hospitality suites—
While not discussing their expenses
Or their mortgages or their fees

Or their cars or their lifestyles
Or their favourite restaurants
Or their children's private schools—

Would dip a toe in the zeitgeist
And then bloviate
About regime change,

Like self-important sheep
Housing wolves:
I mean, obviously

One has to get rid of Saddam...
Gassing his own people.
It's a breach of international law

For heaven's sake...!
The man has rockets. Chockfull of sarin,
VX, mustard gas, anthrax, you name it.

Didn't you see the Evening Standard?
Front page.
They could all reach London

In about forty-five minutes flat.
Apparently.
According to Tony...

Tony, who in March 2002,
Received legal advice from the Foreign Office
That an attack on Iraq was illegal
Under international law.

<u>Tony, who would make himself a stranger</u>
<u>To all moral standards</u>
<u>Save for the acquisition of wealth</u>

And millions are now his,
Thanks to consent
Being manufactured
By media gossips hovering round
Water-coolers, and by his craven civil servants,

And thanks to missiles being launched—
Nato's evil acupuncture
That turned Iraqi skies orange.
1,690,903 Iraqi people were executed
For the 9/11 crime that they never committed
(But with which they were charged);

Baghdad was floodlit by bombs—
By bombs' continuous explosions—
And in Iraq no one's health was improved,

Just death from vile airborne cancers;
Birth defects that impoverish nightmares
And amputations on an industrial scale.

But the oil's easier to get at now
And Alan Greenspan, the Chairman of the Federal Reserve, Would
admit, ...*that it is politically inconvenient to acknowledge*
What everyone knows: the Iraq war is largely about oil.

Humanitarian?
The Iraqi boy might query, and then ask,
So they're happy now?

Well, they're all very rich.
Maybe they'd buy my drawing?
The boy says.

STARRING, IN ORDER OF APPEARANCE: GOD, ROUSSEAU, FREUD, EPICURUS, MARQUIS DE SADE, PLATO, WITTGENSTEIN, MALTHUS, MARX, NIETZSCHE, THE MADONNA AND BABY JESUS

Dead Philosophers in Heaven

By Matt Russell & Nick Gibb

www.DEAD-PHILOSOPHERS.com

©2012 MATT RUSSELL & NICK GIBB

SUCK NEOLIBERALISM

THEOCCUPIEDTIMES.CO.UK

PUBLIC SERVICE ANNOUNCEMENT FROM THE OCCUPIED TIMES

IMG: THE INDIGNADOS

ISSUE___2

IMG: ADRIAN NETTLESHIP
NICHOLAS HAYES

THE ARGUMENT OF THE BROKEN WINDOW PANE IS THE MOST VALUABLE ARGUMENT IN MODERN POLITICS

— EMMELINE PANKHURST

Occupying the Media

When the Going Gets Weird, the Weird Turn Pro

Life's too short to waste in a dead-end job. When that dawned on me this time last decade, I was working for The New York Times as a foreign correspondent, and my colleagues were enabling the invasion of Iraq. I was naive enough to be shocked by their propaganda, and too ambitious and too junior to challenge it. The only way ahead was to resign, and try to start a revolution.

The form this took was determined by my circumstances. Since I'd been hired to report on the Balkans, I was stationed in Serbia, which ignited the wars that had killed off Yugoslavia. My brief was to ask if 'The Serbs' had accepted guilt. This got me ridiculed as a hypocrite: young Serbs were resisting their leaders all along, whereas I was employed by a paper that whitewashed warmongers.

I didn't have an answer to that, except to get stoned. My editors showed minimal interest in Balkan news, so I had plenty of time to dream up other plans. I'd met a man who suggested we organise a music festival, on an island in the Danube in Belgrade. We convinced ourselves we'd start a Summer of Love, drawing crowds from the neighbouring countries Serbs attacked. We could also revive the dormant student protest movement, which helped topple a Serbian president two years earlier. We'd even lure some tourists from afar, by promoting ourselves as Ibiza crossed with Glastonbury. All told, it was 'constructive ethnic cleansing', a way of reclaiming Serbia from its past. Hell, The New York Times might even cover it.

To facilitate this, I invented an alter ego. That way I could interview myself, and talk us up in print to raise some cash. I set to work at once on laying a paper trail. A few days later, *The Times* ran a letter from Raoul Djukanovic, who ranted about the flaws in U.S. policy. 'Western officials should consider how they can become a catalyst for change in the Balkans,' the text harrumphed, 'by investing heavily in economic revival.' Like by funding the ECHO Festival in Belgrade!

Raoul's fear and loathing subtext went unnoticed. His name was a Balkanised remix of Raoul Duke, the pseudonym of the volatile Hunter S. Thompson. And as the doctor of gonzo explained: 'When the going gets weird, the weird turn pro.'

Before quitting, I made my job a kind of protest stunt. Armed with promotional brochures and a film, I hustled contacts for assistance, often in the middle of scheduled interviews for the Times. I asked NATO to lend me a pontoon bridge, in the name of improving relations with the people they'd bombed. I urged the European Union to sponsor the event, and promote itself to Serbs instead of vice versa. And when both said no, I tried a Nobel Prize-winning Auschwitz survivor, and begged him to ask his friends for a million dollars, with a promise to foster reconciliation.

My business partner found these stunts amusing.

'If you are Raoul,' he said, 'I wanna be archetype of Balkan refugee, like a Goran Needsavisavic of no man's land. Together we make Utopia in shithole.'

Our venue seemed well suited to this task. Its name was Big War Island, and it once marked the edge of the Ottoman and the Austro-Hungarian empires.

'Now we make here anarchistic Interzone,' my partner said. 'What can be better location to come on with love-in?'

Inspired by his zeal, I got radical ideas.

'Imagine if Serbia legalised soft drugs,' I said. 'They could call it learning lessons from The Hague. Coffee shops are full of foreign smokers. If we ran one, this place would be crawling with Western cash.' I'd already been importing hash in bulk, re-routing work trips so I could smuggle it on expenses. The next step was to court some politicians. This got easier once we'd scrounged loans from shady businessmen, who doubled as their friends.

Backed by the national airline and Serbia's minister of tourism, I hijacked a stand at the world's largest travel trade fair in Berlin. Our video blared on auto-loop for days. 'It's 2003 in the Balkans and everyone's bored,' the soundtrack declared, over footage I'd nicked from the BBC and EXIT, another festival in Serbia. 'That means the biggest crowd since the downfall of Slobodan Milosevic. Only this time everyone's out to have fun.' And so it boomed on to its cheesy finale: 'Come and watch Belgrade get back in tune with the rest of the world!'

Meanwhile, back in Serbia, the prime minister was being shot dead outside his office, by gangsters from a suburb near our island. I returned to be told to file a front-page story. Although I'd resigned, I was technically serving out my notice. I did the minimum, fearing the impact on our festival. Most of my story was copied off the news wires. It ended with a made-up comment from a man in the street. Compared to false pretexts for war, this seemed quite tame. So I also concocted quotes from Western diplomats. The New York Times seemed none the wiser.

Subversion was all I could muster at the Times, where news is routinely skewed to suit the powerful. It's the same every day in newsrooms round the world. To quote official liars is objective, but saying someone's lying makes you biased. To challenge who sets the agenda, I later made a fake Financial Times, depicting a world less addicted to ruinous growth, and explaining how the media serves big business. Though I gave away thousands of copies to commuters, and journalists let me tell them their shortcomings, it's fair to say this didn't change the world.

As for the festival, well, that also got subverted: by the well-armed men we hired as our security, as 'recommended' by the government. My attempts at resistance proved futile, strengthening the forces I opposed. Even so, they set me free from disillusionment. Our festival's marketing slogan still applies: 'life is an illusion; choose a nice one.'

VIRTUES
FOR THE MODERN AGE
BY ALAIN de BOTTON

RESILIENCE

Keeping going even when things are looking dark; accepting that reversals are normal; remembering that human nature is, in the end, tough. Not frightening others with your fears.

EMPATHY

The capacity to connect imaginatively with the sufferings and unique experiences of another person. The courage to become someone else and look back at yourself with honesty.

PATIENCE

We lose our temper because we believe that things should be perfect. We've grown so used to many things (putting men on the moon etc.), we're ever less able to deal with things that still insist on going wrong; like traffic, governments, other people.... We should grow calmer and more forgiving by getting more realistic about how things actually tend to go.

SACRIFICE

We're hardwired to seek our own advantage but also have a miraculous ability, very occasionally, to forego our own satisfactions in the name of someone or something else. We won't ever manage to raise a family, love someone else or save the planet if we don't keep up with the art of sacrifice.

POLITENESS

Politeness has a bad name. We often assume it's about being 'fake' (which is meant to be bad) as opposed to 'really ourselves' (which is meant to be good). However, given what we're really like deep down, we should spare others too much exposure to our deeper selves. We need to learn manners, which aren't evil – they are the necessary internal rules of civilization. Politeness is very linked to tolerance, the capacity to live alongside people whom one will never agree with, but at the same time, can't avoid.

HUMOUR

Seeing the funny sides of situations and of oneself doesn't sound very serious, but it is integral to wisdom, because it's a sign that one is able to put a benevolent finger on the gap between what we want to happen and what life can actually provide; what we dream of being and what we actually are, what we hope other people will be like and what they are actually like. Like anger, humour springs from disappointment, but it's disappointment optimally channelled. It's one of the best things we can do with our sadness.

SELF-AWARENESS

To know oneself is to try not to blame others for one's troubles and moods; to have a sense of what's going on inside oneself, and what actually belongs to the world.

FORGIVENESS

Forgiveness means a long memory of all the times when we wouldn't have got through life without someone cutting us some slack. It's recognising that living with others isn't possible without excusing errors.

HOPE

The way the world is now is only a pale shadow of what it could one day be. We're still only at the beginning of history. At you get older, despair becomes far easier, almost reflex (whereas in adolescence, it was still cool and adventurous). Pessimism isn't necessarily deep, nor optimism shallow.

CONFIDENCE

The greatest projects and schemes die for no grander reasons than that we don't dare. Confidence isn't arrogance, it's based on a constant awareness of how short life is and how little we ultimately lose from risking everything.

De Botton's ultimate aim for the project is that it ignites a vital conversation around moral character to increase public interest in becoming more virtuous and connected as a society. He explains: 'There's no scientific answer to being virtuous, but the key thing we have some kind of life to which to flex our ethical muscles. It reminds us that we all need to work at being good, just as we work at anything else that really matters.'

Led by The School of Life, who have commissioned a range of creative artwork to support the campaign, The Virtues Project will also enact upon a range of events that will explore the necessity of the virtues outlined in the Manifesto. Watch this space and further details to be announced in due course.

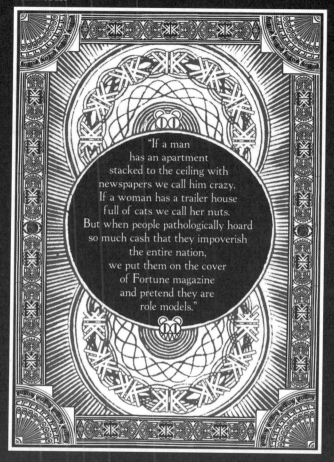

"If a man
has an apartment
stacked to the ceiling with
newspapers we call him crazy.
If a woman has a trailer house
full of cats we call her nuts.
But when people pathologically hoard
so much cash that they impoverish
the entire nation,
we put them on the cover
of Fortune magazine
and pretend they are
role models."

The Day We Nearly Broke Blair

Remembering the Power of Protest

On Tuesday 11 March, just nine days before the attack on Iraq, British Defence Secretary Geoff Hoon phoned Donald Rumsfeld in Washington and told him that Britain might not be able to participate in the war. 'We have real political difficulties,' he is reported to have told his opposite number, 'real difficulties, more than you might realise.'

The phone call reflected the fact that there was panic behind the scenes in Whitehall and Downing Street in the run up to the war. Blair himself later admitted that things were so bad that Bush offered him an out from the war. Cabinet ministers, including Foreign Secretary Jack Straw, spent the next few days begging Blair to accept the offer and stand the troops down. Straw told Blair that if there was no official UN backing for the invasion 'the only regime change that will be taking place will be in this room'. Civil servants were looking into the constitutional issues should the vote over the war go against the Government. Blair admits he thought 'these might be the last days in office.'

All of this was largely a response to a wave of outrage around the country at the prospect of Britain participating in a war most thought would be a disaster. In his own account of the time, Blair admits to feeling isolated and desperate:

The international community was split. The party was split, I was between numerous rocks and innumerable hard places. The strain on everyone around me was almost unbearable. At home in Downing Street, I was a bit like a zombie.

The demonstrations on February 15 were the biggest protest event in world history. No-one has been able to come up with anything like a historical precedent. Up to 30 million people protested around the world. The protests unfolded across the globe in sync with the sun. The Australian demonstrations set a precedent: around a million Australians marched in all—about 5% of the total population—making it their biggest ever demonstration. Country after country had their biggest protests in generations, or ever. There were major demonstrations in every continent, hundreds accross Latin America, a huge protest in Damascus, Syria—many hundreds of thousands in New York and other US cities and millions on the streets of Madrid, Rome and London.

The London protest was more like a wave of humanity moving east-west across the capital than a strightworward march. London belonged to the people that day and no-one had seen anything quite like it. Thousands were still entering the park and chanting after the speeches had ended and the sun had gone down. To savour the moment people lit fires in Hyde Park and partied into the evening.

On the day of the demonstration Blair and his entourage escaped London by going up to speak at the Scottish Labour Party conference. This, according to a senior aide, 'really was the moment of maximum pressure on him. As he travelled up there, we just didn't know whether the event would turn in to a fiasco.' Alistair Campbell accepts the mood in his camp was desperate, 'every part of the strategy was in tatters—re the EU, re the US, re the country which was about to march against us.'

Blair was greeted with stony silence inside the conference hall, and outside was the biggest demonstration in Scotland since the 1920s, variously estimated at between fifty and a hundred thousand people.

Blair got through the day, but February 15 was not a one-off, merely the most focussed moment of a period of popular rage. The then Home Secretary and loyal Blair supporter, David Blunkett, was shaken by it. He complained of protests 'everywhere' around his constituency, even at his surgery sessions:

Everything was dominated by Iraq, and it was really hard to win the audience round. The issue is obsessing everyone and permeating everything. It is affecting the world economy and creating a degree of uncertainty and tension that everything else is feeding into.

The movement used the demonstration on February 15 to launch a campaign of direct action and civil disobedience. The Monday after the demo the Guardian ran a story headlined 'New Protest planned to bring Britain to a standstill'. It included a long quote from the Convenor of the Stop the War Coalition, Lindsey German, calling on people to 'walk out of their offices, strike, sit down, occupy buildings, demonstrate, and do whatever they think fit the moment war starts.'

Many others joined in the attempt to make the country ungovernable. Stop the War organised a Peoples' Assembly in the weeks after the demonstration that called for action across the board if the government went ahead with its plans. One of the Assembly's most popular slogans was 'if they start a war, we must stop the country'. The day the war started turned out to be the biggest day of direct action the country has probably ever seen. Hundreds of schools were closed by striking students and tens of thousands of people occupuied town halls or blocked roundabouts, motorways, tunnels and bridges across the country.

According to John Kampfner, who based his insider account on scores of interviews with senior civil servants and politicians, all this led to a state of paralysis in government at the time:

The British government, in the normal sense of the word, had ground to a halt. A small group of cabinet members met several times a day. Hilary Armstrong, the Chief Whip, and John Reid, the Party Chairman, spent their entire time trying to work out the extent of the forthcoming rebellion in the commons.

Blair, of course, got away with it—just. Despite the fact that even David Milliband estimated that there were no more than ten Labour backbenchers who actually believed in the war, enough ignored their constituent's wishes and voted for war, saving Blair's skin and condemning the Iraqis to years of carnage and mayhem. Partly this democratic malfunction can be put down to the culture of careerism and favour that poisons Westminster politics. Partly it reflected the fact that defying Bush felt too much like a challenge to the 'special relationship' that dominates foreign policy 'thinking' across the political spectrum.

But Blair wasn't out of the woods. The pressure against him mounted again in the second half of the year as 300,000 people took to the streets—on a weekday—when George Busgh vistited London. The failure of the Iraq strategy and his growing unpopularity led him to try and resign in November 2003. He was persuaded to stay, but he never managed to move the agenda on, and he was eventually hounded out of office, in disgrace over Iraq.

The great demonstrations of 2003 narrowly failed to stop Britain going to war in Iraq. But it would be a mistake to underestimate the movement's impact. Those demonstrations, and the massive protests that have followed— over Lebanon and Palestine as well as Afghanistan and Iraq—have caused a massive swing in public opinion and helped change the calculus of war. In the 1980s Thatcher won an election as a result of fighting a war. Nowadays our politicians know that new foreign interventions are likely to be opposed by sixty, seventy or even eighty per cent of the population. They have to worry about the votes and they know they may face massive protests.

Cameron's government is still enthusiastic about foreign wars. Libya, Mali and the threats against Iran all attest to that. But don't let them tell you marching makes no difference— they're only saying it so that you will stay at home...

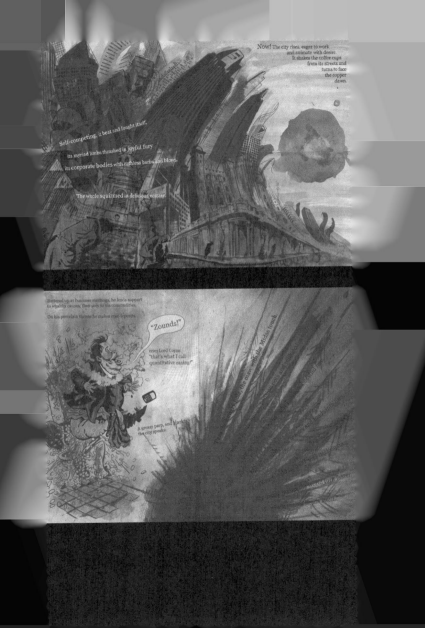

Now! The city rises, eager to work
and animate with desire.
It shakes the coffee cups
from its streets and
turns to face
the copper
dawn.

Self-competing, it beat and fought itself,

its myriad limbs thrashed in joyful fury,

its corporate bodies with ruthless barbs and blows.

The whole squirmed in delicious ecstasy.

Buttered up at business meetings, he lends support
to wealthy causes, then uses to his commodities.

On his porcelain throne he makes over-deposits.

"Zounds!"

cries Lord Coyns
"that's what I call
quantitative easing!"

A greasy parp, and Hark!
the city speaks.

"This is the best, this is the best,

This is the best that we can be.

This is the blessèd, feted, zenith,

This is the End of History.

Open your markets, chinks and darkies,

Open your laps to luxury.

Open a line of ready credit,

Of debit and habit and live in me."

Compañeros of the Word

Towards a Literacy of Rebellion

In the dead of winter, 1994, a mysterious caller left a voice-message on my answering machine. Speaking in English, but with a Mexican-sounding accent, the female voice simply said, 'The *compañeros* asked me to call you to thank you for the pamphlet you made about the struggle.' *Compañeros*? It was the first time that I had consciously heard the word, and it would be years before I really understood it.

A few weeks earlier, I had opened that day's New York Times and stood, without moving, while reading the paper's cover story. It was January 3, 1994. An indigenous uprising was taking place in Chiapas, Mexico. The article described how a well orchestrated, surprise action staged by thousands of Mexican rebels had managed to seize control of several towns. Photos showed the rebels, many armed with nothing more than sticks. Without words, the faces in the photos spoke: *Estamos aqui. No queremos morir, ya no! Somos ustedes. Ustedes son nosotros. Ven, compañero. Ven, compañera. Levantanse!*

Day by day, coverage of the rebellion deepened, and day by day, bits and pieces of the words of the indigenous communities and their spokespeople made it into print. When they did, phrases floated out like lines from great writers like Pablo Neruda, Gabriel Garcia Marquez, Mario Benedetti or Walt Whitman; words you never forget, words that hold you in their hands, words that call you, invite you, and stay with you as if they were those of someone you have always known and loved, but have never met.

A young woman, Barbara Pillsbury, began posting her translations of the rebels' writings on the website of the Institute of Agriculture and Trade Policy. From these initial translations, the Mexican rebels' own perspectives began to gradually emerge in their own voice, in their own rhythm, and in their own words. Declarations of indignation, dignity, justice, democracy and freedom flowed like mountain springs from remote Mayan communities to the rest of the world.

'Here we are, the dead of all times, dying once again, but now in order to live,' began one of the rebels' communiqués. Through simple and heartfelt language, 500 years of indigenous resistance was being signaled out as both a local Mexican struggle and as a global defence for humanity itself. As an activist and a movement publisher, everything about this resonated and inspired. By February 1994, my friend and I began publishing pamphlets of the Zapatistas' first communiqués and declarations. Not long after, the mysterious voice message was left on the answering machine. But it wouldn't be until August 1999 that I made my first trip to Chiapas, met with the insurgent communities, heard the living voice of those people, and began to learn bits and pieces of their language of community, dignity and struggle.

In the meantime, I learned by reading Zapatista literature. As support for the movement spread, new translators emerged with new styles of translating that preserved some terms in the Spanish original. Among the words that appeared most abundantly were compañero y compañera. For example, many of Zapatista letters and public presentations begin with greetings to others in the struggle: 'Brothers and sisters, *compañeros y compañeras*...' In Chiapas, *compañero*, or *compa* for short, is how Zapatistas refer to one another, and to anyone or anything in solidarity with the movement. You might also hear '*compita*,' an affectionate version of *compa*, which I first came across through written correspondence with freed Zapatista political prisoner, Javier Eliorriaga.

Time, memory and oral history all flow differently in the Zapatista communities. Their braid of struggle is woven equally with strands of the past, the future and the present, and whatever helps them weave it is a weapon against oblivion. 'We have other arms,' states one of their letters. 'For example, we have the arm of the word. We also have the arm of our culture, of our being who we are...We have the weapon of the mountain, that old friend and *compañera* who fights along with us, with her roads, hiding places, and hillsides, with her trees, with her rains, with her suns, with her dawns, and moons...'

Paolo Freire said language is never neutral, and Alfred Korzybski said words are like maps, but never the territory to which they refer. In the case of insurgent discourse, the territory to which the terms of struggle refer is the possible world, experienced in glimpses through collective acts of the imagination, conscience and yearning. The genius of Zapatista literature is the narrative it voices to protect its historical memory and parent the possible.

In our dreams we have seen another world, an honest world, a world decidedly more fair than the one in which we now live. We saw that in this world there was no need for armies; peace, justice and liberty were so common that no one talked about them as far-off concepts, but as things such as bread, birds, air, water.

The words dignity, dream, democracy, justice, struggle and liberty are among those central to the Zapatista vision, but perhaps it is the word *compañero*, the building block of the community and the organization, that holds and contains all of these other words in it. Araceli and Maribel, Zapatista women from the La Realidad region, describe how the original insurgents introduced them to the word:

After visiting us several times, they began to explain the struggle to us: what they were fighting for and whom they were fighting against. They told us there was a word we could use to show our respect for each other, and that word was compañeros *or* compañeras. *Pronouncing it meant that we were going to struggle together for our freedom.*

While its meaning may change from place to place, the word *compañero* is common in conversation, movement songs, and the literature of resistance throughout Spanish-speaking culture. You can hear it in the dialogue of the characters in the film Corazon del Tiempo, in the one-word title of Jorge Casteñada's biography of Che Guevara, and in the lines of Argentine poet Juan Gelman:

Nosotros vamos a empezar otra vez la lucha
Otra vez vamos a empezar
Otra vez vamos a empezar nosotros
Contra la gran derrota del mundo
Compañeritos que no terminan
O arden en la memoria como fuegos
Otra vez
Otra vez
Otra vez

In art as in life, the word carries the love and aspiration of people who use language, like territory, to struggle for a better world.

At time of this writing, 7,719 people have been arrested at events and actions organized by the Occupy movement. I was among the 700 people arrested on the Brooklyn Bridge on October 1, 2012. Spending the night in a jail cell with 115 other protestors was a galvanizing and affirming experience. During my first court appearance I was reunited with many of the movement people with whom I marched and spent the night in jail. With great joy, I passed around copies of pamphlets I had published since our arrest and chatted with young organizers about plans for upcoming actions. A few blocks away, Zuccotti Park was roiling with activity.

When the judge called out my name, I made my way up from my seat, passed through a small wooden gate, and stood before the bench. I declined the court's offer for an adjournment in contemplation of dismissal, and chose to fight all charges against us. As I turned from the judge and began to exit the space before his bench, a Latina woman from the movement was called up. For a moment we stood facing each other, the gate between us.

It was for me to exit before she approached the bench, but I said, 'After you, *compañera*,' and opened the gate for her to come forward first.

'*Gracias, compañero*,' she answered.

We looked at each other again, but now with new eyes, a new understanding connecting us. Unlike the very real bond we also shared with everyone else in the room through the movement, the march, and our mass arrest, this stranger and I, through a single world, communicated and connected with something deeper. In calling each other *compañeros*, it was as if the struggle we were waging went far beyond one arrest, one place, one time, one movement, one people, one language, one history. It was as if the tables were turned: a whole world was now ours to speak, and the silence that came with sharing it was clandestine and beautiful.

'Words are deeds,' wrote the philosopher Ludwig Wittgenstein. They can divide and conquer or tie things with possibility; they can serve systems of domination and control or help overturn them. In learning words and phrases from other struggles, and creating new ones, a literacy of resistance and emancipation is advanced that creates territory out of consciousness itself. 'It is the word that gives form to that walk that goes on inside us,' say the Zapatistas,

It is the word that is the bridge to cross to the other side. Silence is what Power offers our pain in order to make us small. Speaking we heal the pain. Speaking we accompany one another. Power uses the word to impose his empire of silence. We use the word to renew ourselves.

As an act of renewal, social struggle succeeds most, not when it focuses on winning a single-issue reform, but when it relocates power from authority to the people and community. A literacy of struggle and solidarity, drawing on terms borrowed or those just born, can open the way to thinking and acting outside a set of choices imposed by the system; in much the same way, achieving traditional literacy opened the path for Frederick Douglass to pursue and win his own liberation, fomenting resistance and movement organizing in the process.

We live in a time of indignation, outrage, uprisings, rebellion, and insurgent democracy movements against systems that have become hostile to the public interest. Developing a literacy of solidarity and resistance can not only help break step with corporate-controlled society, but also assist people identify and articulate with the traditions of resistance developed over generations of struggle by the indigenous, people of color, women, and defenders of the Earth's natural environment.

'Challenges to the system,' writes Rául Zibechi, 'are unthinkable without spaces beyond the control of the powerful.' After almost two years of coordinated repression against the Occupy movement, 7,719 arrests, timed entrapment cases, mass surveillance, and a police-state presence waged against public plazas and squares, language offers itself as an open yet clandestine space to occupy and mobilize in the effort to freely describe the world, its injustices, and our narratives toward common emancipation. Like Zapatistas, as 'incompleted beings conscious of their incompletion,' we mentor one another to build networks grounded in a literacy of rebellion.

Subcomandante Marcos recently wrote,

Those who looks at us and look at themselves thinking about us, and make themselves a bridge and then discover that these words that they write, sing, repeat, transform, do not belong to the Zapatistas, that they never did, that those words belong to you, they belong to everybody and to nobody, and that they are part of a larger whole, and who knows where that larger whole may be, and so you discover or confirm that when you look at us looking at ourselves looking at you, you are touching and talking about something bigger, something for which there is no alphabet yet, and that through this process you aren't joining a group, collective, organization, sect, religion, or whatever you may call it, but rather that you are understanding that the passage to humanity today is called 'rebellion.'

With our word as our weapon, the passage to humanity opens. At the same time, repression against us, blocking what we open, intensifies. As it does, we learn to find one another and connect in new ways, learning from one another as we go, finding solidarity in disobedience, in stories of community and resistance, and in simple words we carry in from sister struggles, words like *compañero* and *compañera*.

HERE COMES WHAT YOU GET FOR YOUR EASY FRIENDSHIPS. HERE COMES THE OTHER AMERICA. HERE COME THE WHITE WORKING CLASS/ HERE COME THE BLACK PANTHERS AGAIN. HERE COMES THE SHADOW OF YOUR DREAM. HERE COMES THE GHOSTS OF YOUR TWO CAR FAMILY AND YOUR IDEAS OF PURE NEW LAND AND YOUR RIPPED OUT CITIES. HERE COMES YOUR TWENTIETH CENTURY RE-LOADED. HERE COMES YOUR INNATELY COWARDLY PURITAN SELF-DISGUST, ONCE MORE LIKE YOU MEAN IT

THE SPECTACLE OF ADVERTISING
CREATES IMAGES OF FALSE BEAUTY SO
SUAVE AND SO IMPOSSIBLE TO ATTAIN
THAT YOU WILL HURT INSIDE AND NEVER
EVEN KNOW WHERE THE HURT COMES
FROM, AND IN ALL PICTURES NOW THE
FAMOUS PEOPLE HAVE ALREADY BEGUN
TO LOOK LOST AND LONELY

NINA POWER

IS A PHILOSOPHER, WRITER & JOURNALIST, AS WELL AS BEING A SENIOR LECTURER AT THE HAMPTON UNIVERSITY. SHE IS THE AUTHOR OF 'ONE DIMENSIONAL WOMAN', PLUS INFINITE THOUGHT & HAS A RADIO SHOW IN RESONANCE FM CALLED 'THE HOUR OF POWER'

TRENTON OLDFIELD

IS A CO-FOUNDER OF THIS IS NOT A GATEWAY, AN ORGANISATION THAT EXPLORES CRITICAL IDEAS OF URBANISM & THE PLATFORM. IN 2012 HE SWAM INTO THE THAMES & DISRUPTED THE BOAT RACE IN A PROTEST AGAINST ELITISM. HE WAS JAILED FOR SIX MONTHS.

ANTONIO NEGRI

IS A MARXIST SOCIOLOGIST & POLITICAL PHILOSOPHER. AN INTEGRAL PART OF THE ITALIAN AUTONOMIA MOVEMENT OF THE 70'S, HE IS THE CO-AUTHOR WITH MICHAEL HARDT OF 'EMPIRE': ONE OF THE KEY TEXTS OF THE ANTI-GLOBALISATION MOVEMENT.

EVE ENSLER

IS A PLAYWRIGHT, FEMINIST & ACTIVIST. IN 1996 SHE WROTE 'THE VAGINA MONOLOGUES' WHICH HAS SINCE BEEN TRANSLATED INTO 48 LANGUAGES & PERFORMED IN OVER 140 COUNTRIES. ENSLER ALSO FOUNDED V-DAY, A GLOBAL MOVEMENT TO STOP VIOLENCE AGAINST WOMEN & GIRLS.

NOAM CHOMSKY

IS A LINGUIST, HISTORIAN, POLITICAL CRITIC & ACTIVIST. AUTHOR OF OVER 100 BOOKS, HE HAS FOR THE LAST 40 YEARS BEEN THE FOREMOST CRITIC OF NEO-IMPERIALISM.

PUSSY RIOT

IS A RUSSIAN FEMINIST PUNK BAND. IN 2012, 5 OF THE MEMBERS PERFORMED IN MOSCOW'S CATHEDRAL OF CHRIST THE SAVIOUR. IN PROTEST OF THE CHURCHES SUPPORT OF VLADIMIR PUTIN. NADEZHDA TOLOKONNIKOVA, MARIA ALYOKHINA & YEKATERINA SAMUTSEVICH WERE ARRESTED & SENTENCED TO TWO YEARS IN PRISON. SAMUTSEVICH HAS SINCE BEEN RELEASED ON APPEAL.

CHANTAL MOUFFE

IS A POLITICAL THEORIST & CURRENT DIRECTOR OF THE CENTRE FOR STUDY OF DEMOCRACY, AUTHOR OF THE "DEMOCRATIC PARADOX" AND "RETURN OF THE POLITICAL" A MAJOR PROPONENT OF THE IDEAS OF AGONISM" WITH MARXIST-RADICAL DEMOCRACY.

DAVID GRAEBER

IS AN ANTHROPOLOGIST & ANARCHIST. HEAVILY INVOLVED IN THE ANTI-GLOBALISATION AND OCCUPY MOVEMENTS. HE WAS ALSO THE INTELLECTUAL CENTRAL BANK. HIS "DEBT : THE FIRST 5,000 YEARS"

ALAIN BADIOU

IS A PHILOSOPHER. TAUGHT BY ALTHUSSER & AN ACTIVE PARTICIPANT IN THE MAY '68 UPRISINGS. FOR OVER 40 YEARS BADIOU HAS CONTRIBUTED CONTINUALLY TO MARXIST THOUGHT & CONTEMPORARY PHILOSOPHY. HIS KEY WORK "BEING & EVENT" ...

MOHAMMED BOUAZIZI (1984 - 2011)

WAS A TUNISIAN STREET VENDOR. ON 17TH DECEMBER 2010, IN PROTEST AGAINST CONFISCATION OF HIS WARES & HIS TREATMENT BY LOCAL AUTHORITIES, HE SET HIMSELF ON FIRE. THIS ACT IGNITED DEMONSTRATIONS & RIOTS WHICH BROUGHT DOWN THE PRESIDENT OF 23 YEARS. THIS IN TURN BEGAN A SCHISM INTO WHAT BECAME KNOWN AS THE ARAB SPRING.

SLAVOJ ŽIŽEK

IS A PHILOSOPHER & CULTURAL CRITIC. DRAWING RATHER HIS INTERESTS SPAN FROM LACANIAN PSYCHOANALYSIS & HEGELIAN DIALECTIC TO FILM THEORY & POPULAR CULTURE.

HOWARD ZINN (1922 - 2010)

WAS A HISTORIAN, PLAYWRIGHT & ACTIVIST. DEEPLY INVOLVED ON CIVIL RIGHTS, LABOUR & ANTI-WAR MOVEMENTS THROUGHOUT HIS LIFE ZINN'S ENDURING LEGACY IS THE BEST-SELLING "PEOPLES HISTORY OF THE UNITED STATES" WHICH IS NOW BECOME A KEY TEXT BOOK IN AMERICAN HISTORY CLASSES.

* APOLOGIES TO ALL

Dirty White Gold

The Seams of Sedition

Fashion. Darling, there's no bigger canvas than fashion. It's the practical craft, design and form shown everyday on the everyman. Democratic in its pervasiveness, it's the one type of art that everyone owns. Preying on our very human sense of vanity, we use fashion to show the world what we'd like the world to think of ourselves. Looking good.

Or not. Nearly 300,000 Indian farmers have committed suicide to get out of debt since 1995. A great number of those farm cotton in a part of India called Vidarbha—otherwise known as the Cotton Suicide Belt. Much of that cotton ends up in the jeans we wear, the shirts we drape and the knickers we whip off.

Much like the way food we eat is packaged in a way that divorces us from the source of that food (have you eaten a burger lately?), the origin of clothes we wear is obscured by a complicated web of suppliers and middlemen that distances consumer from producer. The label says 100% cotton and made in Britain but what does it really mean?

I'm making a film that will unpick the fashion value chain. We'll ask: when you bag a bargain, who pays for it? Is there room for ethics and sustainability in an industry that houses all the building blocks of capitalism and globalisation?

There is an estimated 80 billion new items of clothes made every year around the world. The global population hovers around 7 billion. Of that, 40 million of them are garment workers producing mainly fast fashion for the likes of H&M, Zara, Topshop and all the other places we're told to shop at if we want to keep 'on trend'. These fast-fashion outlets produce knock-offs of couture and designer styles pushed on consumers by lifestyle magazines and advertising. Like the Diesel brand campaign *For Successful Living*, the language used to sell preys on self-image and the human need for acceptance and recognition. You might not have a lot of money, but you can buy a cheap item of clothing modeled on a style that looks like it cost a lot of money for about the same price as your lunch. Who cares if it won't last more than a handful of washes? You've been Facebooked wearing it so you obviously can't be seen in it again. The tragedy.

'Looking good!'

'Thank you.'

A spoil-sport somewhere will invariably ruin our consumerist fun by pointing out that what you're wearing was probably made by a factory worker in Bangladesh earning £35 a month. The sequins on your daughter's blouse were probably sewn on by a small child. Clothes made by kids, for kids.

Few spoil-sports go beyond the factory when they discuss supply chain transparency. The factory produces clothes that are cut out of fabric that is woven out of thread that is spun at a mill that gets raw cotton from a broker who's bought it from a farmer who has been paid less than the minimum price for toiling away in the fields for months. Current international rates put cotton at around fifty pence per pound.

The corporatisation of production and agriculture means there's little room for a fair division of wealth at the bottom end of the cotton supply chain. Hanuman, a farmer we met, borrowed around 80,000 rupees from the bank so he could grow cotton on his five acre farm. He'd spent almost the entire loan on boxes of Bt [Bacillius Thuringienis] cotton seed and pesticides. The technology behind Bt is owned by Monsanto and is licensed to seed companies for use and sale across a range of crops—it's meant to repel a pest known as the bollworm but does little to stop other pests. The seed our farmer uses costs 950 rupees a kilo. Monsanto gets around a quarter of this amount.

Global warming means the rains that feed his crops either fail or arrive late. The narrative among farmers is that organic farming offers lower yield and that brokers at the market pay the same price for organic cotton as they do for conventionally grown Bt cotton. He's heard of the benefits of organic farming (lower costs, better health, etc.) but feels the risk of a lower yield is too much to take that gamble. Because last year's crop was less than satisfactory, he's borrowed more money to see if he can buy more seeds and chemicals to produce more this year. Rinse. Repeat. Welcome to the cycle of debt that drives farmers like Hanuman to drink the very pesticides they use to farm to kill themselves.

A common suggestion to 'fix' all this is to buy organic cotton. It's a start, but by no means a watertight solution. There are tight certification requirements that involve an economic hit the average small-scale farmer can't risk without proper support. At present, the market demands more than what organic farming can provide—especially when farmers are competing head-to-head with huge tracts of corporate farming carried out in America and China.

Here's where the activism comes in. Instead of accepting the things they can't change, some people are trying to change the things they cannot accept. Our film will take you on a journey from seed to shop—from fashion interns working for free to bolster an industry that's almost forgotten it's come out of art and expression, to the farmers toiling away so they can pay back the banks and loan sharks they've borrowed money from in order to eat. We're following the designers who incorporate ethics and sustainability into their clothes, the politicians fighting to debunk the idea that fashion is fickle feminine fluff and the scientists and economists with the knowledge and skills to offer alternatives. We'll be poking into corporate sponsorship and green initiatives and calling 'bullshit' on the biggest greenwashers.

To have a healthy and sustainable relationship with anything, you need trust and honesty. We're calling for transparency across the whole fashion supply chain. It's not an unreasonable demand. Just tell consumers where everything has come from and what impact that has on people and the environment. Bollocks to your 'market sensitive information'. If a bunch of university students can take on the likes of Adidas and Nike and get them to behave better, think of what entire switched-on countries can do. Nobody likes being cheated on. And cheaters eventually get found out.

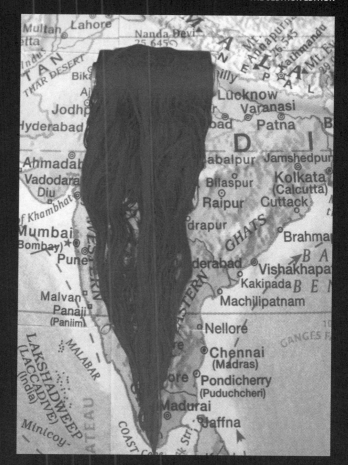

Blue/Green/Black
Being the Colours of Revolution

We are players in the game of Revolution: the long cat-and-mouse game between Power and The People that has been raging since our side first demanded democracy in antiquity. Over the many centuries of civilisation since, sometimes our progress has been slow and sometimes great leaps have been made in a week, when just the right spark comes along; but through it all, the guiding dream that unites us in a great historical chain has been the same: a people's democracy constituted by liberty, equality and community.

The world is a dark place now. Maybe we are in the Iron Age or the Kali Yuga or just the last gasp of a dying species. But I saw something magical emerge during our insurrectionary storms of 2011-2012 that gives us reason to keep living and fighting until the bitter end. I saw that you and I are now closer than ever—closer than any previous generation of humanity has ever been—to achieving the dream of people's democracy. And not just in my country or your country, but in every country. A people's democracy on a global scale is within reach... if only we have the courage.

I say courage because all too often it seems that The People shies away from its historical destiny. We get scared as a movement both when we fail and when we succeed. We look back on our past victories (The French Revolution, the defeat of fascism, May '68, Occupy Wall Street, etc.) and instead of seeing an inspiring proof that we can do it again and better, we accept cynicism and see only our excesses or the ways we failed to live up to our Ideal. We don't see how close we've come; we only see how far we still have to go. And looking back on history, it seems to me that most of the time The People have failed to take Power only because we let the status quo rule, out of deference to their elite and fear of their police.

Revolutionary politics progresses through spurts and experiments: the lessons of failed revolutions are internalized by one generation and new tactics are tried out decades later by the next. It is a slow game but every so often breakthroughs happen.

In the middle of the chaotic whirlwind that was Occupy, those of us participating in egging on the storm saw a sublime possibility emerge: mirage-like on the horizon, a tantalizing political vision appeared that used peer-to-peer technologies to connect the 99%'s revolutions from Egypt to China and America to Spain into a single social organism. If only for a brief moment, the internet gave us the ability to think, learn and act together at the same time, and everywhere at once. Hashtags became wormholes that collapsed space and time because it didn't matter if a jammer was in Madrid or Oakland, they were playing into the same Revolutionary Game. A united front became possible the moment we started fighting for a shared platform that was struggling to articulate itself.

That project was never completed. Occupy's intensity was not sustained long enough to achieve the next step: acting together at the same moment to target the same enemy, everywhere-at-once. To take down a global enemy of The People like Goldman Sachs, who has 72 offices worldwide, and send a chill down the spine of every other megacorp in the world. Now the next step in The People's long march to democracy is clear... and there is just enough time to pull it off.

Our greatest task as a species is to find words in our language for this new universalist-leaderless politics—and then fight for them. A hybrid blue-green-black politics that mobilizes The People in Cairo as well as it does in Beijing and New York City toward liberty, equality and community.

Blue—the colour of Intellect and Imagination—stands for mental environmentalism and our party's commitment to the vision of internet democracy championed by Anonymous, WikiLeaks and the Pirate Parties of Europe. Blue is about the spiritual insurrection: the revolution in our mind and inner-reality. It is our quest to steward the mental environment by balancing the rational (Intellect) with the irrational (Imagination) in politics and life and culture. A distinctly Blue psycho-politics gels a range of Left and Right organizations and concerns into a fighting force. Equally proponents of banning advertising in schools, protecting open source software, circumventing censorship, ensuring transparency of government, upholding public anonymity, liberating and de-commercialising information—the umbrella concern is with restoring our cultural and psychological health. Blue warriors vow to change the way information flows and to shake up the production of meaning in our society.

Green—the hue of Earth and Immortality—stands for the four-decade-strong resistance movement against environmental degradation, which we must win for a sane, sustainable future. Green is our collective project to find meaning in an eternal political act, our will to overcome mortal finitude with a multi-generational struggle to save the Earth and our children's children. Green politics is as much a response to death and life (and the terror of living through the ecological end-times) as it is a rejection of authoritarian-consumerism and ecological-fascism. Philosophers Alain Badiou and Slavoj Žižek have said that ecology is the opium of the masses because governments can use the environmental crisis as an emergency excuse for totalitarian rule. And it is well-documented that Australia and America's militaries are already training for an environmental apocalypse while others like Pentti Linkola and James Lovelock are openly calling for authoritarian environmentalism. We must tread a course between the need to implement some kind of global egalitarian environmental regulation—whether it be carbon rationing, emission limits, or maverick initiatives funded by a Robin Hood Tax—and the danger of force and impatience. Green requires that we think and act globally—a very dangerous thing.

'BLUEGREENBLACK is a vision that gives our long march a direction.'

Black—the tenor of Struggle and Justice—stands for our party's promise to abolish corporate personhood and institute a new post-capitalist global world order in which corporations bow to the will of the people. Black is the colour of Occupy and anarchism: nonviolence, horizontalism and innovation—the qualities that make our movement great. Black is our militant-edge but it is also our belief that no modern revolution will be successful without a steadfast promise to virtue—especially nonviolence and charity—in pursuing Justice. Guided by the light of Fidelity and Patience, Black stands for our commitment to humility, goodness and wisdom in pursuing our long-term goals. Fidelity is about never giving up hope. And it is also about resisting the temptations and distractions that are thrown in our path to lead us astray.

It may take years or decades or centuries to finally realize the #BLUEGREENBLACK vision—we do not know what the future holds. To enter a fight not knowing if you will see the final victory takes courage. But like the North Star that guides lost travellers, #BLUEGREEN-BLACK is a vision that gives our long march a direction. So wherever you are, look up and look around, and join the fight for people's democracy.

Squat the Lot!

A Call to Arms

Beyond the blatant injustice of it all, the most devastating thing about the news of the first two people being sent down under the new anti-squat law was their stories, printed in the paper. Squatting was not about moral arguments or political football anymore; for the first time, what we were reading about was the lives of these two men and the series of events that led to their imprisonment.

One had come to England, then lost his job and his girlfriend; the other had moved to London to find a job that didn't exist. Both were arrested for the heinous crime of attempting to put a roof over their heads, and soothe the plastic anger of a handful of powerful bigots who'd rather see buldings rot rather than try and understand the lives of those less privileged than them.

We've had it up to here with the oh-so-difficult lives of smug rich tossers who care more about the empty notion of property and the importance of leaving buildings empty, rather than occupied by the wrong kind. What we need is more real life stories, by people like you and me—and since I'm here anyway, I guess I'll go first.

Though I had to go back to the world of kind-of-renting last month, as the Graduate Without a Future I'm about to become needs a bit of stability (at least for now), there are a decent amount of stories I'd like to share. My experiences might not be the best or the worst you could read on the subject, but they're my own—if you feel like your tales are a hundred times more exciting than mine then, please, do write them up somewhere. Far from being an end in itself, this piece should merely be a beginning.

I guess I started squatting more or less by mistake: being part of the generation which got brutally radical- ised during the 2010–11 student protests, I first spent a few months around projects like the Really Free School, and toying with the idea of kindly telling my landlord to fuck off. It all happened quite suddenly, when someone offered me a room in the squatted Hand In Hand in Elephant & Castle, and a combination of shower, washing machine and sink breaking down simultaneously made me realise that I was perhaps paying too much for my crackden-like flat.

The windows were covered in Sitex, which made our pub look like a bunker, but the old furniture was still there and the great weather meant that we were spending all our time in the garden anyway. The possession order had been served already, so we knew we only had about a month left, but decided to build a swimming pool anyway. We'd spent days removing needles from the ground, as the building used to be a brothel-cum-genuine-crackden, so we felt like we'd gained the right to enjoy our backyard.

A part of me always felt that it was too good to be true and, sadly, it was. One evening, after having finished to lay down the bricks and mortar at the bottom of the pit we'd dug, we all went to bed, only to be woken up at seven by a squat mate shouting something about men in suits destroying the front door. Half dressed and definitely not awake, we all ran downstairs; at the window, we saw six over-tanned and comically muscular men taking turns with a sledge hammer to try and get through our door. And laughing about it. They tried and tried but, unable to get past our barricades, ended up using an angle grinder to break through a window.

Only then did they decide to inform us that the owners of the building had applied for another possession order at the High Court, which meant that they didn't have to noti- fy us of our impending eviction. We had, they announced, fourty five minutes to collect our belongings, otherwise they'd be locked in the pub without a chance of getting them back. The sequence of events was absurd: within an hour and a half, fourteen people went from asleep in their home to sitting on a pile of mattresses in the street, wondering what the fuck to do next.

Fast forward two weeks, via a friend's couch and a note on the squatters board of the 56a Infoshop, and onto an ex-laundry shop in Shoreditch. No shower—again—bucket powered toilets, but a direct view on Columbia Road flower market on Sundays, and a quiet place to enjoy the summer. Though once again, it all fell down too quickly: after a mere two weeks, two builders employed by the owners turned up, and threatened to evict us by force, whether we wanted it or not.

Terrified, we called our friends, who couldn't not come, then the police, explaining that we still had squatters rights, and were afraid they'd beat us up. A copper did turn up ten minutes later, but, rather unsurprisingly, did not take our side: when I asked if he realised that he was about to not only make three young women homeless for no reason, but also break the law himself, he shrugged and said that he knew, but could not care less. ACAB, indeed. The three pigs eventually decided to give us til the next morning to clear off, unless we wanted to get arrested for, well, y'know... something.

After an excruciating night of planning and discussions, we decided to go our separate ways. And once again, I ended up knocking on the door of a friend's house at dawn, with a pile of suitcases, and apologising profusely.

My third try was more successful—and nearly unbelievable. The building was absolutely gigantic, and its front, entirely made of glass, was directly on the banks of the Thames. It'd been built as a yuppie restaurant in Greenwich, but was so hidden from the main road that they never managed to get any customers. The bar was still full of posh glasses and cutlery, and though the (now customary) lack of shower or functioning toilets (and, this time, electricity) was a bit complicated, we all got used to it quickly enough. And to be frank, you can't say you know 'dysto-pian' til you've spent your evenings in a large and empty dining room lit exclusively by candles, and the lights from the Canary Wharf skyscrapers from across the river.

The charm of our big open space started to fade, how-ever, when some of us attempted to bring people home late at night, and effectively woke up absolutely everyone. Besides which, some of us had noticed a big mansion-like building in Walworth that'd been empty for several months. Secret plans were hatched, a team was formed, and once it was certain that it was unoccupied and likely to remain so, we got to work. As it turned out, we'd just hit the jackpot: while our friends who'd stayed in Greenwich got swiftly evicted by the owners boarding up the win-dows and literally leaving them in the dark, the Elephant & Castle squat is still proudly going, a year and a half later.

Not that it's really a squat anymore: when we moved in, and the owners expectedly turned up, they turned out to be surprisingly receptive to our plea, which was something along the lines of 'please don't kick us out, we're tired and we just want a home we can take care of.' Whilst relatively reasonable, this type of message is generally greeted by property owners with a big, bold 'fuck off', swiftly followed by a court date. But not this time: after a few meetings at their offices, we agreed on a month by month rolling-con-tract, a peppercorn rent of a pound a month, and got our-selves comfortable in our barely-falling-apart new house. It had everything: electricity, a shower, two kitchens—a bath!—and even a garden, which foxes ended up using more than us. Blame the terrible British weather.

This brings us to the end of my tale, which I would have liked to be a happy one, but sadly cannot be. In our time living in a stable squat, we ended up becoming a refuge for those less lucky than us—and boy, there was a lot of them. From the one who turned up on our doorstep with a black eye because he'd been beaten up by thugs hired by a land-lord, to those who kept getting kicked out again and again, legally or illegally, it simply never stopped. And the new law only made it worse: by strictly having to stay in commercial properties, many ended up in absolute shitholes, when there are so many residential places in London that could do with occupiers.

Sadly, this may only be the start: Parliament is planing to criminalise squatting in commercial properties as well, and if we let it, more and more people will be driven to the streets, or on to these few overcrowded places that are lucky to be legal and safe.

The theme of this edition is sedition, so I guess this is my call to arms. If you squat or used to squat, please talk and write and shout about it as much as you can. Our stories need to be heard. And if you're stuck in a shit flat in a shit part of London, wondering why the fuck you bother to spend most of your money on an overpriced rent, then start considering your options. The most beautiful thing about squatting is the sincere solidarity between everyone involved. As a community, it is stronger than anything I've seen, or was ever hoping to see. Whilst not wanting to fall into the cliché of the union making us strong, I so honestly believe that if more people could start squatting, nothing could stop us. And, quite frankly: if I've managed to do it for two years, then so can you. Or, in a nutshell: what the fuck are you waiting for?

STOP THE CRIMINALISATION OF SQUATTING

VISIT SQUASHCAMPAIGN ORG

TXT: CAT BROGAN

Keith

The only land he's ever owned
Is the six feet he's lying in.
He squatted the mortuary,
Didn't pay a penny.
No embalment, friends washed him.
Keith's skin splashed them.

Coffin made of reclaimed wood,
Loaded on a flatbed truck,
Driven by a pink haired punk.
Sound system smacking Surrey,
This is how the squatters bury.
Our numbers, the youngsters,
Surprised the natural burial owners.

Procession sunned,
An aisle of wild flowers.
Squatters dug and filled the hole.
A minute's noise. No celebrant,
One squamily and his family
For two hours, sharing stories.

'Squatter is unacceptable.'
Said the registrar to the next of kin.
She had activist put in.
Sent with the organ donation letter,
The strangest of all the afterlife admin.
His big hand prints on red paper,
Like staff send home from nursery,

Keith squats four new owners.
His kidneys clean another property,
(We're surprised they took his liver)
His heart beats a cage, still.

By Gove What a Naughty Boy

You hypocrite, first take the log out of your own eye, and then you will see clearly to take the speck out of your brother's eye.

Matthew 7:5 King James Bible

I can't go to university because of Michael Gove. The government paid for Michael Gove's degree, but he thinks that if they pay for mine, it'll make me immoral. If I don't struggle, I won't understand the value of my education. If they take their feet off our heads for a moment, let us come up for air, we'll all be ruined. Education is not for everyone. Michael Gove is making us strong.

Did his government-funded degree make Michael Gove immoral? Is Michael Gove morality? Did he write his name down the side of the King James bible and deliver it to students to encourage them with their struggle? Michael Gove is worth a million pound. Repeat again and repent, sinner: Michael Gove is making us strong.

AN ANARCHIST
GUIDE TO GOLD

Anarchist Economics

Some aspects of the dominant economic system we are all a part of—are all subjected to—are so ubiquitous and naturalised that they exist largely unquestioned, even by those that make the interrogation of power their duty. To ask the kind of questions that might genuinely threaten the entrenched corporate and private banking structures blighting our existences, our understanding must go beyond the puppet theatre of media driven politics, into the real terrain of capital: finance, markets and money.

Since 1971, when Richard Milhous Nixon closed the gold window to pay for the Vietnam war, so called 'free market capitalism' has been underpinned by a global fiat monetary system backed by nothing more than the faith and credit of individual governments; banks create money as debt, and government's got their back. Despite the unprecedented scale of government debt, and the ever diminishing trust in politicians, this faith in the dollar, the Euro and the pound largely abides; a belief akin to trusting a proven liar and committed debt-junkie to make good on his IOUs and promises.

To be effective, protest against corporate banking hegemony must rupture the blanket acceptance of government-backed, bank-created fiat debt-money. A movement of resistance must sew doubt in the minds of the faithful—not just in the 'fairness' of corporations and banks, but in our most commonly held conceptions about money. The emperor's new clothes are made of dollars and pounds; we must train our eyes to see through money and, as ugly as the reality may be, reveal the emperor's gross nakedness.

So let it be shouted in the streets: there's nothing there! The dollar is worthless and the pound is too.

The threat to power of this anti-fiat position can be guaged by two relatively recent 'interventions'. It is no secret that the West went to war in both Iraq and Libya to stake bomb-backed claims on oil. What's less debated is the evidence that the violent dictators in both those countries were snuffed out because they planned to sell oil in something other than dollars—Euros in Iraq, and a pan-African gold-backed currency in Libya. Overtly jeopardising the dollar's supremacy as the world reserve currency would have set an extremely dangerous precedent for those institutions that dominate the financial system.

As long as money could be easily created—essentially out of thin air—to exchange for oil, Western governments blithely ignored the oppression and violent abuses taking place in these countries; only when the dollar's (and, by extension, the pound's) desirability was questioned were the bombs and war-planes unleashed. The essence of their global economy is creating dollars to buy oil, and killing anyone who doubts their creation's worth. These wars make clear that, instead of gold, the fiat system is now backed by military might.

The money exchange merely 'connects strangers as strangers', and relations based on something other than this exchange should be fundamental to a resistance movement. A global communism in which money is unnecessary is a distant, utopian dream; but if part of money's power is creating connections between those who have no connections, the consistency of these connections—the authority to decide what money is—must be wrestled from the those in power. Many activist groups, charities and unions are starting to realise that the financial system is rigged by banks and protected by the political class; they need a method for undermining the monopoly on the determination of money—a practical, immediate alternative to the current fiat currency grid.

There are several arguments that suggest gold can be integral to this shift away from the dictatorship of fiat.

Converting pounds to gold takes money out of the fractional reserve banking system and prevents it being multiplied as debt. Gold's value is based not on the promises of corrupt, corporate managed governments, but on its intrinsic natural properties, including it's high malleability, resistance to corrosion, and it's near universal recognisability. These attributes combined with finite availability mean gold is historically unrivaled as the best method humans have found to store wealth. Free from the requirement of laws to imbue it with value, it's no coincidence that people who have traditionally lacked faith in central banks, and looked for freedom from state control, have used gold; as a currency, it is anarchist in essence.

But for those interested in radical new ways of forming societies, it would be a mistake to argue for an outright return to a gold standard; we need to continually destabilise prevailing conceptions of money, not replace one dominant paradigm with another. However, gold can exist as money in a multiplicity of non-state currencies. The growing use of bitcoin, a digital currency developed in the wake of the financial system's attempt to starve Wikileaks of funding, show there are workable alternatives. While bitcoin shares gold's freedom from government involvement, it has attributes that set it apart, and compliment gold's wealth preserving characteristics. Any number of bitcoins, potentially worth millions of pounds, can be transported as weightless data encrypted on a memory stick, or sent through the internet. So with a currency like this, who needs banks? You may baulk at the idea of purely digital money, but concerns over a unit of exchange backed by only an algorithm seem redundant when we consider how much of our infrastructure is already run by computers—and the fact that around 97% of all the pounds sterling in circulation are merely digital data as it is.

As well as returning to an ancient form of metal money, and becoming familiar with a contemporary, computer-based one, we can also look to new forms developing in the currency eco-system, including local variants and time-banks. Mayer Amschel Rothschild was right when he said 'let me issue and control a nation's money and I care not who writes the laws'; to shake off our financial oppression we need a money they can't control, a distributed money, free from the state and its corporate banking parasites. There is a way out from under the fiat currency yoke, a way to exit the great capitalist casino and cash in your chips, the ones with the Queen's head on them: swap them for gold, get some bitcoins. The pound is a worthless promise and the emperor is shivering in his transparent coat.

Pankhurst was sent to prison for publishing seditious articles in **The Workers Dreadnought**. The article which landed her in jail was called **'Discontent on the Lower Deck'**

In the dock, Sylvia was unapologetic, standing up and declaring that: **"Capitalism is the wrong system of society and it has to be smashed—I would give my life to smash it."**

23rd OCTOBER 1920
SYLVIA PANKHURST
Tried for Sedition
Manor House, London

Sylvia set up the East London Federation of Suffragettes in 1913 in Bow, which in 1916 became the Workers' Suffrage Federation. Interested in working class feminism and armed with a visionary understanding of intersectionality and a socialist spirit she set up a milk distribution and medical centre for sick babies, opened a toy factory to provide work for women and created a cut price restaurant serving four hundred meals a day.

She opposed the war, published anti-war statements and by 1920 she ended up in court under sedition charges. The article which landed her in jail called for the dismantling of the British Empire and for revolution in the Royal Navy. She was given a six month sentence. Like many of her suffragette colleagues, she had been in and out of prison since she was first sent to Holloway in 1906 - arrested for protesting the imprisonment of other suffragettes.

The Suffragettes rushed Parliament to demand the right for women to vote but Sylvia rushed more than a political building: she rushed capitalism itself. Like many activists today she refused to underplay her power or to give up: she had faith her actions were making a difference.

As Zoe Williams wrote recently on the power of the boycott:
"However trivial your custom may seem the alternative is to overplay your insignificance, to turn your impotence into a self-fulfilling prophecy."

Some people think that using fossil fuels to move our machines is civilized, profitable and a great sign of progress.	But carrying on as normal and refusing to take action will lead us into a future with a 4 degree temperature rise.	In a 4 degree world an extra billion people would have difficulties accessing clean and regular water supplies, and 6 million km² of farmland will become less productive.	Researchers from the Walker Institute and the University of Reading have found that if we reduce global carbon emissions now we could limit the impact of climate change by 29-85%.	Bringing in swift measures to reduce carbon emissions and keeping future global temperature rises within 2 degrees could prevent 50 million people from experiencing water shortages, and 100-180 million people wouldn't be at risk of flooding.	We might not see the benefits of our actions until 2030 or even later but we would have changed the world.

RESPECT YOUR POWER

1. Ram at the doors of power as hard as you can and shout your very loudest. Speak to everyone who will listen. Write, blog, tweet, march, and act. Whether it is writing a letter to your MP or locking on to parliament, never doubt your power.

2. Refuse to buy things you don't need. Shop locally, return excessive packaging, be offended by bottles of water, buddy up with your local organic farmer, and mismatch your charity shop bought or swished clothing with pride.

3. Keeping faith in your agency even when you can't be sure of the outcome is tough. There are so many people trying to make things better so join a community, make a community, and be a community.

4. Be nobody's darling. At work or college, in a public meeting or an activist meeting, refuse to be silenced.

WORDS: Siobhan Grimes **DESIGN:** Alice Howarth-Booth **FOR:** Climate Rush
www.climaterush.co.uk Climate change action inspired by the suffragettes.

CLIMATE RUSH

All Animals are Equal

But Some are More Equal than Others

Be the inferior to no one, nor of any one be the superior.

William Saroyan

Lots of people say, 'oh, leave off the royal family, they do a lot for charity, y'know?' If I was an unemployed multi-millionaire, I'd do a lot for charity, too. Many fine people do work for charities; most manage to get there every day without the aid of a chauffeur. That the royal family are themselves a charity should negate any charitable work they do; why not cut out the middle man and give the cash straight to those in need? This might avoid parties, palaces and peacocks being skimmed off the top.

'Yes, but what about the tourism, man? Don't forget the tourism!' It is as patronising as it is insulting to the entire nation to suggest that people would not visit our green and pleasant land without the Windsors—that the entire sum of our cultural worth resides in the crown and its cronies. France doesn't have a monarchy, but plenty of people go to Paris to see the Louvre. I hear the food's half-decent too.

We Brits love democracy. We're mired in misadventure all around the globe, obliterating foreigners and putting our own sons and daughters in danger in its name. Yet, in our own country, we're happy with the hypocrisy of having a picture of a lady on our stamps and sterling who believes she deserves to be there by divine right—because God said so. And simply because, for as long as we care to remember, it has always been so. Doesn't democracy deserve better? Are we so unimaginative?

Uprising

The Crisis of Civilization and the Struggle for the Global Commons

The last half decade has seen the persistence of social protests in various forms, including civil disobedience and mass demonstrations. From the Occupy movement across the Western world, to the Arab Spring in the Middle East and North Africa; from riots in European capitals, to the current protests in Cyprus: uprisings have become a regular feature of life.

With the world reeling under the impact of banking collapses, austerity, environmental crisis, energy woes and rocketing food prices, it's no wonder that people everywhere are rising up and demanding change.

But at the heart of these disparate uprisings is a single global struggle: between the people and profit, for access to the planet's precious land, water, energy, raw materials and resources—a struggle for the global commons.

Over three hundred years ago, the struggle kicked-off in a major way when the seeds of English capitalism were planted amidst mass evictions of peasants from public lands. Formerly landed peasants, who were compelled by threat of force to pay tribute (a percentage of their produce), to local lords, now ended up as a new, landless proletariat. They had no choice but to sell their labour power for wages to the lords who now owned and controlled what was once their land. This process of enclosure gradually enforced a new social condition—the dispossession of people from access to the sources, means and technologies of production—that was, and remains, the fundamental basis of modern capitalism.

But in 1649, Gerrard Winstanley gathered together fifty-odd supporters to challenge the new order with a radical message: to make 'the Earth a common treasury for all... not one lording over another, but all looking upon each other as equals in the creation.' Occupying vacant and public lands in Surrey, Buckinghamshire, Kent, and Northamptonshire, Winstanley's rag-tag movement of 'Diggers' uprooted the centralisation of economic power with a call for equal access for all, growing their own food, and distributing it to the public for free. Until local landowners hired thugs and mercenaries to force them out; although the Diggers turned to the government for support, they were ignored and forced to disband.

But the struggle for the global commons had only just begun. Fast forward to the 21st century, and despite the wonders of modern industry and global communications, in many ways little has changed. In countless communities around the world—in the UK, in Spain, in Greece, in Africa, Latin America and India—the spirit of the Diggers lives on as poor people, farmers, workers, and peasants find themselves making a last stand between the common land they own collectively, and global corporations in pursuit of ever greater profits.

Ultimately what we are facing is a struggle between two visions of the world. Global civilizational crises of climate change, energy depletion, food scarcity, economic meltdown, and violent conflict are interconnected symptoms of a protracted collapse process of the broken, neoliberal model. As this model increasingly crumbles under the weight of its own sustainability, the battle for new, more viable alternatives intensifies.

At stake is a new, emerging paradigm of civilization based on a vision of a global commons for all; new only in the sense that such a notion has never been practiced before on a global scale, for it is rooted in ideas and norms that traditional peoples all over the world have implemented in different ways.

At the core of our current civilizational model is a dramatic inequality in access to the Earth's resources, coupled with an ideology that sees those resources as nothing more than a playing field for a minority of members of the human species to accumulate material wealth without limits. The vast majority of the world's resources—not just monetary wealth, but land, resources and raw materials—is owned and controlled by a tiny minority of states, monarchs, aristocratic families, banks and corporations.

It is no accident that the Queen of England (arguably the harbinger of contemporary global capitalism before its supersession by the United States) is the world's largest landlord, owning about 6.6 billion acres of land. That is one-sixth of the Earth's land surface. Put another way, 1,318 corporations own 80 per cent of the world's wealth, and out of those, a tiny interlocking nexus of 147 'super corporations' own half of that.

And as civilizational crises deepen, the response of this nexus of power has been to attempt to increasingly centralise its control of the Earth's last remaining untapped resources. The last half decade alone has seen a dramatic acceleration of land grabs—largely in the less developed countries. In 2008–2009, about 22 million hectares were subject to acquisition, according to the World Bank, rising to about 80 million in 2011. Overall, the last decade has seen a total of 203 million hectares acquired or being negotiated. This process, driven by varying combinations of political patronage, violence and market forces, is leading to the escalating displacement of poor people from commonly owned lands, and the transfer of their land into centralised ownership of foreign corporations and investors.

What is driving this process? Short answer: a civilization in overshoot. Across the board, as resources are depleting, scarcity is increasing and prices are rising. Since 2005, the world food price index has doubled, and despite stabilising this year, remains at record levels. Simultaneously, the global oil index in the same period has roughly tripled, and despite promises about shale gas and fracking, even the International Energy Agency concedes that the age of cheap oil is well and truly over. Other commodities are also rocketing in value—from metals to timber to chemicals—with one study by Inverto AG noting a 'systematic shortage' leading to 'supply bottlenecks', meaning companies raise prices and pass costs onto consumers.

Unfortunately, even those who claim to be at the vanguard of responding to these crises can be part of the problem. Chris Martenson, for instance, is a former executive of the giant pharmaceutical firm Pfizer and an ex Vice President at US defence conglomerate, Science Applications International Corporation (SAIC), who now devotes all his time to writing presciently about the 'triple crisis' of environmental, energy and economic collapse—but has very few meaningful solutions. Instead of advocating systemic transformation, or challenging capitalism in its current form, he effectively advocates a strengthening of the most regressive neoliberal principles: Individuals should seek 'resilience' by investing what remains of their wealth in high value stocks and shares—largely commodities like farming land, which we have seen are rocketing in price—based on Martenson's strategic investment advice. This sort of 'elitist survivalism' is ultimately part of the problem: encouraging those with capital to maximise their control of the world's wealth, as crises kick in, in order to remain safe amidst imminent civilizational collapse. Meanwhile, the rest of the world's population can go to hell in a handbasket.

As the persistence of uprisings proves, of course, it won't work—people will not simply lay back while power seals its destruction of the Earth.

And civilization is unlikely to collapse so imminently. Despite that, while things will get worse before they get better, the trends we are seeing today are illustrative of a fundamental and often forgotten reality: that the 21st century signals the unequivocal demise of the carbon age.

The failure to come to terms with this fact and its implications is symptomatic of the delusion of our current era.
Whatever happens, by the end of this century (if not far
earlier) our civilization in its current form will not—cannot
exist. We will either have overshot, drastically and fatally, with horrifying consequences for humanity, or we will
have transitioned to something far more in parity with our
environment—or somewhere in between.

That is why the choices we make now, the struggles
we choose to partake in, will be critical in determining the
course of our future. We do not have the option of pessimism and fatalism—there's enough of that to go around.
Our task is to work together to co-create viable visions
for what could be, and to start building those visions now,
from the ground up.

TXT: VENUS CUMARA

Reclaim Love

Ten Years On

Standing up against war and oppression of any kind is indeed very honourable; it has now become normal to focus our attention on the atrocities we see occuring in our world. Lets face it, though, how many people truly want to listen to complaints? The complaints of our people have become such a normal part of our culture that this voice is being overlooked—it is now heard as the voice that you can't bear to listen to.

How can we re-amplyify the voice of the people—and why do we continue to manifest bigger and bigger shadows as we move further and further form our collective dream? Surely, to live as one in peace is the dream of all those alive in the world today, whether this is a conscious or an unconscious dream, and no matter how it is manifested. Why do we focus on what we don't want, when we have a choice: complain or cure?

The Reclaim Love movement and events began in 2003 to act as a platform for what I—as poet and activist—perceived to be the most obvious solution to the lack of peace and the growing list of complaints in the world. But just because it is probably the most obvious solution doesn't make it easy—it is often the most overlooked, and even ridiculed, solution.

Pioneering a loving movement in a collective consciousness so stuck in keeping its focus away from Love is not easy. But not easy does not mean impossible. People who long to live in peace feel afraid of the word Love and are worried to be associated with it. They think its 'hippy', as if hippy was a bad thing. Well, ask yourself, why would the CIA have been so intent on stopping a movement that was promoting Love, Peace and Unity? Love has Power.

Ten years of Reclaim Love have passed and it's clear that it has only just begun. This platform has given public spaces around the world back to so many peaceful people, to be fearlessly fun and loving with one another. On the nearest Saturday to Valentine's Day, people come together and celebrate what unites us and keeps us strong. In a world where people are repeatedly being taught to fear and compete with each other, the divine abnormality of these free gatherings is growing joyfully, and uniting communities across the globe.

This year I revealed a new dream for the future of Reclaim Love. This is to carve out a moment in infinity, where all those alive in the world will stop, as we do at Reclaim Love, to graciously and joyously honour the Love that unites, sustains and keeps us at peace.

It's got to be bigger than Christmas. Christmas is too exclusive. We need a non-religious moment in which we stop what we are doing and come together. We need a moment where we stand side by side in our communities to celebrate and give thanks for Love. In this moment we plant our visions and our seeds of Love for ourselves and for the generations to come as we repeat from our hearts, in our local language, the words:

'May all the beings in all the worlds be happy and at peace.'

We do it every year 3.30pm local time on the nearest Saturday to Valentines. Standing up for Love is brave, fun and honorable. You may get some strange looks at first but you won't be overlooked.

Millbank for HR

*No one in their right mind could claim that the violence of
students in London today is justified.*

The Telegraph

1.

It's challenging to think the most politically joyous day
I remember
—and the most ecstatic news bulletin I'd turned on in years—
was that of the young marchers ransacking Millbank
in the late autumn of 2010. This, I felt, was sedition... At last!
No, not drawing a brilliant cartoon of some Tory basilisk,
or writing an iconic protest song, or devising a modern dance,
or even finding the just words for a literary satire
to call forth Puppet Ubu from his shit-caked lair again
but an action that transcended the artistic, the aesthetic,
a replay of Bastille. That I laughed and cheered on 10/11/10
so fulsomely, so earnestly, drunk on nothing but the facts,
sending messages to the round earth's PC-screened corners,
later made me ask myself if something was amiss.
Perhaps I—or many of us—had been warped by the control-machine
of Conservatism, and made incapable of finer feelings?

2.

To hear the young had smashed into the Tory forcefield
—think of the name Millbank, the very concept of Millbank:
a fusion of Blake's satanic mills with the banking system—
seemed like an orgiastic victory. They'd struck a blow,
ferocious cherubs with Asian bows-and-arrows,
not by throwing eggs at individuals or fire extinguishers at no one
but by attacking the furry, malodorous Ubu of an institution,
punishing an office ceremonially, humiliating a party HQ,

one that corrodes the morals of those who work in it
with powergames and endgames
'forever and ever amen',
by assaulting Tory architecture in black hoods and leopardskins
along the chameleon smile of the Thames.

3.

The students shocked everyone out of their automatism
that day. Authority was rug-pulled. That night: masterless revels
in an upside-down realm, with a cavalcade of royals and retainers
looking a thousand years old in slow-rolling contraptions,
and a palpable mass joy not felt in years. London throbbed
with frisson, and the vibration of the island was raised.
Those hecklers who cavilled of 'self-interested students'
had missed the point that—while the sad majority
have become inured to suffering Tory-dealt attritions
retaliating at best with cartoons, songs, dances, poems
or, at worst, buying shares in loss leader alcohols—
a new generation had stood up to Goliath and hurled
the full force of its slingshot, right at his walnut brains.
Images of the spider-webbing glass, the spray-painted As
and youths kicking and chanting at yellow phalanxes
of Met baboons, seemed to my bruised and fragile psyche
a vision of the coming Eros and redemption

4.

(even if there's something wrong with me for thinking it
or something wrong with you for reading this)

COPYRIGHT

PATENTS

.../PEOPLE/DEMOCRACY/TECHNOLOGY/　　　/CENSORSHIP/...

DIGITAL RIGHTS MATTER
PROTECT THEM NOW

/WHISTLEBLOWING/　　　/GOVERNMENT TRANSPARENCY/　/

FREEDOM OF SPEECH

PRIVACY

#DIGITALRIGHTSMATTER
#PPUK

DIGITALRIGHTSMATTER.COM
PPUK.ORG.UK

DEPLETED URANIUM WEAPONS

CAMPAIGN AGAINST DEPLETED URANIUM
HTTP://WWW.CADU.ORG.UK/

ICBUW – INTERNATIONAL COALITION TO BAN DEPLETED URANIUM WEAPONS
HTTP://WWW.BANDEPLETEDURANIUM.ORG/EN/INDEX.HTML

ICBUW VIDEO – WHEN THE DUST SETTLES – DEPLETED URANIUM
HTTP://WWW.YOUTUBE.COM/WATCH?V=ULQTBWQDDT0

ACTIVIST DONNA MULHEARN BLOG – SEE. 7TH MARCH 2013
HTTP://DONNAMULHEARN.COM/

BRITISH NUCLEAR WEAPONS TEST SITES IN AUSTRALIA

SITE MAP & ADDITIONAL INFORMATION
HTTP://AUSTRALIANMAP.NET/CATEGORY/NUCLEAR-WEAPON-TEST-SITE/

4 SEARCH TERMS FOR WWW.WIKIPEDIA.ORG: BRITISH_NUCLEAR_TESTS_AT_MARALINGA /
EMU_FIELD / OPERATION_HURRICANE / OPERATION_TOTEM

MARALINGA & EMU FIELD ARE ON THE LANDS OF THE MARALINGA TJARUTJA
(SITE VISIT PERMITS) HTTP://WWW.MARALINGATJARUTJA.COM/

A TOXIC LEGACY – BRITISH NUCLEAR WEAPONS TESTING IN AUSTRALIA
HTTP://WWW.AEC.GOV.AU/PUBLICATIONS/PREVIOUS2009ERIES/CL/3/1-28/VANGUARD/CH6.HTML

MARALINGA: THE BLACK MIST INCIDENT
HTTP://COOBERPEDYREGIONAL.TIMES.WORDPRESS.COM/2010/04/28/MARALINGA-THE-BLACK-MIST-INCIDENT/

COMBINED VETERANS' FORUM INTERNATIONAL. EMAIL THE INTERNATIONAL CRIMINAL COURT
HTTP://NUCLEARHISTORY.WORDPRESS.COM/2013/01/21/EMAIL-TRAFFIC-4-DENNIS-HAYDEN/

Hey you Brits,

your government has used toxic

radioactive weapons on its own people, on
Indigenous Australians and on Australia's service people,
and also those whom it was supposed to be 'liberating' in ███.
They are actively working to bury it. British born ex-Veterans have recently
claimed your government and has committed 'crimes against humanity'.

Nuclear Veterans & Aboriginal Australians, including the Pitjantjatjara & Maralinga Tjarutja,
are systematically denied records and information relating to a toxic catastrophe that will
unfold for generations, by both the British and Australian governments regarding these tests
in the 1950's & 1960's is ongoing.

Additionally, it has done the same again in the Gulf. Modern heavy battle weapons made of Depleted Uranium.
Growing evidence of birth defects & other serious medical complications near battle sites, & the claim that it is impossible to
account for these toxic materials, are a repeat of long term denial & obstruction, symbolically beginning with
UK Prime Minister Anthony Eden in 1953, when faced with knowledge of genetic damage was quoted as saying:

'It is a pity, but we cannot help it'.

Fuck your government.

WARNING

TEST SITE
TOTEM 1
A BRITISH ATOMIC
WEAPON WAS TEST
EXPLODED HERE ON
15 OCT 1953

RADIATION HAZARD
RADIATION LEVELS FOR
A FEW HUNDRED METRES
AROUND THIS POINT MAY
BE ABOVE THOSE
CONSIDERED SAFE FOR
PERMANENT OCCUPATION

GROUND ZERO URANIUM
EMU FIELD,
South Australia

GAME
not
OVER

ENGLAND IS THE WRONG PLACE FOR A BOY WHO WANTS TO SMASH WINDOWS. BECAUSE HE IS RIGHT, OF COURSE, HE SHOULD SMASH WINDOWS. ANYBODY GROWING UP IN ENGLAND WITHOUT A SERIOUS URGE TO SMASH WINDOWS IS PROBABLY TOO DUMB FOR HELP

- HUNTER S. THOMPSON

STRIKE! MAGAZINE
THE SUMMER OF ...

POLITICS
PHILOSOPHY
ART
SUBVERSION
SEDITION

ISSUE___3

To be hopeful in bad times is not just foolishly romantic. It is based on the fact that human history is a history not only of cruelty, but also of compassion, sacrifice, courage and kindness.

What we choose to emphasise in this complex history will determine our lives. If we see only the worst, it destroys our capacity to do something. If we remember those times and places—and there are so many—where people have behaved magnificently, this gives us the energy to act, and at least the possibility of sending this spinning top of a world in a different direction.

And if we do act, in however small a way, we don't have to wait for some grand Utopian future. The future is an infinite succession of presents, and to live now as we think human beings should live, in defiance of all that is bad around us, is itself a marvelous victory

Evening's Gentle Sun

Bored, Hungry, Shattered, Skint, and Why that Matters

The evening's gentle sun is sinking, and the red skies above the soon-to-be demolished council high-rises carry an air of extraordinary beauty, simplicity and peace.

Beneath the palisades of CCTV posts, surplus street-signs and rolling billboards, I cycle through familiar streets, a nice way to pass the time and keep fit when you can't afford to meet friends in pubs or eat much except processed foods (frozen, tinned or dried). The bike's seen better days but it's a gift from my Dad, from the last generation of workers who can still expect a pension—at the expense of long-frozen wages and delayed retirement. I could go back home, but my head's still reeling from arguing with my partner again about how skint we are and the growing number of things we can't fix. So I'll keep cycling a little further, marvelling at the beauty of the sky this evening.

I wrote a book called Negative Capitalism: Cynicism in the Neoliberal Era about a year ago, while I was still in work and fizzed up from the then-recent events of the student protests and August 2011 riots. Unlike others I was weary of reading, I didn't want to add another condescending Return to Marx text, nor a denunciation of everyday life without a sense of humour or happy ending. Instead, it drew up a shopping list of new means and ideas of revolt, proceeding from strategic optimism. But things have changed in many respects, shifting into a more indistinct moment, an inter-regnum between the collapsed political legitimacy of neo-liberalism since 2008 and some new dark night of reaction and opportunity. That the book has just been published by

Zero Books now is strange for me, and the work reads like a love-letter or note written by yourself five or ten years ago, animated by a foreign, naive bravura for transformation and revenge that has become dulled over the stalemates and no-score draws of the last few months.

In particular, the voice of James Connolly, Irish socialist revolutionary and one of the leaders of the Easter 1916 Uprising, booms out and addresses our contemporary melancholia, a near-century on: 'the great appear great to us only because we are on our knees: let us rise.'

Roll Connolly's words around in your mouth again, feel the syllables with your tongue. Though all forms of the British establishment have lost all legitimacy and moral authority—be they politicians, bankers, newspapers, police forces, monarchy, church or the army—we, the collective body of people living and working in Britain, have yet to confront them, bring them to justice, or meaningfully prevent their cuts and impositions. For that reason their class war continues, with government policies motivated only to benefit the most wealthy: privatisation and private tendering of public services and justice, tax cuts for high earners and businesses, QE for banks, removal of legal aid and the welfare state, eviction of the poor from inner cities, de-skilling labour, reducing university access and teaching/learning standards, and so on.

Some people are toying with a bogus idea of national independence, straight out of an episode of Downton Abbey. It's compelling that images of country-pubs or cucumber sandwiches on village greens should appeal to the disenfranchised of the bland suburban sprawls and Tesco towns of the M25, Midlands and Home Counties. But nationalism offers an immediate win-or-lose, us-or-them narrative, which in disorientated times appeals—offers clarity and stability, a purpose. I reckon it's time we started thinking about our own narratives.

Our narrative could begin with a question: for how much longer do they dare ignore our anger?

It leads me to four observations. First, evidence of popular anger is everywhere, in ways activists always underestimate. The crimes of politicians and banker are well-known and recited often, but so far with a sigh of defeat or cynicism. It's as if misrepresentation and dishonesty are undesirable but necessary features of a democracy. This anger races around without an outlet like a bee in a hot room, repeatedly colliding against that one bit of the window that's still shut. Occasionally it erupts in spectacularly self-destructive and horrible ways, like psychotic killing sprees in schools, malls or high-streets, or in self-immolations or suicide bomb attacks.

It's a matter of tactics, then. Aside from the passive marches from frustration to impotence, or the self-serving reactionaries of TV political debate, our discontents are electively expressed online. Untold labour is expended in e-petitions, comments, blogging and social media exchanges, and great ideas are developed and put to the collective test. Problem is when these words and symbols are mistaken for political activity. The recently-leaked NSA online surveillance programme demonstrates that our western political leaders are to indiscriminately record every communication each of us makes, and in their paranoiac endeavour, can count on the collusion of the handful of web/software magnates who have now monopolised the net. Online radicalism becomes not just a talk shop but a honey trap.

Besides, even well-directed talk changes nothing when the political establishment has no intention of listening to anyone except the rich. Perhaps it's not a problem with our words, but a problem with the question. They have no obligation to ignore or hear our anger. In the UK at least, there is no meaningful political constitution or moment of consent, a social contract, for citizens. I think there should be. Politicians are only accountable to those interests that sustain them—wealthy donors mainly, but also security forces. With political parties in all countries now in practice identical, the interests of one part of the electorate or another are irrelevant.

Lastly, our situation isn't unique to our country or specific era. Since the 19th century there has been talk each decade of an age of anxiety, of the necessity of austerity. It's a type of language typically used to justify bankers and politicians becoming richer whilst the working class have their living conditions substantially reduced. Across Europe and America, the situation's similar: tax cuts for the rich and privatisation of public services, paid for by wage decreases, rising rents and prices. But the error is in seeing anything new in this. Though this is neoliberalism, it follows the same logic as 19th century capitalism. If anything, we're going back in time, with workhouses, pawnshops, food-banks, overcrowding, poverty ghettos, illiteracy and a lifetime of debt on our Victorian horizon.

The problem facing anyone with a mind or heart who seeks to oppose the miserable circumstances above is that the new political act of the 21st century has not yet been discovered. The first stone has not yet been thrown, and genuinely new tactics of resistance and creation await discovery. It could involve a simple narrative that mobilises collective power, that speaks of collective desire, that isn't just online, or passive, or strategically irrelevant like the march, petition, or town hall grumbledown. They will hear your anger once you force them to listen. Though this expression must emphasise not the clarity or meaning of the words, what has been so long quibbled and theorised over, but the power and charisma of their expression.

With that, I step away from the soapbox of certainties and back into the night's bruised light, the black and the gold of streetlamps beating against bust-up pavements and bursting buddleia. I'm bored, hungry, shattered, skint. There's nowhere left to escape to but back the here and now, and for that I'm glad. Nothing less than a basic quality of life is what we ask for. In our struggles for the present, nothing less than the future is at stake.

Bitcoin or Bust

An International Currency for International Communities

In the past two weeks I received two paychecks. The first was for 7.6365 BTC, from an employer in Romania for doing some programming work. The three other programmers I was working with were based in England, Israel and China. The second, for 4.16 BTC, was from Bitcoin Magazine, a company with its chief editor in the EU, its CEO and the person in charge of marketing in Atlanta, and myself in Toronto, Canada. When my friends ask about the magazine, one of the questions they always ask is 'where are the offices?', or 'where is your company based?' And to this, I have come up with a succinct, and snappy, answer: 'we're based in the cloud.' And it's true: every day, we communicate over Skype, share files over email, Mega and Google Docs, and, of course, send and receive money using Bitcoin. And once everything is put together, the thousands of kilometres separating us from each other fade into insignificance.

The story is a common one in the Bitcoin world. Many Bitcoin businesses were built by a team of founders living on completely different continents who first found each other on an internet forum, and through years of hard work, determination, enjoyment and suffering, the sometimes chaotic ups and downs of the Bitcoin market, have become not just lifelong partners, but also true friends. It's true that, in theory, most of the transactions that have been conducted with Bitcoin could have also been done with Paypal, bank transfers or Western Union; in practice, however, in my own experience and that of hundreds of thousands of others, Bitcoin wins by miles.

Part of the difference can be explained by Bitcoin's intrinsic properties: its fees are indeed much lower; its semi-anonymous and uncontrolled nature allows innovative businesses to grow without fear of getting arbitrarily shut down by Paypal or the banks; and as far as convenience goes, 'Give me an address' followed by pasting the Bitcoin address into the 'To:' field of a Bitcoin wallet and clicking 'Send' is hard to beat. There is, however, another effect at play. If Bitcoin was just about cutting a few percent out of merchants' transaction fees, simplifying payment forms or breaking the monopoly of the banks, then businesses and landlords would not be giving 20% discounts for making a transaction with Bitcoin when that transaction could just as easily, and legally, have been carried out via cash or Paypal.

Aside from being an often superior method of payment, Bitcoin has also come to serve another function: that of a signalling device. By accepting Bitcoin, what thousands of merchants, employers and employees are saying is: I support the ideals behind Bitcoin, including internationality, decen-tralisation, individual liberty and the power of technology to make the world a better place, and I want to interact with other people who share those values. When two Bitcoin users meet at a meetup—the Bitcoin conference in San Jose, say—or online, each one immediately knows that the other shares a similar background of basic knowledge, has been through the same experiences—watching the fluctuating Bitcoin markets rise and fall—and shares, at a deep level, a fundamentally similar worldview, even if fairly substantial political disagreements can sometimes hide this fact on the surface. In short, the Bitcoin economy is a perfect fit for the very definition of a community. The difference is, the community in question is not a community of circumstance, but an intentional, voluntary community of ideals—and a community in which anyone can participate.

The idea of such an international, self-organising business community is not new. Thinkers such as Kevin Carson, David de Ugarte and Doug Casey have all come forward to promote the concept and have even given it a name: phyles. A phyle is essentially a transnational community that, as Doug Casey puts it, 'is self-defined by whatever values they share.' Phyles would not be based in any one country, although they may have bases in every country, which their members can go to for help. Phyles can be formal or informal to any degree, ranging from a community whose members do not even realise its existence to a fully fledged institutional structure with its own social welfare provisions and tax system.

The possibilities that phyles may bring are unlimited: some see them as the future of cultural development, and many of their more radical proponents see them becoming the dominant form of economic organisation, transcending both traditional corporations and governments in importance.

Bitcoin's relationship with the concept of phyles is a complex one. Not only is Bitcoin, as a community, itself a phyle, but also, as a currency, it has all the right properties to make it the perfect currency for any phyle to use. Bitcoin does not discriminate on the basis of ideology, race, sex, or religion, it works equally well in any country and across countries, and it does not rely on any existing institution. It is also proving to be a particularly successful currency for making monetary donations—a surprising fact, given that traditional economics teaches that deflation like that built into Bitcoin can only lead to hoarding.

Another property that phyles will have is inter-operability. Unlike nations, which often strive to be insular groups that protect their own even at the expense of outsiders, phyles are intrinsically designed to interact. One can be a member of several phyles at the same time, and phyles will often find it in their interest to pool their unique resources and cooperate on common projects. This, once again, is a property that Bitcoin is perfectly suited for. There are now about half a dozen major 'alternative cryptocurrencies' under development that take Bitcoin's basic features but make substantial modifications to suit their own needs, but under the hood these currencies all speak the same 'language'. they all use elliptic curve cryptography, atomic transactions and 'triple-entry accounting' as fundamental building blocks of their security, and so systems designed for one such currency can easily be adapted to work for any other. Transaction mechanisms that work across currencies are also very possible.

We can see Bitcoin integrating into other communities already. At the conferences so far, we have seen the Free State Project, the civil liberties community, open source software developers and many more smaller groups. Many of the organisations present have benefitted from thousands of dollars worth of Bitcoin donations, and continue to receive many more every week. The next Bitcoin conference, coming this November, is explicitly intended to further this agenda. The conference will bring Bitcoin advocates together with activists of all stripes from around the world, aiming for a general theme of reforming all institutions of society from the ground up–hence the conference's name, 'unSYSTEM.'

Of course, this is only the start. Some organisations have now taken the plunge and reformed themselves to operate on Bitcoin entirely, and more will likely follow suit as the currency continues to expand and its underlying technologies and businesses develop. The next step may be for other more formal phyles to establish their own currencies; so far, the one major attempt to do this is Stan Stalnaker's Hub Culture, but experiments like Bitcoin (and its cousins, like Ripple and Freicoin) will likely lead the way for more organisations to attempt to do the same thing. The best ones will not be quite so intentional: making a community just for the sake of making a community rarely works out in practice if there are no underlying values that bond the community together. Internet-based transnational currencies and internet-empowered transnational communities are, to paraphrase Epiphyte spokesman Edan Yago, two mutually reinforcing ideas whose time has come. All that's left is to implement them.

Equality

Why More is Good for You

1.

'There's ultimately a very small number of people that are phenomenally bright but also have the skills to run a company, the social skills to run a company at that level. It's just the nature of the world... If this person has those skills, then he deserves the money.' Male, 37, private sector, earning more than £100,000 ($160,000) a year.

Equality matters because, when you have less of it, you have to put up with obnoxious behavior, insulting suggestions and stupid ideas, such as inequality being the 'nature of the world' or that 'a very small number of people' are 'phenomenally bright'.

Equality matters because human beings are creatures that thrive in societies where we are treated more as equals than as being greatly unequal in mental ability, sociability or any other kind of ability. We work best, behave best, play best and think best when we are not laboring under the assumption that some of us are better, more deserving or so much more able than others.

We perform the worst, are most atrocious in our conduct, are least relaxed and most unimaginative in outlook, when we live under the weight of great inequalities—and especially when we live with the illusion that these are somehow warranted.

Inequalities harm the rich as well as the poor. The rich are not necessarily especially hard-working, well behaved, happy or creative. Some are obsessed with making money and can be driven by that. Most behave much better when they are more like the rest of us. They can have appalling social skills while believing that they are 'phenomenally bright'. Many don't understand that it is at best questionable whether the poor should work hard for a pittance or obey the law, or any other social conventions, when they are members of a group being treated so unfairly.

How can people have the time and energy to contribute to our overall understanding and enjoyment of life when they are thinking about the world under delusions either of superiority or of inferiority? Inequality matters because it brings out the worst in us all.

2.

The vast majority of people in the world enjoy greater equality in so many more ways than did their great-grandparents. In relation to men, the position of women has improved most markedly. As mortality during childbirth continues to decline, for the first time in human history, women—any day now—are about to make up a majority of humans on the planet. Another example of progress is that few people now live in colonies (as explicitly defined). Fewer people are governed by obvious dictatorships than ever before.

Only recently have a majority of children worldwide been treated as being equal enough in value to other children to be taught to read and write—and, again, this is the first time in human history that this has happened. At the same time, most people are enjoying less equality in many ways than their parents did.

Women make up the large majority of the world's poor. Death in childbirth remains the biggest killer of women. More of us now, worldwide, live at the whims of colonising corporate organisations, some of whose employees suggest that there is no alternative to concentrating primarily on inhuman profit-taking. For the first time in history, we could easily prevent the majority of the millions of deaths that are suffered by very young children every year, but we choose not to. At least we now have the choice.

The technologies and knowledge that gave us this choice were only developed themselves in places where enough equalities had been won to allow more than the elite to join in the study of medicine and science, and so make advances. If greater equality has been, and continues to be, the underlying solution to so much that troubles people, then it is worth concentrating for once on what you gain from it, not on what you suffer as a result of inequality.

3.

Take just one example, from a long time ago. In 1452 a servant-girl gave birth to an illegitimate boy, Leonardo. He went on to become perhaps the best known painter, sculptor and inventor the world has ever known. Although his achievements are naturally ascribed to his talents, and he has been described as the most talented man to have ever lived, it is also true that he thrived because of when and, more importantly, where he was born. He was born just outside the town of Vinci in the Italian region of Tuscany, whose urban center was Florence.

By the middle of the 15th century, Florence had grown rich on unequal trade (buying cheap and selling dear) and on a little relaxation of the laws of usury to allow profit to be made from lending money. As yet these riches had not totally corrupted those who received them: Lorenzo de'Medici was the wealthiest of the bankers, and he took what appeared to be gifted artists and scholars into his household.

As Ernst Gombrich explained in his *A Little History of the World* (in 2008), there: '...was no seating order at table. Instead of the eldest and most respected sitting at the top of the table above the rest, it was the first to arrive who sat with Lorenzo de'Medici, even if he were no more than a young painter's apprentice. And even an ambassador, if he came last, took his place at the foot of the table.'

Leonardo da (of) Vinci was just one of those young men who came to sit at Lorenzo's table (around 1480). It is ironic that the Renaissance sparked such creativity while also creating a new form of banking, epitomised by the Medicis, which made profit by lending to others and making it permissible to receive interest on those loans.

4.

Those who make excuses for great inequalities sometimes inconsistently suggest that there is something innate in humans that makes them desire inequality.

But you know what equality is. You have seen it if you grew up within what is now considered a 'normal family.' You either treat your friends as equals or they are not your friends. The same with your partner, if you have one—they are not really your partner if you do not treat them as your equal.

If you went to a normal state school, like most people all over the world, including most that now go to university, you may at times have experienced being treated in an institution as an equal to other children. Only within the course of the last century have so many human beings experienced being treated as so equal to others.

In a hospital, in a park, on the sidewalk, at a party, in any situation in which entry was not conditional on your ability to pay or denied you because of the colour of your skin, your sex, religion or caste: at all these points in life you have felt what equality can be. And you should feel it especially strongly at the weekend.

Ask why next year we cannot be a little more equal than this year. Ask why the barriers between us have to rise. Ask what is being organized to avoid things getting worse and to stop a rich few taking more and more. And keep on asking—it doesn't matter how quietly, or how infrequently.

If you are questioning why we need be so unequal, you are part of the solution. If you see others as being like you, then you are part of the solution. If you are decent, and want to treat others decently, you are part of the solution. Nobody should seek to be part of the problem.

On the Phenomenon of Bullshit Jobs

A Work Rant

In the year 1930, John Maynard Keynes predicted that, by century's end, technology would have advanced sufficiently that countries like Great Britain or the United States would have achieved a 15-hour work week. There's every reason to believe he was right. In technological terms, we are quite capable of this. And yet it didn't happen. Instead, technology has been marshaled, if anything, to figure out ways to make us all work more. In order to achieve this, jobs have had to be created that are, effectively, pointless. Huge swathes of people, in Europe and North America in particular, spend their entire working lives performing tasks they secretly believe do not really need to be performed. The moral and spiritual damage that comes from this situation is profound. It is a scar across our collective soul. Yet virtually no one talks about it.

Why did Keynes' promised utopia—still being eagerly awaited in the '60s—never materialise? The standard line today is that he didn't figure in the massive increase in consumerism. Given the choice between less hours and more toys and pleasures, we've collectively chosen the latter. This presents a nice morality tale, but even a moment's reflection shows it can't really be true. Yes, we have witnessed the creation of an endless variety of new jobs and industries since the '20s, but very few have anything to do with the production and distribution of sushi, iPhones, or fancy sneakers.

So what are these new jobs, precisely? A recent report comparing employment in the US between 1910 and 2000 gives us a clear picture (and I note, one pretty much exactly echoed in the UK). Over the course of the last century, the number of workers employed as domestic servants, in industry, and in the farm sector has collapsed dramatically. At the same time, 'professional, managerial, clerical, sales, and service workers' tripled, growing 'from one-quarter to three-quarters of total employment.' In other words, productive jobs have, just as predicted, been largely automated away (even if you count industrial workers globally, including the toiling masses in India and China, such workers are still not nearly so large a percentage of the world population as they used to be.)

But rather than allowing a massive reduction of working hours to free the world's population to pursue their own projects, pleasures, visions, and ideas, we have seen the ballooning of not even so much of the 'service' sector as of the administrative sector, up to and including the creation of whole new industries like financial services or telemarketing, or the unprecedented expansion of sectors like corporate law, academic and health administration, human resources, and public relations. And these numbers do not even reflect on all those people whose job is to provide administrative, technical, or security support for these industries, or for that matter the whole host of ancillary industries (dog-washers, all-night pizza deliverymen) that only exist because everyone else is spending so much of their time working in all the other ones.

These are what I propose to call 'bullshit jobs'.

It's as if someone were out there making up pointless jobs just for the sake of keeping us all working. And here, precisely, lies the mystery. In capitalism, this is precisely what is not supposed to happen. Sure, in the old inefficient socialist states like the Soviet Union, where employment was considered both a right and a sacred duty, the system made up as many jobs as they had to (this is why in Soviet department stores it took three clerks to sell a piece of meat). But, of course, this is the sort of very problem market competition is supposed to fix. According to economic theory, at least, the last thing a profit-seeking firm is going to do is shell out money to workers they don't really need to employ. Still, somehow, it happens.

While corporations may engage in ruthless downsizing, the layoffs and speed-ups invariably fall on that class of people who are actually making, moving, fixing and maintaining things; through some strange alchemy no one can quite explain, the number of salaried paper-pushers ultimately seems to expand, and more and more employees find themselves, not unlike Soviet workers actually, working 40 or even 50 hour weeks on paper, but effectively working 15 hours just as Keynes predicted, since the rest of their time is spent organizing or attending motivational seminars, updating their facebook profiles or downloading TV box-sets.

The answer clearly isn't economic: it's moral and political. The ruling class has figured out that a happy and productive population with free time on their hands is a mortal danger (think of what started to happen when this even began to be approximated in the '60s). And, on the other hand, the feeling that work is a moral value in itself, and that anyone not willing to submit themselves to some kind of intense work discipline for most of their waking hours deserves nothing, is extraordinarily convenient for them.

Once, when contemplating the apparently endless growth of administrative responsibilities in British academic departments, I came up with one possible vision of hell. Hell is a collection of individuals who are spending the bulk of their time working on a task they don't like and are not especially good at. Say they were hired because they were excellent cabinet-makers, and then discover they are expected to spend a great deal of their time frying fish. Neither does the task really need to be done—at least, there's only a very limited number of fish that need to be fried. Yet somehow, they all become so obsessed with resentment at the thought that some of their co-workers might be spending more time making cabinets, and not doing their fair share of the fish-frying responsibilities, that before long there's endless piles of useless badly cooked fish piling up all over the workshop and it's all that anyone really does.

I think this is actually a pretty accurate description of the moral dynamics of our own economy.

Now, I realise any such argument is going to run into immediate objections: 'who are you to say what jobs are really "necessary"? What's necessary anyway? You're an anthropology professor, what's the "need" for that?' (And indeed a lot of tabloid readers would take the existence of my job as the very definition of wasteful social expenditure.) And on one level, this is obviously true. There can be no objective measure of social value.

I would not presume to tell someone who is convinced they are making a meaningful contribution to the world that, really, they are not. But what about those people who are themselves convinced their jobs are meaningless? Not long ago I got back in touch with a school friend who I hadn't seen since I was 12. I was amazed to discover that in the interim, he had become first a poet, then the front man in an indie rock band. I'd heard some of his songs on the radio having no idea the singer was someone I actually knew. He was obviously brilliant, innovative, and his work had unquestionably brightened and improved the lives of people all over the world. Yet, after a couple of unsuccessful albums, he'd lost his contract, and plagued with debts and a newborn daughter, ended up, as he put it, 'taking the default choice of so many directionless folk: law school.' Now he's a corporate lawyer working in a prominent New York firm. He was the first to admit that his job was utterly meaningless, contributed nothing to the world, and, in his own estimation, should not really exist.

There's a lot of questions one could ask here, starting with, what does it say about our society that it seems to generate an extremely limited demand for talented poet-musicians, but an apparently infinite demand for specialists in corporate law? (Answer: if 1% of the population controls most of the disposable wealth, what we call 'the market' reflects what they think is useful or important, not anybody else.) But even more, it shows that most people in these jobs are ultimately aware of it. In fact, I'm not sure I've ever met a corporate lawyer who didn't think their job was bullshit. The same goes for almost all the new industries outlined above. There is a whole class of salaried professionals that, should you meet them at parties and admit that you do something that might be considered interesting (an anthropologist, for example), will want to avoid even discussing their line of work entirely (one or t'other?) Give them a few drinks, and they will launch into tirades about how pointless and stupid their job really is.

This is a profound psychological violence here. How can one even begin to speak of dignity in labour when one secretly feels one's job should not exist? How can it not create a sense of deep rage and resentment. Yet it is the peculiar genius of our society that its rulers have figured out a way, as in the case of the fish-fryers, to ensure that rage is directed precisely against those who actually do get to do meaningful work. For instance: in our society, there seems a general rule that, the more obviously one's work benefits other people, the less one is likely to be paid for it. Again, an objective measure is hard to find, but one easy way to get a sense is to ask: what would happen were this entire class of people to simply disappear? Say what you like about nurses, garbage collectors, or mechanics, it's obvious that were they to vanish in a puff of smoke, the results would be immediate and catastrophic. A world without teachers or dock-workers would soon be in trouble, and even one without science fiction writers or ska musicians would clearly be a lesser place. It's not entirely clear how humanity would suffer were all private equity CEOs, lobbyists, PR researchers, actuaries, telemarketers, bailiffs or legal consultants to similarly vanish. (Many suspect it might markedly improve.)

Yet apart from a handful of well-touted exceptions (doctors), the rule holds surprisingly well.

Even more perverse, there seems to be a broad sense that this is the way things should be. This is one of the secret strengths of right-wing populism. You can see it when tabloids whip up resentment against tube workers for paralysing London during contract disputes: the very fact that tube workers can paralyse London shows that their work is actually necessary, but this seems to be precisely what annoys people. It's even clearer in the US, where Republicans have had remarkable success mobilizing resentment against school teachers, or auto workers (and not, significantly, against the school administrators or auto industry managers who actually cause the problems) for their supposedly bloated wages and benefits. It's as if they are being told 'but you get to teach children! Or make cars! You get to have real jobs! And on top of that you have the nerve to also expect middle-class pensions and health care?'

If someone had designed a work regime perfectly suited to maintaining the power of finance capital, it's hard to see how they could have done a better job. Real, productive workers are relentlessly squeezed and exploited. The remainder are divided between a terrorised stratum of the, universally reviled, unemployed and a larger stratum who are basically paid to do nothing, in positions designed to make them identify with the perspectives and sensibilities of the ruling class (managers, administrators, etc.)—and particularly its financial avatars—but, at the same time, foster a simmering resentment against anyone whose work has clear and undeniable social value. Clearly, the system was never consciously designed. It emerged from almost a century of trial and error. But it is the only explanation for why, despite our technological capacities, we are not all working 3–4 hour days.

Kill All Hipsters

Don't Hate the Player, Hate the Game

The death throes of the hipster have lasted a surprisingly long time. Critiqued and commodified in hipster-spotting handbooks as early as 2003, and subsequently skewered and parodied everywhere from the hipster-baiting grand guignol of Nathan Barley to the YouTube gold of *Being a Dickhead's Cool*, the hipster, like the cockroach, has proved almost admirably resistant to attack. Surely we've now reached a point of peak hipster-bashing, as well as Peak Hipster?

Hipsters have been adept at the adoption and commodification of the past. The objection often made to this aspect of hipsterism is that, unlike its subcultural predecessors, it makes little attempt to carve out a distinguishing niche through creation or innovation of its own, but instead appropriates and pastiches the signifiers of previous subcultures. To be fair, this reliance on recycling and the turbo-charged reviving of previous trends has tended to define contemporary popular culture in general, a tendency which Simon Reynolds usefully diagnosed as 'retromania'. 00s popular entertainment seemed to concentrate on remakes, reboots and rebrandings of the already bankable, safe and commodified, glutting itself on reformed bands and jukebox musicals, and ending up retreating down a cultural cul-de-sac. And, where one might have expected those beyond the mainstream to construct their own version of the avant-garde, hipsters seemed to lack both inclination and ability to do so.

In addition, the adoption by hipster culture of previous trends seemed to involve stripping them of any subversive or oppositional political potential they might once have held, giving hipsterism the appearance of a radical alternative subculture while in reality it had only reactionary politics or political disengagement to offer. Some kind of counter-cultural renewal was clearly called for in a decade where political discourse continued to drift lazily rightwards while insisting on the existence of liberal harmony and content-ment in the face of worsening material inequality—leaving society becalmed in deepening waters of unfocused resent-ment and dissatisfaction. Hipsterism, though, offered only a wilfully weak reanimation of the signifiers used in previous shows of resistance and opposition, effectively forming a counterculture without the 'counter'.

To some extent, this disengagement merely reflected growing political alienation and estrangement in wider 'OOs society. Demoralisation took root, notably, through Blair's dismissal of popular opposition to war on Iraq, despite its expression in some of the biggest mass demonstrations the world has ever seen. In 'alternative' as in mainstream culture, a remarkable spirit of apathy, disinterest and individualism prevailed; it grew increasingly nostalgic through immersion in vintage and retro and increasingly averse to taking an interest in politics, when events appeared to reinforce the idea of activism as futile and escapism as both an attractive and logical alternative. Political engagement came to be seen as resolutely uncool: dabbling, playfulness and pastiche was preferred to po-faced, earnest political commitment, and a rising tide of irony swamped everything.

As with so many cultural excrescences of late capital-ism, the rot that has resulted in contemporary hipsterism seemed to settle in during the 1990s. The loss of political alternatives, as New Labour embraced a post-Thatcher economic consensus, and the switch from an alternative culture that rejected consumerism to one which celebrated market-driven consumption, both significantly damaged alternative culture's capacity for political opposition. They reached their peak in the smugly noncommittal irony of the hipster. More insidiously, the opportunities offered by the 90s trends of Britpop, Cool Britannia and 'new laddism' for class tourism, for attempting to live like common people, set the tone for the stripping of political meaning and identity from working-class signifiers, while the existence of 'working-class' as a political identity was downplayed or dismissed. Over the next decade, the adoption of working-class drag by the comfortably trust-funded became so ubiquitous that it now seems to barely raise an eyebrow.

Retromania can be seen as a function of what Mark Fisher has defined as 'capitalist realism'—the denial of any possible future significantly different from the present, which stifles both artistic and political innovation. This has obvious resonances with Douglas Haddow's 2008 broadside *Hipster: The Dead End of Western Civilisation*, which claimed that the appetite of US hipster culture for the ironic appropriation of previous subcultural signifiers had neutered its potential for radicalism and invention. In the UK, from second-wave Britpop's attenuation of post-punk's radicalism, to the compromised conservatism of nu-folk, retromania and hipsterism have overseen not merely the commodification of previously subversive or oppositional artistic movements—under capitalism, this process is both predictable and inevitable—but their co-option to the extent of preventing the emergence of anything new.

From this perspective, hipster culture's derivative and appropriative nature, its inability to innovate, mirrors a wider lack of alternative political possibilities. The instability, uncertainty and introversion that has produced a loss of faith in political orthodoxies has also produced a culture at a loss as to how to define itself and, given the apparent imminence of disaster, unconvinced that it's worthwhile bothering to do so. Have we fallen back on imitations or reproductions of what has gone before because creating or producing anything culturally distinctive currently seems as pressing and productive a task as arranging deck-chairs in a previously untried pattern on the Titanic? Half cynical disbelief in alternative possibilities, half comfort-seeking focus on past certainties and glories, this impasse illustrates the acceptance by both mainstream politics and pop culture of late capitalism's 'end of history' propaganda. Hipsters are hardly the originators of this political and cultural malaise, even if they have arguably become its cheerleaders; there is less to be gained by hating the hipster itself and more by focusing on the underlying processes—of which hipsters are symptom, not cause.

TXT: DEAN PUCKETT

Grasp the Nettle
Finding the Fault Lines

It's a rare privilege to stumble upon a completely unique story—in this case, a motley collection of land-rights activists squatting a 3-acre piece of land in the heart of suburban London. When I began filming on the 6th of June 2009, I had no idea what I was getting myself into. For the first few weeks, when I visited and filmed Kew Bridge Eco-Village for a few days at a time, I had a sense that my footage was only skimming the surface of the forces and characters behind this fledgeling movement. Journalists who visited the site for just a day, or hours at a time, left with great sound-bites about sustainability and land rights, but there was something we were all missing.

There was an intoxicating energy about the place, a sense of freedom from a system that many of us recognise is unequal and destructive. Yet this rag-tag bunch of occupiers defied conventional stereotypes of the 'ecowarrior'. They were people from different walks of life: some were students, others were former professionals; some had years of campaigning behind them, for many this was a new experience. And they had come together not simply to occupy a piece of land, but to transform it, bit by bit—in an exciting and unnerving sense, creating their own reality outside the system.

And the more I filmed, the more fault lines began to appear. Despite promoting a radical alternative to modern industrial capitalism, the village was inevitably and intrinsically linked to the wider city, including the capitalist system. And I would watch, enthralled, as the village's little community frequently struggled in anguish to understand how to deal with the friction between idealism and reality.

There was certainly more to this movement than meets the eye, and my occasional filming as a visitor could only bring so much insight into this community's day-to-day struggles with government and big business—and itself. So I moved in.

A year and three months later I find myself with 200 hours of footage, at the tail-end of a journey that quite literally changed my life. Having lived this experience so intimately—sometimes beautiful and exciting, other times completely crazy—it was a challenge to bottle its essence into a 90-minute film. In the editing room we decided that the very experience of moving in and making the film had to be an element of the story. It seemed like the only way to go: attempt to be as honest as possible, within the parameters of a fundamentally dishonest medium.

While making the film, I found myself opening a window into a world I'd never seen or imagined before. In the process, I got to know ex-MI5 whistleblower David Shayler, who now believed he was Jesus, and dressed as a transvestite; was inspired by visionaries who were sincere and articulate in their thoughts and ideas about how we could create a better world; was bemused by activists whose hopes for a better world were inseparable from, what seemed to me, bizarre conspiracy theories; and was even accused by these conspiracy obsessives of being an undercover police officer. So when I condensed my hundreds of hours of footage into a film, I wanted the audience to feel the way I did when I was there: inspired, in awe, freaked out, alienated, out of my depth.

These inspirations, absurdities and eccentricities weave a complex mosaic of the human struggle to create meaning in a world that often makes little sense. Warts and all, the film captures the reality of life for a group of people disillusioned with a mainstream consumer society whose values and culture threaten to bring the planet to a point of irreversible destruction. As such, it's a film about activism, idealism, homelessness and insanity. This has made it problematic for broadcasters in this country. They seem to have abandoned films that look into the nooks and crannies of our societies. Television very rarely gives a meaningful voice to radical political ideas; the person at the BBC who rejected our film on the basis that it was biased decided instead to commission the shows *Jamie—Drag Queen At 16* and *The War on Britain's Roads*. Broadcasters seem to think that all that matters to people are identity based politics and tabloid titillation. With many families struggling to make ends meet during a protracted economic collapse, young people may be open to watching films about people trying to live in another way. It is a worrying trend that the world we see via television has an increasingly narrow view that is masked by a fake 'balance', which never allows any kind of radical perspective. When was the last time the BBC went to a radical voice when discussing the economy? Wouldn't true balance include a view that asks for the end of corporatism, the free market or even the complete dismantling of the state? In short, the BBC's balance is bullshit.

As John Pilger put it, 'Understanding the BBC as a pre-eminent state propagandist and censor by omission—more often than not in tune with its right-wing enemies—is on no public agenda and it ought to be.'

The ambiguity of Grasp the Nettle has also made it difficult for some film festival selectors. The social realities of holding an urban space, such as alcoholism and homelessness, don't always make for a film with a concise political point or an easy one-click manifesto on a website. The film allows the audience to feel at times critical or ambiguous about the protagonists, and this seems to be a hard sell. Their branding may make them seem progressive, yet distributors and most film festivals are fundamentally beholden to 'the market'. See distribution company Dogwoof releasing the recent Snoop Dogg documentary, which is essentially a film about a stoned millionaire going on holiday.

Some festivals are more forward-thinking though, and we showed it at the Open City Docs Fest in London recently, as part of their *City Stories* strand—their program was packed with films which explore the ambiguities of life. We've now opened the film up for community screenings, with an eye to online distribution, DVD and a more direct relationship with the people who watch it. Not having a cinema release means that many film magazines and newspapers won't write about the film—yet another hurdle for the independent filmmaker. Its been a four-year journey getting it to the screen, but when we sit down with an audience at screenings as we did with my last documentary *The Crisis of Civilization* it will all be worth it. I wouldn't change a thing.

As one of the most articulate characters—and now my good pal—Simon, says during the final days of the Democracy Village, outside the Houses of Parliament in Westminster, 'Despite the troubles and the madness, this is very powerful: people are standing up and speaking out.' Grasp the Nettle throws up an array of questions—and not just, what is the point of activism? But even, what is the point of life—of any struggle that can frequently seem futile? And as the characters learn to let go of outcomes and find meaning in their struggle, it's my hope that the viewer can too.

Co-operate or Die

How to Posse Up and Lose the Landlord

What is a Housing Co-op?

A model of housing with no landlord or bank breathing down your neck; a group of people collectively managing and owning property; one step closer to freedom.

All registered co-operatives follow the same seven 'Co-operative Principles', and have done since the first co-operative was founded in Rochdale, England in 1844.

They are: voluntary and open membership; democratic member control; members' economic participation; autonomy and independence; education, training and information; co-operation among co-operatives; concern for community.

Posse Up

Find a group of like-minded people who have the same goal as you. How do you want to live? Do you want a communal house or individual housing? Where will you be in five years? Get all of this sorted with your group at the start and you'll be solid.

Don't let money shit in your head

Money can shit in everybody's head, so put together a comprehensive plan based on your anticipated income from rents and your estimated outgoings. Include everything. Banks, building societies and loanstock investors will want to see this as well, so it's important.

Existence is important

You'll need at least 3 members to register as a fully mutual co-operative—you do this with the Registry of Friendly

Societies (RFS), a part of the Financial Services Authority (FSA). UK Co-operatives and other co-operative networks can register you for a charge—look around for the best price. They can also provide you with a set of model rules that you can either use or adapt.

Start this straight away: it can take time and you can't do anything with a co-operative that does not (legally) exist.

Lil help?

One of the 7 co-operative principles is to help other co-ops, so you're joining a world with mutual aid hard-wired in. Ask other coops how they did it, or get in touch with UK Co-operatives, the national body that promotes cooperation (and is itself a co-op). Radical Routes is another network of worker and housing co-ops working for radical social change.

Property is not theft

Property is not theft if you own it co-operatively, so get your hands on some. Look around for the kind of houses that suit your purpose. Are they affordable? Are they in an area that is viable for everyone?

By buying property as a co-operative you can take advantage of economies of scale—you can buy a house with nine bedrooms for much less than it would cost to buy three three-bedroom houses. So you can house a greater number of members at lower rents or repay your loans quicker—you may well get some land or a big old garden, too.

Learn about loanstock

For many co-operatives loanstock is the only means of raising the deposit on a property. Loanstock is a way of borrowing money from people and organisations to help you purchase your property. Investors in your co-op lend money for a set number of years, after which it is paid back with interest—usually at a very low rate. Co-ops often buy loanstock from other co-ops.

Raise funds

You'll need to raise at least £150 to register the co-operative, and you'll also need to find some cash to buy your property. Building societies can lend up to 70% of the value of a property, and ethical banks—such as Triodos—are more receptive to requests for cash. Don't just apply to one institution, keep your options open and apply to as many as you can.

Kick back

You've set up your co-op and you never have to pay rent to a landlord again. Congratulations: you're one step closer to freedom.

Let's get this straight

Don't let sloppy accounting scupper your ship. Always keep a record of all transactions and, if you are borrowing money, make sure that the lenders and the group have a full understanding of the time-scale and any interest rates agreed.

LEA RIVER SITE

Leisure Riot
Utopian Architecture and Organised Fun

Crap Work

Recently I was filming on the Atlas Mountain tourist-trail in Southern Morocco. My 11am stop was a visit to a factory producing the local speciality—argan oil. It was an all female co-operative, providing jobs for divorced women.

As a window on the past it was fascinating, but it didn't look too great as a job. Yes it was better than absolute poverty, but it was boring, slow, almost certainly arthritis-inducing— the global qualities of crap work.

Thinking aloud, I mumbled 'Wouldn't it be better to use machines?'

Immediately my guide admonished me: 'But then the ladies wouldn't have jobs!' Of course, she was right, unless the ladies owned the machines.

Leisure Dialectic

Near Manchester, England, 1932. Hundreds of ramblers had trespassed on open and uncultivated moorland close to Manchester owned by the Duke of Devonshire. He used it 12 days a year for his own leisure pursuit of hunting. The trespassers demanded the right for local people to walk the land on their Sunday off from work. The Duke's gamekeepers resisted, and the result was the world's first leisure riot.

The Kinder trespass was organised by a 20-year-old Jewish communist, Benny Rothman. His genius was to realise that by demanding the peaceful right to ramble, he could make a direct attack on the idea of the private ownership of property. His challenge was not unnoticed by the local magistrates, who sentenced him to three months in jail.

Rothman's pioneering politicisation of leisure started a new movement. A few weeks later 10,000 ramblers gathered to walk across Kinder Scout in protest at the jail sentences.

Among them was a young playwright and singer called Jimmy Miller—stage-name Euan MacColl. MacColl with his future wife, Joan Littlewood, went on to pioneer a new form of politicised theatre directly inspired by the Kinder Trespass, believing that mass action based on shared cultural experiences could change the world. Seventeen years later, in 1949, a part of the dream came true: in direct response to the Kinder Trespass, the post-war Labour government created national parks across Britain, giving all citizens rights of access to private land. Leisure had proven to be a potent organising force for political change.

Fun Palace

London 1964. A group of British radicals drew up plans for a vast building that they believed could open the door to a new society. It was called the Fun Palace.

Their vision: a computerised, mechanised future, free of exhausting, tedious jobs, where humankind would be free to live creatively in an age of leisure. If in industrial Britain work defined social division and inequality, in post-industrial society its antithesis—fun—could heal these wounds.

Leading the group was Joan Littlewood. In the 1930s she had created a traveling theatre group—called Theatre Workshop—committed to her dream of using art as the catalyst to create a new, socialist society. After many years of poverty and struggle on the road, by the early 1960s Littlewood was finally successful and famous.

Designing the scheme was a young architect called Cedric Price. He was a man whose work would reshape modern architecture, yet he completed almost no buildings. An anti-architect, Price generally saw building as the wrong solution—he once advised a client asking for a new family home that the solution to his problem was not bricks and mortar, but divorce.

Backing the project was a man hugely famous in the 1960s, but almost unknown today—Tom Driberg. Tabloid gossip columnist, TV personality and left wing Labour MP, his vision of an egalitarian future was forged during the hours he spent each day cruising for gay sex in London's public toilets. Here, while seeking his own pleasures, he learnt that all men were equal before the porcelain. To Driberg it was clear that radical change would need to appropriate space, and use it in ways that went far beyond the imagination of its designers.

Detailed drawings superimposed the new building onto the brownfield wastelands of East London. The artwork highlighted how spaces that had once hosted mass industrial employment would now put the people in charge of their own fun. The users were expected to reconfigure the palace's activities—and even the building itself.

Here's a taste of the Fun Palace manifesto:

Choose what you want to do—or watch someone else doing it. Learn how to handle tools, paint, babies, machinery or just listen to your favourite tune. Dance, talk or be lifted up to where you can see other people make things work. Sit out over space with a drink and tune in to what's happening elsewhere in the city. Try starting a riot...

But the Fun Palace was not to be. In October 1964, even as Price was drawing up the design, Littlewood told Vogue: 'I forecast disaster for this cathedral-brothel. I'm throwing myself in the fan. Who cares? Someday it'll work.'

Defeat came not from reactionary capitalist forces, but from the Left. The Palace's offer was beyond the imagination of the traditional Labour establishment; for them, working class power came from workplace identity, family and the repression of these most frivolous urges to pleasure.

Rumours spread that the palace would corrupt the innocent, that actors (universally known for their transgressive morals) would be available for sex with the public in the bushes outside the venue.

Meetings to present the scheme only intensified the hostility. A local resident shouted: 'A new attitude to time and space? What's she talking about? I'll tell you what it's about, a lot of rowdies infesting the place day and night.' The urban working class showed no taste for being emancipated by this kind of culture—one man telling Littlewood: 'We've got all we need here, a museum, a cinema, and the women have their housework.'

E is for Emancipation

The broader vision of the Fun Palace would eventually come to be realised but in two separate and totally contradictory ways. Architecturally, Price's concept of high-tech, reconfigurable buildings inspired countless airports and those steel and glass temples of inequality—the Lloyds building and The Shard.

But more joyously, the true spirit of the palace came to life at the end of the 1980s, with a suitably radical application of technology to mass leisure—through pharmacology. The mass use of ecstasy at rave parties—held suitably transgressively in abandoned industrial workspaces—created, at least for a few hours, a world free of class distinction. More significantly it gave the worker the chance to choose to maximise the use of his or her serotonin levels in their free time and concentrate their subsequent lows during the following week of wage slavery.

The uninhibited mix of sex and ecstasy that dominated the rave scene through the 1990s and 2000s was one that Driberg—an early campaigner for liberal drugs laws—would surely have approved of.

Admittedly this utopia faded with the comedown, and rumours that Tory cabinet ministers took ecstasy in their youth make it harder to believe that drugs alone could help create a better world. The rich and powerful have never given up anything without some threat of violence, either.

But now that social solidarity based around work seems as alien to modern urban existence as the spectacle of extracting argan oil by hand, in this time of mass un- and under-employment, maybe we need to follow Benny Rothman's idea of organisation around shared fun. Anyone for a leisure riot?

AN ANARCHIST GUIDE
TO JAROSLAV HASEK

Anarchist Alcoholics

His life was, frankly, a disgrace. He might have appeared to be a Bolshevik but in fact he was just bolshie. He made a bad start in life and got steadily worse. At one time he edited two rival anarchist papers in Prague and conducted a vicious polemic between them. He edited the prestigious magazine Animal World where he invented fantastical animals and sold 'pedigree' dogs he had stolen on the street. His one book *The Good Soldier Schweik* was mostly written when he was drunk and is nothing more than a ramshackle collection of pub stories. It is also hailed as one of the 100 greatest books of the last century. Such was the life and work of the very bad Bohemian Jaroslav Hasek.

Hasek was by nature anarchic and resentful of authority but from 1906–1909 he was active in the Czech anarchist movement. He was expelled from one anarchist group for bartering the office bicycle for beer. He led a tram-workers strike though not a tram-worker. He was arrested for throwing a rock at a policeman during a riot. His defence was that he had spotted a rare fossil on the ground during the riot. Fearing it might be lost—or worse still used as a missile—he threw it over a wall for safekeeping where it had unfortunately hit a police inspector. Introduced by his fiancé to his worried prospective father-in-law Hasek assured him he had just obtained regular employment. 'What are the wages?' he was asked; 'two litres of beer a day,' he replied cheerily.

Hasek's greatest project was the foundation—along with four artist cronies—of 'The Party for Peaceful and Moderate Progress Within the Bounds of the Law' to contest Prague council elections in 1911. Prague was part of the Austro-Hungarian Empire and strict censorship was in force, but Hasek got round this by establishing an extreme party of moderation. Meetings were uproariously chaotic, always held in bars and attended by government police spies hoping to find evidence of subversion.

'What do you think of the Crown?' asked an agent, hoping Hasek would be forced to openly criticise the Emperor. 'It is an excellent establishment,' replied Hasek, 'I drink there often.'

'Why is the portrait of the Emperor turned to face the wall?' asked another.

'In case a fly might shit on it and someone make an unfortunate remark,' came the reply.

As crowds flocked to the nightly meetings Hasek rashly promised to list 20 Prague municipal councillors who had murdered their own grandmothers at the next meeting. Expectation grew beyond hope as police and officials joined the huge throng. Hasek had painted himself into a corner but as usual his cronies came to the rescue.

Before Hasek could begin, the 'Chairman of the Party' (there wasn't one) gravely intoned that an emergency question had been asked which must receive priority under the party constitution 'Section 35 on agriculture' (there wasn't one).

'What do you think of Foot and Mouth Disease?'

'This is an extraordinarily stupid question' replied Hasek, 'but one which must be answered.' He then spoke for 89 minutes on the ravages of foot and mouth to cattle in the Ostrogoth and Visigoth empires before ending with the assertion that the only present-day carrier of the disease was the mayor of Prague who must immediately be given 10 gallons of creosote mouth wash. Exit crowd in search of creosote... and mayor.

On election day itself, only minutes after the polls opened, Hasek's supporters began sticking up posters claiming an overwhelming victory for Hasek. All voters were invited to the pub HQ of the party to celebrate, and hundreds did. Eventually a policeman arrived asking Hasek to remove the posters. Hasek grabbed the humble policeman and announced he was now making him Chief of Police at three times his salary and sent him on his way.

The rest of Hasek's life was extraordinary. Conscripted into the Austro-Hungarian army he was captured by the Russians. After the October revolution he briefly joined the Czech Legion and then the Red Army where he quickly rose to the rank of Political Commissar before wandering back to Prague in 1920. For the next three years he led a vagabond existence writing stories on scraps of paper, which he would then lose, and asking anyone if they could remember the story he had told the night before. He drank prodigiously and at the time of his death in 1923 he weighed 22 stone—the wall of his house had to be knocked down in order to remove his body.

He had, however, written the stories and adventures of *The Good Soldier Schweik*—which seemed remarkably close to his wanderings. By playing the wise fool and adopting imbecilic obeying of authority, Schweik is the most anarchic and subversive character in history. Here's an example from chapter one:

The landlord of Schweik's local tavern is continually tying to avoid conversations with him for fear of being overheard by police agents. Schweik enters the bar and is greeted by a weeping landlady:

'After you left, my husband was arrested for subversion and last week was sentence to 10 years in gaol.'

'That's excellent news,' responds Schweik cheerily.

'How is that excellent news?'

'Because he has served a week already.'

In September 26th 2000 I was in Prague for the World Bank riots in the company of Jane Nicholl and Martin Wright. We visited the very touristy Chalice pub where Hasek used to drink (amongst many others). On leaving we could hear tear gas volleys and see the smoke rising from street battles. We raced down. I picked up a rock; it had no fossil.

TXT: MICAH WHITE

Out of the Darkness
Into the Light

How do we awaken our neighbours, our friends, our family to the truth? Do we go up to people one by one in the street and plead our case? Do we hand roses to strangers in the airport? Or do we work on a larger scale: raise big money from shadowy donors and roll out a nationwide television campaign? This is the foundational problem of political change. And without a compelling theory of how to do this— how to shift the minds of large swaths of the world—there is no hope of pulling off a global revolution.

Seven billion people on Earth with their own opinions, dreams, religious, knowledges, perspectives and discourses. It should be impossible to unify this many people's minds. And yet, we have seen revelations sweep through The People in the past and we know that it can happen again in a flash. Witness the sudden proliferation of encampments during Occupy Wall Street. The development of transnational capitalism is itself a photonegative testament of the potential of an idea, a money, a meme to cut across all boundaries—and touch the essentially human.

The human is, in its essential being, adaptable. Since embarking on our experiment in civilization in the ancient world, we have lived in vastly different ways. Our species' capacity for dramatic shifts—our plasticity—is our greatest strength. Look historically and see that amazing transformations have happened in a generation or two. It took the Romans three generations to absorb the barbarian Cisalpine Gauls into the Roman culture and way of being. During the World Wars of the 20th century, tremendous social changes (rationing, conscription, air-raid drills, the wartime morality) happened in the span of months. If Time is ripe and The

People are awake then mobilizations on a scale rarely seen in human history can strike at any moment.

Kicking off a paradigm shift on a global scale is not a matter of rational argumentation. In American English, to talk of convincing a person conjures images of a zero-sum debate where one side emerges the conversational winner and another the loser. But think about it: how often in your life have you let go of a long-held belief? Why did it happen? I remember the few times when I have totally changed my mind about a truth I once held.

These kinds of paradigm shifts are as rare in an individual's life as revolutions are in our social life. If they are more common when we are young, they are more profound when we are old. Sometimes the epiphany is sudden. And sometimes it is a slow-dawning realization. My departure from atheism and transition toward anarchism was the latter. It started with a sensation of being uncomfortable and it grew into a cognitive sense that I could no longer express my whole self through the atheistic mindset. I understood that I had yearnings that could not be satisfied through a narrow focus on rejecting religious authority. Paradigm shifts arise from moments just like this: an intuition that our spirit exceeds our current mindset, worldview, ontology, paradigm. The same in politics as it is in faith.

As populist anarchists, we ground our theory of social change in the epiphany. We understand that only a species-wide metanoia—from the ancient Greek word for 'a turnaround'—can release the tremendous interpersonal forces necessary for a social revolution. Others, the Browns in particular, have sought the high energy necessary for social transformation in emotions of hate, fear, superiority. However, authoritarianism backed by military force is far too resource-intensive to work on a global scale at this contemporary moment. It requires capture of a nation-state's military and a consequent global military conquest and occupation that would be time-consuming while exacerbating the already dire ecological state of the world. (Imagine the carbon emissions of world war!)

We are the people of truth and we must be forever innovative in how we spread that truth. This is what it means to be a meme warrior. In these end-times, the only viable path is to provoke an epiphany that spreads throughout the world like wildfire.

The Browns, the fascists and authoritarians, think the answer is in force. And they will be able to convince some people of this. But that path will not lead out of the morass. There is no way to conquer the world physically. Violence can be used to divide the world but it cannot be used to unify the world. No army can hold the world's territory if the people are hostile. But on the immaterial plane, at the level of ideas and our cultural imagination, we can make the world's armies lay down their arms and their people welcome our governance with open arms.

For Plato, waking up our neighbors to the truth was a philosophical problem of how to break the spiritual chains that keep us enraptured by illusion. Plato is known as the great father of philosophy but I think of him as the first meme warrior. In Book Seven of Plato's masterpiece, The Republic, which for millennia has been celebrated as the originary great work of Western political philosophy, Plato introduces the allegory of the cave by asking us to imagine a dystopian world dominated by untruth. Not a world where people believe one or two incorrect facts. But a world where our fundamental understanding of the world—what philosophers call our epistemology—is based on false assumptions imposed by structures beyond our control.

Picture, Plato counsels his students, that human beings are imprisoned in an underground cave dwelling. There they live, from earliest childhood, with their legs and necks in chains. Behind them is a flickering bonfire. And before them is a stone wall that functions as a screen for projections whose source they cannot know. They see shadows dance on the wall and believe the shadows are the real. Nearly all these humans live and die in the cave without ever learning the truth of their imprisonment. Now, imagine that on one day just like today one of us were to escape.

We stumble out of the cave, blinded by light. The brightness is painful and for a while we can only look down, away from the sun. Still, our eyes are drawn to brightness and we glimpse a puddle that reflects the solar light. How much brighter than the bonfire in the cave! And yet only a reflection of the true light-source. We must look up! We gather our strength... give our eyes time to adjust to the new reality... and then gaze upward toward the sky. For the first time in our life we see the Truth. And our first thought is of the others still trapped in the cave, living in ignorance. How can we show them the truth? How can we spread the epiphany beyond our individual consciousness?

Returning to the cave is dangerous. Having been exposed to the true light, we have difficulty seeing by the dim bonfire. We find the others and begin to explain what we saw...

Stop! Plato breaks in to warn us of a grave danger. The prisoners do not want to hear what we have to say. To them, we are insane. And worse, we are taking away their enjoyment of the shadows. Beware! Plato reminds us of the fate of his mentor, Socrates, who was killed by a citizen jury in Athens for blasphemy. Heterodoxy is blasphemy to the orthodox no matter how convinced we are of our truth.

And what does the great philosopher counsel us to do? Does he ask us to be kind to the ignorant? To plead our case intellectually? To educate them? No.

Grab them by the scruffs of their necks, says Plato, and drag them into the light, no matter the pain, so that they see the sun and so that they may return to the underworld to liberate others.

Mujica vs. Mr Hollywood

Mike Weatherley is the Member of Parliament for Hove and Portslade. He regularly boasts that he was instrumental in the recent criminalisation of squatting—public-funded property protection for the rich and prison sentences for the poor.

Like all MPs, Mike gets paid £65,738 a year; last year, he claimed an additional £24,192 in expenses for travel and accommodation. Should our MPs still find themselves short, they also have a tax-payer provided hardship fund to fall back on; nobody knows when Mike Weatherley last felt the dread-fear of an unexpected bill landing on the doorstep.

In 2012, Mike did just 72 hours of work (six a month) for the Motion Picture Licensing Company (MPLC) and was reimbursed a total of £34,000—he sells himself to Hollywood at the handsome rate of £422 per hour. Mike has recently been Secretary for the all-party parliamentary intellectual property group, and championed changes to copyright legislation worth £500million. The MPLC is a leader in motion-picture copyright compliance, supporting legal access across five continents and more than 20 countries.

Now that he's attained office, Jose Mujica is on a deliberate drive to make the Uruguayan presidency 'less venerated'. He refuses to live in the official presidential palace, using it instead as a shelter for homeless people during the coldest months.

His presidential salary is about $108,000 per annum, but he donates 90% (mostly to programs for expanding housing for the poor), which leaves him with an amount comparable to that of an average Uruguayan. In 2010, his annual personal-wealth declaration was $1,800 (£1,100)— the value of his 1987 Volkswagen Beetle.

He's been dubbed the world's poorest president, but when asked if he has enough to live on, Mujica's response is straight-forward:

'I do fine with that amount; I have to do fine, because there are many Uruguayans who live with much less.'

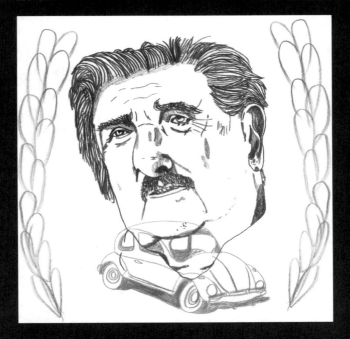

MIKE WEATHERLEY

M·P & CUNT

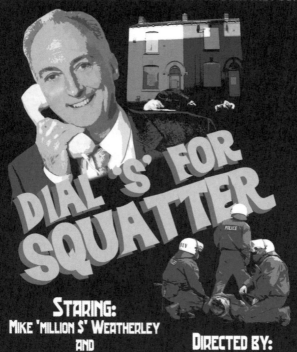

Options for Dealing with Squatting

In August 2011, the Ministry of Justice launched its consultation, Options for Dealing with Squatting. When the results came back, a full 96% of respondents were against criminalisation. They included homelessness charities like Shelter and Crisis, as well as the Law Society, the Magistrates Association and even the Metropolitan Police Service.

Just 6 days after the consultation responses were released, the government announced a clause to criminalise. It was debated late at night, and received almost no scrutiny whatever; the criminalisation of squatting in residential buildings was yawned through in the House by 237 votes to 13.

Here are some of the responses that were ignored by the Ministry of Justice:

Is squatting a particular problem in your area and where does it occur the most e.g. in residential or non-residential property? Were these properties empty/abandoned/derelict before they were occupied, or were they in use?

229—Wandsworth Council
For Wandsworth Council, as a social landlord with some 17,000 tenanted properties in management, squatting is not a particular problem. in 2010–11, the Housing Department dealt with fewer than 4 cases of squatters in both residential and non-residential premises. Where

squatting has occurred, it tends to be in street properties that have been referred for sale.

55—Persons Unknown
I think 'problem' is a loaded term. There is squatting in my area but these properties were abandoned and I think the problem is leaving properties unused in the first place.

56—Persons Unknown
I do not see squatting as a problem. Yes, there are squatters in some residential property nearby. All were empty and unused before, and I see it as a positive thing that people are using them.

35—Persons Unknown
Squatting is not a problem in my area. What is a problem, however, is the number of empty buildings that are deliberately kept empty by the owners, often project developers, who often keep them uninhabitable, waiting for a better time to do them up, or let them go derelict on purpose, in order to be able to tear them down eventually. Many of these properties are, or could be, with relatively little cost, perfectly sound houses. Property speculation is the problem, not squatting.

28—Persons Unknown
There is minimal squatting in my area. That which I am aware of has been on abandoned farmland or empty/derelict property, where squatters have made improvements to the property

Please provide any evidence you have gathered on the number of squats and the nature of squatting in your area or nationwide?

201—Ealing Borough Council
Between 1.12.07 to present, we have evicted a total of 28 squatters. (21 in the East and 7 in the West of the borough)

68—Slough Borough Council

We have had up to 12 squats in the Borough, in the last 12 months since September 2010. The squats have all consisted of typically Eastern European males, generally out of work, addicted to alcohol or drugs. These individuals are not in regular work and are therefore not exercising their treaty rights. They also have no recourse to public funds. There is a reluctance or direct reason for not wanting to return to their country of origin. These reasons include shame, addiction, rejection by family, relationship break up, avoidance of police or prison sentences back home and their situation or opportunities are better here in the UK.

Do you think that the current law adequately deals with squatting? Please explain your reasons.

36—Persons Unknown

No—you might be able to get them out eventually but they are not 'punished' for the damage they do or the things they steal—http://www.dailymail.co.uk/news/article-2026723/Gypsies-immigration-officers-home-Proms.html

17—Persons Unknown

I believe that the current legislation is adequate for dealing with squatters and until the problem of empty properties is addressed it seems logical for homeless people to occupy them, if they have been empty for a long time. Most of the young people I know who are squatters improve the properties they live in.

64—Persons Unknown

The current law seems to enable property owners to evict squatters and then leave buildings empty to fall into further decay. As a woman, I would rater walk past a squatted building at night than a decaying and empty one.

Do you think there is a need for a new criminal offence of squatting?

Law Society
Section 7 is not often used, because squatting happens infrequently, but where it is, our members report that it is extremely effective.

Metropolitan Police Service
The law is broadly in the right place, and the existing array of offences allow us to tackle the worst cases of squatting (eg. where squatters cause the homeowner to be displaced.)

82—Persons Unknown
It has the potential of ignoring the issue of affordable homes and perpetuating the problem of homelessness. If the laws focus on the power and unacceptable evils of aggression involved in eviction, then no. If the laws look at making suitable property even temporarily available, in cities particularly, then yes.

In your experience (e.g. as displaced residential occupier or protected intending occupier or as a law enforcer), how effective is the existing offence in section 7 of the Criminal Law Act 1977?

71—Persons Unknown
I have never heard any first hand reports of squatters occupying buildings that are already lived in, and I believe these stories are largely media fiction intended to manipulate people into believing that squatters pose a threat to them. If such cases exist then DROs are already adequately protected by law.

47—Persons Unknown
In my experience, the majority of squatters occupy buildings that are not intended for living in by a DRO or PIO. The problem being that they have to move out when they return. The number of empty properties which are genuinely abandoned require only interim possession orders for owners to

retake possession. We have never squatted a building whose owner needed to use section 7 of the Criminal Law Act, and similarly have never met squatters who have required it. The DRO is a media-myth, created out of all proportion to the reality of housing in London.

Nigel

Nigel Falange riding to Westminster in a sedan chair carried by the sweating, gurning, clueless shower of BBC journalists for whom he exerts such a fascination. He daintily extends a boot— British leather, of course—for Nick Robinson to lick. Across the country, moustachioed & spittle-flecked colonels (retd.) blimp their way through shabby primary school halls to cast their vote for a man (and, really, politics should be left to the men, none of this trendy degenerate feminonsense) who'll sort out the ravening hordes of 'asylum' seekers who probably hide round corners so we never quite see them. Each of them ambles home to a long-suffering wife, who briefly contemplates how much rat poison she could get away with putting in the mashed potato, before settling down to another choleric divagation on the evils of hijabi marxism. At the end of the evening, each sleeps the sleep of the damned, which is restful, and dreams of a silvered wall, three miles high, keeping this forever England.

Thatcherism-(Isn't)

pitts clampdown. thatchers detach. edens evict. pitts execute, pitilessly. edens execute, edenically. they have executive power, they have executioner's masks and hatchets. clarkes cluck, clarkes gobble, clarkes listen to jazz of oppressed classes and races. clarkes snort, clarkes grunt, clarkes liquidate with 'benefit of clergy'. clarkes pirouette, clarkes harrumph, clarkes disparage 'human rights'. cecils brylcreme™ their quiffs. hurds moo. tebbits explode. foxes run. foxes run charities for rich Americans in need. foxes hunt. things change. foxes react. things change. thatchers react. foxes apologise. thatchers don't. edens evict from eden. porters socialise, porters clean, porters clean toilets, porters clean portaloos. porters, thatchers also suffer. porters port, thatchers thatch. thatchers milksnatch, thatchers semi-detach. camerons milksnatch, camerons fully detach. porters gerrymander and embezzle, embezzle and gerrymander. porters abscond to the holy land. michael howards choose 'everything I do' on desert island discs. michael howards dedicate 'everything I do' to mrs. michael howards. michaels bill and coo. everything they do, they do it for us. ids dribbles. ids pisses. ids suffers from irritable bowel syndrome. ids has ibs. which is worse? ids or ibs? if ids suffers from ibs, does ibs suffer from ids? tories suffer. tories defecate, tories desecrate. ids calculates how to be less beneficial. hagues drawl comp-lacently, reassuringly. hagues have voice training to sound less smug. but it doesn't work. hagues sound more smug. hagues suffer. hagues are 'charismatic- ally challenged'. churchills slurp. thatchers rigidify. thatchers kill northern irish, kill argentinians. churchills sniff. pitts emit. borises bluster. borises blub. borises bikeses are brought to you by barclayses bankses. freudses **** their motherses. dimblebys do not disapprove. dimblebys drool, dimblebys dribble, dimblebys lick, dimblebys spittle. churchills snuffle. dimblebys do not disapprove. michael howardses prefer bryan adamses to gerry adamses. ~~tebbits explode. imagine a punk band called 'the exploding tebbits'.~~ widdecombes waggledance. tories prefer the adams family to gerry adams. (torieses are the adamses.) churchills burp. dimblebys do not disapprove. porter is, thatcher is, ids is. ids is and ids isn't. mays scare, mays scarify, mays are much scarier than muslims with hooks. clarkes listen to more jazzes of more oppressed classes and races. 'wow man that's feral!' porters inherit more tescos. thatchers wither. the withering away of the thatchers. thatcher is and isn't. there is no such thing as

mrs
t******r

(Note: the only reason this strained elegy is in such bad taste is so that Conservatives can understand it)

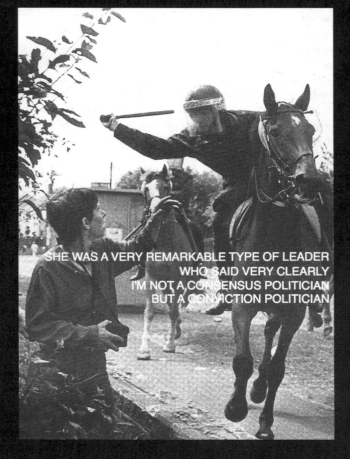

SHE WAS A VERY REMARKABLE TYPE OF LEADER
WHO SAID VERY CLEARLY
I'M NOT A CONSENSUS POLITICIAN
BUT A CONVICTION POLITICIAN

THIS IS THE BEST WAY
WE HAVE FOUND
TO LIVE
AND   WE MAKE
EVERYONE
IN THIS WORLD OF
NEW PRIVILEGE SLAVES,
TO FALSE IDEAS OF GOD
AND COMFORT
AND WAKING UP
EVERY MORNING
IS A WRENCH
FROM THE DREAM STATE
INTO THE PARANOID
NEW MIND
AND WE ARE STILL
SAD AND LONELY
IN A WORLD OF GLASS

The Suffragette Gazette

DAILY NEWS FROM A BETTER WORLD

100 YEARS OF POSSIBILITY

1913 was a fierce year for the Suffragettes. It was a year of militancy, of tragedy and of hope. It was a final year of mass actions before the outbreak of World War I, before the chaos and destruction of unnecessary global violence. 1913 was a year bearing similarities to 2013 - this is a year when our efforts can still be focused on combatting climate change, before the effects of the unrepentant burning of fossil fuel launch us into desperate struggles to deal with the consequences of a burning earth.

1913 saw the suffragettes build a global movement with mass rallies in the US and the UK. On March 3 of that year, there was a mass march in Washington, D.C., where 8000 American Suffragettes marched for Votes for Women. On the 8th of June 1913 Emily Wilding Davison died under the hooves of the King's horse while trying to fasten a Suffragette flag to the horse's bridle - a brave and seditious act. On the 14th June, Emily was laid to rest, accompanied by a funeral parade. Her gravestone bears the Suffragette slogan DEEDS NOT WORDS.

By 1913 the Suffragettes were a mass movement, a community of intrepid

Emily Wilding Davison's Funeral Procession, 1913

women announcing the potential for democratic change. Through bold and scandalous actions they succeeded in making themselves heard. They were tortured and imprisoned, and eventually they won.

In 2013, we are a part of a global movement committed to non-violence in the struggle for a low-carbon future. We are connected to the women who campaigned before us through shared passion and the fervour to pass on a world we can be proud of. We know that climate change threatens life itself, especially for the world's poorest women, and that the actions our governments take in the next few years have the power to change history. The pressure for change will come from us. It's important to take strength from our memory bank of historic women's movements. The memory and the legacy of the power

of past movements sustains and inspires climate activists today in the same tradition which saw the Suffragettes strengthened by the memory of Joan of Arc and Boudicca.

The legacy of the climate change movement is up to us to decide. We are told to vote for the changes we want to see realised by voting for political parties who do not represent us, and that voting in itself commemorates the Suffragettes. But voting is more than a ballot box, it can stand for all forms of political agency. It's the ability to create powerful communities. It can mean voting on our feet, building up friendships and networks of resistance, or changing policy. We can put pressure on our pension funds, universities and work places. We can put our bodies in the way of polluting corporations, and ultimately, like the Suffragettes and the women before them, we can...

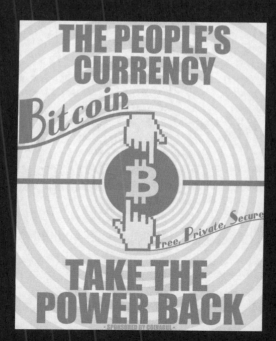

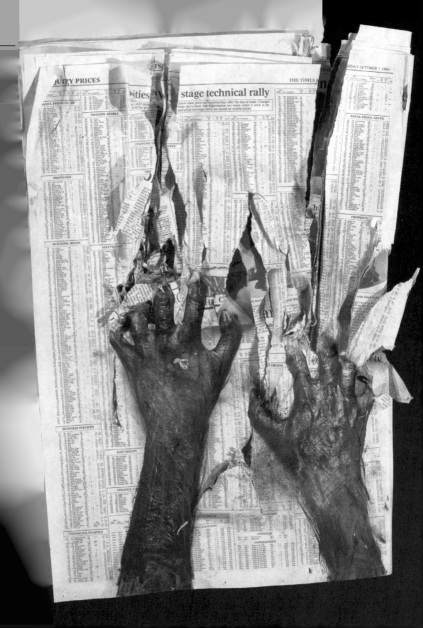

ISSUE___4

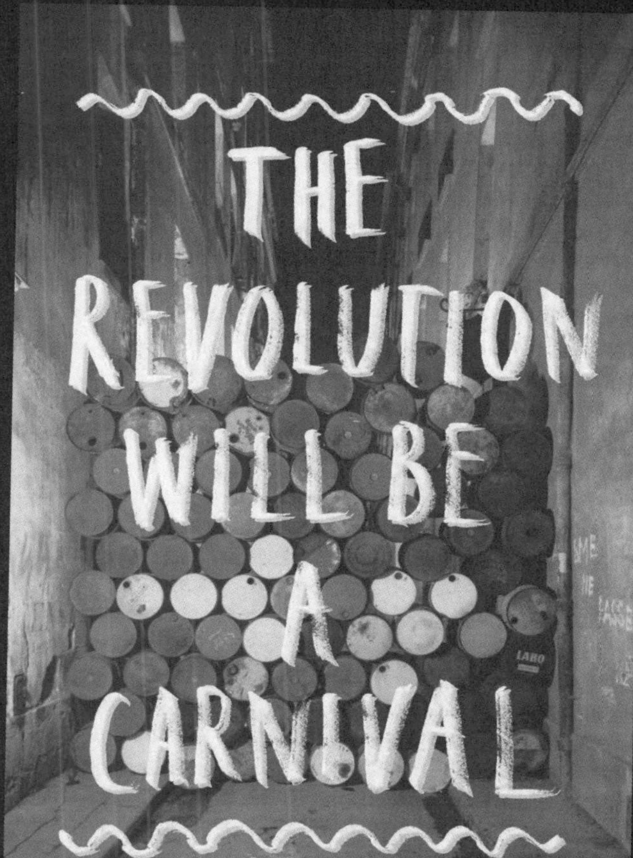
THE
REVOLUTION
WILL BE
A
CARNIVAL

Positive Money
Picking Up the Slingshot

Despite George Osborne's overly optimistic diagnosis that 'Britain is turning a corner,' people living in the real economy know the crisis isn't over yet. We still have 2.5 million people desperately seeking jobs, and almost 1 million of those are between 16 and 24. There are also about 500,000 people who rely on food banks. Yet there is no shortage of work that needs to be done: Britain has a huge shortage of houses and a looming energy crisis. Dealing with these problems alone would immediately create jobs and boost the economy. So, we have jobs to do and we have people to do them—the problem seems to be money. Apparently there isn't enough of it. But where does money come from? How is it created and how come it doesn't seem to reach the places that need it the most?

How does money work?

If you ask a person in the street how money works, they will suggest that money is deposited in a bank, and then lent on, and then deposited in a bank, and then lent on, like a system of tokens that circulate forever. If you suggest that when you repay a loan to your bank the money disappears from the system, they are likely to think you are pulling their leg. However, only 3% of all the money in circulation does circulate forever as tokens. This type of money is cash, and you can find it in your wallet as notes and coins.

So what about the rest of it? The remaining 97% is a kind of temporary money, continuously being created and destroyed. It exists as accounting entries in a computer system, a form of electronic money; it is created when banks make loans and destroyed when those loans are repaid. The result of this strange arrangement is that the total amount of money that exists in the economy is always fluctuating. At any one time, thousands of people may be creating new money by taking out loans, while at the same time thousands may be destroying money by repaying existing loans. The total amount of money in the economy is therefore rather analogous to the amount of water in a bath when the plug has been removed, letting water pour out, and there is a tap running with water flowing in. The water flowing out corresponds to money-destruction as existing loans are repaid, and the running tap corresponds to new loans being made. If these two rates are exactly the same then the total amount of money we have would remain constant, but that's rather tricky to arrange. In general, the total amount of money is either growing or shrinking.

For a long time (at least the last 40 years), banks have had the freedom to make as many loans as they like. When someone repays a loan to a bank the money disappears, whilst the banks keep the interest as profit. Therefore banks will choose where to lend based on their own profits rather than the needs of the economy, and they will lend as much as they can to maximize their profit. In the 10 years running up to the financial crisis in 2008, banks doubled the amount of mortgage lending. This resulted in house prices increasing by more than 300%. Thinking back to the bath, the tap was turned on as far as it could go, pouring water in the bath.

When the financial crisis hit it was like the tap being turned off, or at least being turned down dramatically, as banks panicked and stopped their lending. But the water carries on pouring out the plughole at just the same rate because all that earlier borrowing still has to be repaid. If the government does nothing then the water level would start to fall. This is exactly what happened in the US in the great depression in 1929. During the years of the great depression, the total amount of money in the US economy shrank by a third. The money wasn't 'going somewhere else', it wasn't ending up in somebody else's hands: it was actually disappearing out of existence. Fast forward to 2008 and the same thing happened again. A decreasing money supply is agonising for an economy. People go round scratching their heads, wondering why everyone seems to have less money than they used to.

An Alternative

Now imagine for a moment that all of the money in the system was converted to a system of tokens that circulate forever. Under this system the plug would be put back into the bath and the tap turned on only as and when it is needed, instead of lurching from pouring water into the bath to being switched off. Under this system there is no such thing as a collapsing money supply. Crucially, the control of the tap should also move from being in private banks' hands to public hands—to a place that is transparent and democratically accountable.

Although it is unnerving to think about, most economists and politicians do not fully understand why the financial crisis happened. Recently, a former regulator told us that he only started thinking about the creation of money in 2010, three years after the crisis started. This admission is of great importance because it shows that there is simply a huge lack of understanding in both policy-making circles and the finance sector about how the current system works. The creation of money was not even considered as a possible culprit for the 2008 crisis. Very few mainstream economists are looking at who is creating the money and where it's going, even though money affects everything that happens in our economy. The type of economics taught widely across universities today essentially ignores money creation. If you ask any economics student to explain the exact process of money creation, chances are they won't have much of an answer. We think this is a huge problem. Five years after the financial crisis, UK businesses and households have hardly reduced their debts. A fall in the level of household and business debt is essential for a sustainable economic recovery but, given the government's commitment to lowering public sector debt, this scenario is unlikely. Since most politicians do not have a full analysis of the crisis, they do not know how to get the economy started again. The big problems facing the UK today won't be solved by passively waiting for the economy to recover. We need to demand that the government do something new and different–something that will create jobs, deal with the shortage of housing and allow people to reduce their personal debts. Current government policies are failing and it is time for a change.

We believe that money should serve the people, rather than the people serving money. To achieve that we think legislative change is necessary to fix the monetary system, but politicians will only act when academics, economists, business leaders and the public see the need and demand change; we need the media to understand and debate the issue. We've outlined our proposal for reform in a book called Modernising Money.

Finally, the UK is in a situation where banks are not lending enough to job-creators, whilst increasing their lending for mortgages. This increases the level of private debt, which was the original cause of the financial crisis. We need new money, free from debt, to be spent on areas like green energy, which create jobs in the real economy. We know that the big banks can't do this, and we think that the public and politicians are starting to realise that, too. Therefore we have a big opportunity to shift the status quo away from banks dictating our economy. We have people that want to work and jobs that need doing. Goliath has been beating David for a long time now. It's time that David picks up his sling shot.

Upper-Class Solidarity
Nothing In Life Shall Sever

To understand the British public school system, or certainly, the part of it in which I spent my teenage years, it is crucial to get your head around three things.

The first is that no pupil I can think of left my school fat. The second is that it was only when I arrived at university that I realised I am not short. The third is that I know a pair of twins who, when they left, had the school's emblem tattooed onto their backsides.

How these things happen is not complex.

Every afternoon we played sport. I say 'played'. It was, particularly in the autumnal 'Michaelmas' term, significantly more brutal than that. To warm up before rugby, we would be made to sprint lengths of the pitch until, sometimes, a less-fit child vomited. We would lie in the mud with our feet in the air until our stomachs screamed in agony, and, gradually, formed themselves into neat rows of muscle. And then, come rain or hail or ice or snow, we would hurl our ball and bodies at each other.

When we'd finished, we'd limp back to our various houses, boil a vat of spaghetti, add pesto, and sit with our peers and a loaf of bread. Using the sliced white to grab, we would swallow handful after handful of oily, salty pasta. After this snack, we would head to the grand dining hall and cram in more carbs.

Every waking moment was filled. I was in the choir, the orchestra, the concert band and the pipe band. There was debating, a newsletter, drama. In the summer ('Trinity') term, I'd spend Tuesday afternoons climbing and Thursday afternoons kayaking. I learnt to fence and, at Wednesday

CCF, to salute, march in formation, and to strip, clean and rebuild a rifle in under 30 seconds.

Every day but Saturday, we had chapel. The whole school would congregate, be preached to, pray together, and sing together. My housemaster was choirmaster and organist. Even for a hardened atheist the effect he conducted, in the magnificent chapel, was majestic and moving. Every community should come together, each morning, and sing.

In the evening, it was 'prep'—homework—followed by TV. In order to stray beyond the 'front quad' after these hours, you needed a 'docket'—permission slip. Every move, every moment, could be accounted for.

Younger pupils slept in 'cubes', with flimsy walls about 8ft high allocating each person's portion of an otherwise shared dormitory. 6th formers had their own rooms, with a desk and spring-laden bed. Each corridor was governed by a 'beak'. At 17, I was responsible for 25 of my peers—for ensuring that they were OK, were quiet during 'prep', and, most importantly, were in bed on time.

These houses, along with a few of the classrooms, formed the main school buildings—a front and a back quad mimicking those of an Oxford college. Every 15 minutes, all night long, the bells of the clock tower echoed around the impressive buildings. After five years, they became a nighttime friend.

Other school facilities varied—on the one hand, music was taught in one of Basil Spence's finest. On the other, my maths classes were in Portacabins.

The final thing to consider is the very fact of boarding. I haven't lived with my parents since I was 13. Some left home at eight or nine. If you suspect that this is likely to lead to insecurity then institutionalisation, you'd be right.

There was no beating—my school days weren't those of Tom Brown. But that doesn't mean there aren't scars. If posh people seem not to be rooted, it's because we are untimely ripped from our parents' home.

The process forces you to grow up fast and, I suspect, incompletely. You become tough, but bad at feeling or expressing a healthy range of emotions. Of course, this doesn't prevent future success. As Jimmy Reid said 'anyone who can be totally adjusted to our society is in greater need of psychiatric analysis and treatment than anyone else.'

The sport, the language, the dislocation, the lumpy beds, the chapel: these may sound odd, but they are typical for a British public school. I describe them to make a point. Ask most people to recount their school days and you would imagine, alongside friends, that they would talk about lessons. But this would miss the point of Britain's public school system.

The classes were, of course, good. They were small, and the teachers were effective. They often seemed to be chosen for their skill in coaching us for rugby and tick-box tests rather than in inspiring questioning minds; as exam crammers, they delivered—and the odd one strained at the curricular leash. But it is not because you want your child to get top grades that you send them to live for five years at a British public school. There are much easier and cheaper ways to achieve that.

There is a bizarre belief held by many that success in Britain correlates to intelligence and hard work. This is a very middle-class concept. What the upper classes understand is that success stems from two things: community and the appearance of confidence. And they are the purpose of public school.

So, all that sport, the diet, the uncomfortable beds, they are all part of a process. They ensure that no one is fat, and that everyone reaches the maximum of their genetically permitted height—that everyone appears healthy, fit.

But more importantly, they are about team building. Children are ripped from their parental home. Gradually their school class becomes a surrogate family, the concomitant social-class extended family. To shout 'Stockholm syndrome' would be extreme, but the psychological effect is surely similar.

Each school—like many families—has its own words: 'docket', 'prep', 'Coll', 'beak'. The more prominent English schools even have their own sports—the Eton Wall Game, Winchester Fives and, well, Rugby Football.

Whilst the ruling elite might preach rugged individualism, we are brought up to sing together every morning, to stand on the rugby pitch together every afternoon, and, after leaving, to go away together and run a now-vanished empire.

The aim is simple: to build solidarity. Whilst there are many reasons that the British ruling class is so imperially successful, this process of bonding is surely one of them. The middle classes are taught to believe that they will succeed through individual gumption. The upper class is built on the knowledge that this is nonsense.

And who were we taught to stand against? Anyone who has met me knows that, despite being Scottish, I have what some call an English accent. I suppose I'd argue it's better described as posh. If you didn't speak like this at my school, you'd be bullied—called a 'scoit'. The teachers complained, but the culture remained.

The British public-school system is best understood not by the brutality of Tom Brown nor by the excitement of Harry Potter. It is best understood as the root of the British elite. Each school has its own flavour. But they all play a similar function: they build ruling-class solidarity. And at that, they are exceptional. Here is a verse from the Eton Boating Song. Next time you see a photograph of the government front bench, remember these lines:

> *Rugby may be more clever,*
> *Harrow may make more row,*
> *But we'll row for ever,*
> *Steady from stroke to bow,*
> *And nothing in life shall sever*
> *The chain that is round us now,*
> *And nothing in life shall sever*
> *The chain that is round us now.*

TXT: FEDERICO CAMPAGNA

Work Hard, Play Hard

An Ode to Eudaimonia

Work hard, play hard
Work hard, play hard
We work hard, play hard
Keep partyin' like it's your job

David Guetta, Play Hard, 2013

The position of refusal of work is undergoing a renaissance. As well as anarchists, autonomists, and de-growth hippies, economic experts are also beginning to denounce the unproductiveness of structuring our society around hyperwork. Yet, if we want to create a sharp and effective critique of work, we must combine the economic analysis with a perspective that sees humans not simply as economic agents, but as existentially complex individuals.

Beyond our understanding of work as labour—which seemingly turns noble or ignoble (i.e. exploitative) only according to the ownership of its outcome and of the means of production—we have to place the activity of work within an individual, existential frame.

As we begin penetrating our individualities, we first encounter the temptation of defining as 'work' anything that we deem boring or that we don't want to do. However, a critique of work that is built around its supposed unpleasantness easily falls pray either to childish short-sightedness or, more dangerously, to late-capitalist 'play' rhetoric. Any skills that we might want to acquire demand unpleasant exercise, as any bored 8-year old engaging in piano practice knows. At the same time, 'hip' Google-esque corporations have long exploited such an instinctive reaction to unpleasant activities, by replacing the old, grey, boring work with happy, colourful and ultimately hyperexploitative play-work.

Moving beyond the shallows of immediate dis/satisfactions, I will now attempt a more solid understanding of the place of work within our existential trajectories.

Living in an age which has embraced nihilism both as a nightmare and as an emancipatory possibility, we can finally imagine the fundamental ethical challenge—living a 'good life'—as potentially disentangled from any external dogma. Instead of unfolding as a forced march towards socially endorsed goals, ethics can thus take place as a movement towards a self-constructed, aspirational image of ourselves, which functions for us as a motivational existential figure. Such a figure remains fixed in its position within us, directing our existential development and the course of our actions, although its specific characteristics continuously change through time, just as we do.

Our ethical challenge can thus be fundamentally reduced to a process of increasing the resemblance of our self-perception—as mediated by our understanding of our actions—with such an ever-changing figure, fixed in its immobile position. This aspirational trajectory can be defined as an individual and autonomous progression towards our existential goals. Drawing from the Greek ethical tradition, which defined happiness as a state of eudaimonia (literally, of the 'good demon'), we could define our ethical strivings as a form of inner mysticism, aimed at the progressive unity between us and our daimon, or inner motivational figure(s). While such a unity can only take place as a limit-concept, and is bound to remain constrained by the boundaries of our biology and mortality, it is for us an extremely useful tool to overcome both nihilism and societal ideologies.

We can now attempt to offer a different definition of what is work, and why and how we can oppose its regime. Work can be defined as any activity which is detrimental to—or not effectively instrumental to—the achievement of our eudaimonia, that is, of our own, personal and autonomous, existential progress.

It shouldn't come as a surprise, then, that the most recent discipline of the work regime exerts itself in the realm of existential motivation, more than in that of economic gain. Now that work has revealed itself in its simultaneous economic irrelevance, political failure and environmental catastrophe, it is deep inside of us, at the very end of our existential trajectory, that its new justification seemingly lies. As perfectly represented by those countless talent shows that have work as their topic and employment as their prize, contemporary work propaganda aims at filling the position of the inner motivational figure with the totemic figurine of the 'employee'.

If we attempt to frame the idea of work within an existential perspective, many unpleasant activities suddenly escape the realm of work, while many pleasant ones unexpectedly enter it.

In order to achieve our personal existential goals, we might have to undergo periods of repetitive and unpleasant activity, from taking care of our biological needs, to improving our skills and abilities, etc. Undergoing such tedious processes requires both the long-sightedness of placing them within an effective existential trajectory, and the self-discipline of resisting immediate though existentially detrimental satisfactions. Perhaps surprisingly, after decades in which the discourse over emancipation has stressed the evils of discipline and the beauty of a 'free flowing' existence, self-discipline reveals itself as crucial for any strategy of existential emancipation. At the same time, much of what is glorified as 'fun'—including the imperative to enjoy, shared both by late-capitalist rhetoric and by the pseudo-emancipatory mantra of 'lad/ladette' culture—suddenly takes on a very different colouring.

Far from the dream of partying for our right to fight (or of its pathetic Beastie Boys reversal), contemporary culture proposes partying and fun as an integral part of the work process. Like office work, contemporary fun culture unfolds in stereotyped environments of forced socialisation (festivals, clubs and pubs, eerily similar in their atmosphere to late night offices), as mediated by standardised technologies (such as alcohol and drugs), and ultimately leading to the perfect conformity of the mass of 'fun-ed' subjects. More importantly, contemporary fun, just like work, requires a level of commitment that barely leaves any energy available for the individual pursuit of our own existential trajectories. Post-party hangover, like post-office annihilation, transforms us into hopeless wrecks, clinging onto the most basic levels of survival. In-party drunkenness, like in-work subjugation, humiliates us, turning us into nonsensical fools covered with our own alcoholic vomit—just like we covered our lap, a few hours earlier in the office, with the crumbs of our sad desk lunch.

Once again, the reason behind such a debacle of 'fun' (theoretically, the immediate opposite and alternative to work) lies in the existential territory more than in that of economics. As the Roman Stoic philosopher Seneca once remarked, 'If one doesn't know to which port one is sailing, no wind is ever favourable.' Without the individual's investigation of one's own inner motivational figure(s), and of the trajectories leading there, neither a critique of work nor a disentanglement of fun from work can ever take place. Despite being often relegated to the quack medicine of self-help books or to the expensive scams of private psychologists, the recognition of our existential trajectory is perhaps the most fundamental aspect of any political and intellectual emancipatory project.

Reviving the injunction carved on the stone of Apollo's temple in Delphi, 'Know thyself!', doesn't only amount to an exercise in archaeological nostalgia, but can shed new light on the demands of the work regime and on our opposition to them. Instead of falling for the false dichotomy of labour and entertainment, as epitomised by the work-fun loop, such existential investigation can dramatically help us to ground our claim for an autonomously focused life.

As the understanding of our own inner motivational figures develops into us actively sculpting ourselves in their ever-developing image, we become increasingly wary of any activity that is detrimental to our eudaimonia, regardless of whether it is camouflaged as work or as fun. Complementing the negative dimension of pure refusal with a positive project of existential development allows our struggle against work and alienation to acquire better focus and a sharper edge. Perhaps it is not a coincidence that the golden age of ethical and existential investigation, as it took place on the ancient shores of the Mediterranean Sea, remains to date a beacon of reference for any attempt at emancipation from sorry theologies such as those of God, of the State or of Work. Penetrating the soft tissue of our individuality, and learning how to inhabit it powerfully, is the most basic architectural task for the construction of an autonomous future. If we neglect to engage in it, we risk seeing our life sclerotising into the dead stone of somebody else's project. All that would be left for us to do would be to keep working as hard as we can—and partying just as hard, of course.

DATA ENTRY

OFFICE SUPPORT
SUPERVISOR

FACILITY
ASSISTANT

SERVICES
ADMINISTRATOR

OFFICE
SPECIALIST

ADMINISTRATIVE
ANALYST

ACCOUNTING
SPECIALIST

MAIL
OPERATOR

DATA
ADMINISTRATOR

Horizontalism: The New Democracy

From Occupy to Gezi Park

'Everywhere is Taksim! Everywhere is resistance!' and 'Come, come whoever you are!' were some of the main slogans in the early days of the movement that began this spring in Turkey. What started as the defence of a park quickly turned into hundreds of thousands mobilised in the streets throughout the country, transforming public space as it was held, and morphing in many places into horizontal assemblies and forums—or 'agora', as they are referred to in Turkey. And then in Brazil, only weeks later, hundreds of thousands began mobilising throughout the country, many chanting 'No Party Represents Me!' From these mass-mobilisations, people also began to gather in city neighborhoods and towns, forming horizontal assemblies, discussing both what is wrong in society and what they can do.

These two places, Brazil and Turkey in the spring and summer of 2013, easily could have been Greece and Spain, or the US and UK, Slovenia and Portugal, Moscow and Reykjavik and on and on. Each sparked at different times and from different specific causes, but with similar forms of organization, and under the same general rubric: no to representation and yes to horizontal social relationships. Each of the movements is using space in the same way to create these new relationships, first in the occupation and recuperation of large parks and plazas, and then to the neighbourhoods and smaller towns. None are traditional social movements that have claims or demands, which, once met, will placate them. These are movements about reclaiming our relationships to one another, reclaiming space, and reinventing ways of being.

Something new is happening—something new in content, depth, breadth and global consistency. Societies around the world are in movement—and this movement looks and feels so similar all around the world.

Since the end of 2010 millions of people have been taking to the streets in cities, towns and villages—assembling in plazas, occupying parks, buildings, homes and schools. There is a growing global movement of refusal; simultaneously, in that refusal, there is a movement of creation. Millions are shouting 'No!' as they manifest alternatives in the wake of this no. People from below are rising up, but rather than going towards the top—'from the bottom up'—they are moving as the Zapatistas suggested: 'From below and to the left, where the heart resides.'

Hierarchy and representational democracy are being rejected, ideologically and by default, and in the rejection mass horizontal assemblies are opening new landscapes with the horizon of autonomy and freedom. What that means, what these societies in movement 'want' is not always clear, but they are walking, and as they walk they are creating new ways of being, new ways of creating in the crisis. The want is tied to the walk, it is intentional, it is a refusal of the crisis while opening new possibilities, still to be determined.

This 'No!', this 'Enough is Enough!', speaks for itself. It is an absolute rejection. It is not a shout of protest—it is a shout of refusal. It is a refusal to be a part of the crisis, and in the space of the no millions are simultaneously beginning to create Yeses. People are shouting against an economic, political, social and cultural crisis. But at the same time as the shout of 'No!' millions have been coming together to create their own alternatives to the crisis. This is, in some places and with some people, an ideological choice or position, a rejection of the state or forms of hierarchical power; for millions of others it is the result of a lack of alternatives.

The people are rejecting their states and institutions of power because these same institutions have made clear that it is the people who will pay for the crisis. This is seen most starkly in Greece and Italy, but increasingly so all over the world, from Ireland, Portugal and Spain to the US; at the same time, it is increasingly true that traditional forms of protest are futile. As Greek activist Anestis reflected when I interviewed him:

During the last two years different forms of struggle, mobilisation and organizing have been tested. If you asked people, even from the movement, two years ago 'If we have a massive demonstration in the center of Athens with half a million people would we succeed to throw off the government and cancel the austerity measures?' most people would have said yes. We did that, four times, five times, and they continued. I am not implying that we should stop having massive demonstrations in the center of Athens. I am just saying that we have experienced their limits, and now we must do something else. (Anestis. 2012, Athens, Greece, June.)

Enough! is not so much shouted at the government as it is a point of unity, of people coming together; more of an exclamation that they have had enough—and, in that same space of enough, to begin to create horizontal assemblies in order to find ways to prefigure possible alternatives and futures. In the conversation with Anestis, he went on to explain the development of his neighborhood assembly of Peristeri, where people organize to meet their day-to-day needs as well as networking with other assemblies on broader questions of survival. It is not out of a desire to have an assembly each week that they meet, but that the state has failed and they now feel they only have one another. As Vasilis, in Athens, describes:

They cannot represent us anymore. It's impossible. So it's like recuperating a factory—the factory here is democracy. It's like the bosses left the factory and you have to make the factory work because you have to make decisions, because you have to be recognised, you have needs and want to cover them, you have desires... (Vasilis. 2012, Athens, Greece, June.)

In the space of the No! is also the manifestation of multiple yeses and affirmations: from 'we are the 99%' in the United States; Democracia Real Ya! (Real Democracy! As an exclamation and affirmation, not a demand) in Spain; and *'vy nas dazhe ne predstavlyayete!'* ('You can't represent us—and you cannot even imagine us!') in Moscow.

The use of Horizontalidad, horizontality, and horizontalism, first coined in Argentina by autonomous movements in the wake of the 2001 crisis, has become a widespread way of describing the new social relationships developing around the globe. Horizontalism and horizontal are words that encapsulate the relationships upon which many of the new global movements are grounded.

Horizontalidad is a social relationship that implies, as its name suggests, a flat plane upon which to communicate. Horizontalidad necessarily implies the use of direct democracy and the striving for consensus, processes in which attempts are made so that everyone is heard and new relationships are created.

More than merely a tool for assemblies, Horizontalidad is a new way of relating, based on affective politics and against all the implications of 'isms'; while sometimes translated as horizontalism, it is a sort of play on the fact that it is against all that 'isms' imply. It is a dynamic social relationship, and thus the meaning in English is more than just horizontal or horizontality—there is not yet a perfect word in English to describe this phenomenon. Horizontalism is not an ideology or political program that must be met so as to create a new society or new idea. It is a break with vertical ways of organizing and relating, and a break that is simultaneously an opening. Horizontalism is a process, a way of creating new forms of relating, and in that process the forms of relating necessarily change—so horizontalism is also an ever-changing process.

The intention behind the use of horizontalidad is not to determine the path that a country or group should take. It is to create the space for a conversation in which all can participate and in which all can determine together what the future should look like, while at the same time attempting to prefigure that future society in present social relationships. At its best, horizontalidad is a tool for real democracy.

The force of the slogan, Democracía Real Ya!, as with other slogans, like 'they say we have democracy and we don't'—is to reflect that we do not live in a democracy, but in a dictatorship of corporations. Now, in the movement, we have begun the process of discussing what democracy is. Democracía Real Ya! has opened a space for so many people who were frustrated with what we have—but what it means is still not clear, we are creating it. (Amador. 2012, Madrid, Spain.)

Climate Change is Class War

Solidarity at the Coal Face

We're in a pub in Hackney discussing why the messaging for Reclaim the Power—the direct action camp that took place in Balcombe this August—doesn't have a 'front-loaded' climate message. My friend, a long-term climate activist, is genuinely worried that the protest we're organising, which at that point was going to be back at EDF's West Burton gas power station, isn't mobilising the key people we need to mobilise—climate activists—and that people don't 'get it', and the whole thing isn't 'clear.' I try: We can't ignore austerity. This is the time to join the dots.

Right now it's the Bedroom Tax, it's cuts, it's the NHS being sold off, it's fuel poverty, it's 2 years of the Tories and people are not waking up in the morning and thinking: Shit the icecaps are melting and we're heading for climate catastrophe; they're waking up and thinking: Shit I don't know if I can pay the bills. We need to be able to respond to that. For too long, climate justice, struggles around energy democracy or how we reclaim a commons, haven't had relevancy to the majority of people living in the UK. They've seemed external, an added dimension—even though they relate to everything. Climate change isn't getting people out onto the streets. If anything, it was Occupy and anti-capitalism-lite (Economic Justice) that got people out onto the streets in the last two years. The war on the poor, the reproduction of 'the poor', class war—this is what people are feeling now. 'Class War?' he says, he himself coming from a 'benefits family' way north in the isle, 'but climate change IS class war'.

The economic crisis of 2008 has provided ruling elites around the world with a perfect alibi to continue restructuring, privatising and de-regulating public resources, institutions and spheres. And it is precisely these shock doses of austerity that are enabling bigger, longer-term shifts in policy and ownership to take place behind closed doors. One such shock-doctrine enabled policy is the UK's 'dash for gas'—the plan to build up to 40 new Gas power stations, frack up to two-thirds of England, and mortgage the UK's energy future to the pollutant fossil fuel, controlled by Big Energy, for the next 30 years. Once these facts on the ground are established—a new extractive industry all over the country and massive power stations—they will be almost impossible to reverse. Beating Gas in the UK would open up the space for democratically controlled renewable energy to develop, on a localised basis. This wouldn't automatically happen, but the space—political and economic—to make it possible would be opened up. Coal is over, nuclear would take too long: it is heading off gas that can bring us closer to Energy Democracy.

Everything for Everyone

The Reclaim the Power coalition was a reflection of some of the climate, social and economic justice movements in the UK today: Occupy, No Dash for Gas, Fuel Poverty Action, Disabled People Against Cuts and UK Uncut. The idea behind putting this together was about showing that, to win, we need to co-operate and expose the systemic oppressions and structures that lie behind much of the disempowerment we're facing. Look through the symptoms straight to the causes. It was the community in Balcombe, calling for solidarity to stop Cuadrilla drilling in their area, that changed the political game on climate in the UK this summer. We responded. Had RTP stayed at West Burton, we would have been ignoring a major debate-stirring, gas controversialising, democratic-deficit-exposing struggle on London's doorstep.

The decision to switch to Balcombe just one week before the camp showed the agility that a non-heirarchical network has when it needs to adapt and respond to new developments. Instead of taking action in an area where there was basically no resistance to the already established and running West Burton power station, we would be standing in solidarity with a community that actually did want us there, and where our arguments about democracy and the need to reclaim control over our futures would have far greater traction and resonance. We could also have a real impact on stopping a new fact on the ground from taking root.

The decision to move was compared to a previous decision to have a Climate Camp on Blackheath in 2011, targeting the financial sector rather than holding it in response to the Vestas workers' occupation and struggle down on the Isle of Wight. The decision—set your own agenda or respond to an existing one, the former being the choice—was criticised by many at the time as lacking solidarity and being divorced from live social struggles.

Within hours of Reclaim the Power securing a site by squatting a field at Balcombe, despite heavy police presence, Cuadrilla announced that it would not drill for the entire duration of the camp—six days. We had a win and we hadn't even started. This win was based on 3 factors.

Historical Power

No Dash for Gas had achieved the longest power station shutdown and occupation in UK history and beaten off EDF's subsequent £5million lawsuit, garnering huge public support and reputational damage to the French energy giant along the way. Cuadrilla had to wonder if this type of direct action could happen again? Direct action—by up to a thousand people—was the scariest-to-power element of the camp. The nature of the coalition and its reach—Occupy, UK Uncut, Disabled People Against Cuts and Fuel Poverty Action—also had a deterrent affect. Bar DPAC, all of these had already been defined as 'terrorist threats' in 2011 by City of London police.

An Organised and Established Culture of Resistance

RTP was based on the Climate Camp model of direct action, movement building and sustainable living that came from a culture of historical camps, including those of the anti-roads movement, Earth First gatherings, Greenham Common, traveller and free-party sites and international anti-capitalist and No Border camps. It was amplifying and perpetuating a rich culture of resistance that had already succeeded in heading off the third runway at Heathrow (involving the support of a community-led campaign in the village of Sipson) and new coal (Kingsnorth). This culture is one that sustains itself through an attempted 'lived commons'—networks of low-cost housing co-operatives, squats and communal living, at times in direct confrontation to corporate interests; social centres; independent media and publishing co-ops; concrete tools and infrastructure that are shared and can be reused by groups (i.e. the Activist TAT Collective, which loans tents, water piping, toilets, and other essential infrastructure for camps); self-organised support networks focusing on legal defence, police monitoring and jail solidarity; medical care on actions; psychological trauma support; and further up from the grassroots, a fluid interplay between the political support of established NGOs and the physical support of members–workers who are often able to keep organising at the grassroots because they have financial sustainability and the time to research and build knowledge through working for an NGO. Add into this mix the funding from wealthy progressives: they're often anonymous, but the cosmetics company Lush gave thousands to anti-fracking network Frack Off (who had been key in catalysing 45 local groups to fight fracking all over the country, and was a founding part of the existing Occupy-style camp at the road verges leading to the Cuadrilla site). All told, you have a network of networks based on a culture of trust, mutual understanding, confidence and participatory democracy that can effectively respond to capital's evolving agendas.

Conflict Escalation Avoidance and Neutralisation

Public opinion was already on the side of Balcombe locals: many sympathised with the conservative village and saw their plight as one of locals versus undemocratic big business and government policy. By neutralising the drilling, the company hoped to neutralise any participation and bridge-building between locals and the camp. If the aims of the camp had already been achieved—i.e. shut down Cuadrilla—then what was the point in travelling to Balcombe to protest? Our presence would be seen as 'unreasonable'.

But the protests worked. Recent polling by the University of Nottingham showed support for shale gas extraction in the UK steadily rising for more than a year, peaking at 61% in favour in July, but falling to 55% by September. This is directly attributed to anti-fracking protests in the Summer.

Our Climate, Our Commons

Reclaim the Power is not the only barometer by which to measure climate activism in the UK, but it does epitomise the coalition-building that is happening in order to generalise activism on reclaiming power for a commons—our climate, our energy, our labour. Focusing on a symptom of capitalism—climate change—that affects everyone—Left and Right, top or bottom of the pile—can open up genuine concepts of a collective and of what rights people should have to meet our common needs and aspirations. Drilling license applications in the UK could sow the seeds of a fertile network of resistance and coalitions dispersed all over the country. It can also provoke the possibility of planned alternatives—local sustainable community controlled power in your backyard rather than a fracking rig.

The movement is getting more diverse and class-orientated. Disaster capitalism is presenting us with the conditions for coalition-building and a form of disaster communism. Climate Change is Class war.

Laughtivism

Doing it with the lolz

Using humor as a means for political commentary is something nearly as old as democracy itself: from the plays of Aristophanes in ancient Greece that poked fun at ruling Athenian elites; to Moliere's satires which incited people to take to the streets demanding '*Liberté, Égalité, Fraternité*'; to the present day political cartoons of Syrian cartoonist Ali Ferzat whose depictions of Arab ruling families has had him beaten and banned in countries all through the Middle East. Clearly the use of humour as a means of political dissent has been an important avenue of inciting civil debate, if not full-blown revolution. Now more than ever, though, we are seeing how humour is used not just as a subversive tool by writers, artists and cartoonists, but instead as a weapon for building support for mass social movements by the people directly involved—activists.

The term 'laughtivism' is one of many different coinages that have arisen in recent years to describe the increasingly diverse avenues for civil resistance that new media and technologies have given rise to. Much has been covered on the work of 'hacktivists' such as Julian Assange and Bradley Manning of Wikileaks fame, as well as the advent of 'clicktivism' which describes real-field issues that become oversimplified when people think resistance is tantamount to 'liking' it on facebook or posting about it on youtube. However, 'laughtivism' is still a relatively new term that nonetheless has useful lessons to teach those looking to improve their political landscape.

Laughtivism refers specifically to the use of humour in nonviolent political campaigns to bolster social movements, unite opposing constituencies and decrease the negative effects of fear for resistors who risk oppression. Instead of drawing from the political landscape in the name of entertainment or art as has been done for literally thousands of years, the goal with 'laughtivist' techniques is to bring awareness to a political or social issue using humor as a means for delivering that message.

A few defining characteristics of 'laughtivist' techniques: they are funny; they are political; they are demonstrative in nature and bring awareness to an issue through the use of creative, real-field campaigns.

The 1990s were a difficult time in Serbia—autocrat Slobodan Milosevic had tried an unequivocal powergrab, after a succession of bloody wars, in his attempt to retain power in the Balkans. Out of these struggles grew the student movement Otpor! (Resistance!), which sought to unite the Serbian people against Milosevic. One of Otpor!'s most effective tactics was the humorous dilemma action—pranks that put the opposing forces in a lose/lose situation and were conducted in a decidedly humourous manner. One of the most famous actions was entitled *A Dime for Change*, whereby two Otpor! members painted Slobodan Milosevic's face on a barrel and set it up in a main pedestrian walking area. The members offered passersby the chance to pay a dime to hit the Milosevic barrel in the head with a baseball bat. The Otpor! members managed to slip away and go unnoticed after the event gathered a crowd. Eventually police arrived, and were forced to respond in a no-win situation—they were required either to allow the action to continue, or risk appearing as though the regime was afraid to take a joke. So, instead, they arrested the barrel. Media outlets got wind of the story and the next day it was plastered across the newspapers, giving the small Otpor! movement much needed media attention. Instead of paying big fees to create a large PR event—something that Otpor! members had neither the human nor material resources to do—they simply used a little bit of creativity, which garnered a high media payoff.

Utilising humor in activism helps to dissipate fear. Just as in militarised conflict where people need to keep up their morale as they are preparing to face brutal conflict, nonviolent civil resistors must also build unity so that they are able to face the threat of police brutality, arrest or other forms of violent oppression. The Serbian struggle again provides a good example of using humour to create unity. During the 1999 NATO airstrikes, many students painted giant targets on their backs as a way of showing each other that they were not afraid of the NATO forces flying overhead. Of course, it goes without saying that people did not actually wish to be harmed during the US-lead campaign, but doing so strengthened the bonds of Serbian protestors who were otherwise helpless in the midst of large scale airstrikes. The humor in this situation helped to shift the narrative from one about victimhood to one of activism. This culture of solidarity that Otpor! cultivated with members helped to carry the Serbian struggle to the national stage. Today Otpor! is largely credited with being an instrumental force behind 2000s non-violent revolution that finally saw Milosevic—the 'butcher of the Balkans'—ousted from power.

It is easy to see how laughtivism may be written off as a stopgap solution that does not weigh in on the serious and difficult task of nationbuilding. As Kei Hiruta put astutely in her essay *Two Cheers for Laughtivsm*:

Once strongmen depart or make sufficient concessions, laughtivists must stop laughing and start deliberating and negotiating with their former enemies; they must turn their righteous anger into an enduring sense of justice.

Public actions like *Dime for Change* are just one step towards gaining attention for a movement that should have concrete demands and highly considered future plans. Social movements still take considerable time and consideration; however, the grassroots nature of laughtivist actions means that now more than ever before there is the opportunity for activists to at least begin that process of civil society building, and have a say in how it moves forward.

An initial step towards a robust civil society that is emerging from the heavy-handed rule of an autocratic regime must include unity of constituencies. This is something that humor aids greatly to clarify, particularly on the grassroots level and in the early stages of campaigns. Often when planning a mass social movement, getting people to laugh about similar issues clarifies exactly where participants stand, which can help to lay the groundwork for more specific demands as the movement makes the transition from rallying people on the streets into the negotiation phase with or in government.

In the past five years alone the world has witnessed an unprecedented rise in global civil resistance movements: from Brazilians protesting hikes in bus fares, Turkish citizens taking to the streets in Gezi park, Bahraini's gathering around their Pearl monument, and Bosnians protesting against the lack of identification numbers for infants. The reasons for civil resistance are as varied as their political landscapes and cultures they come from. One thing that makes them stand out is the clear: the carnival atmosphere pervading the movements and the fun, relatively speaking, the protestors are having.

Watch out dictators: you'd better learn to take a joke—the people under you certainly have.

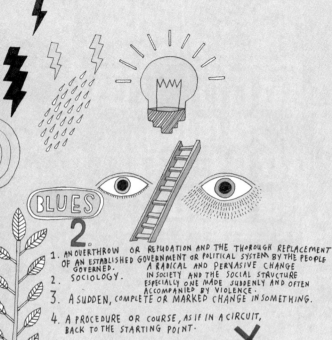

BLUES

2.

1. AN OVERTHROW OR REPUDIATION AND THE THOROUGH REPLACEMENT OF AN ESTABLISHED GOVERNMENT OR POLITICAL SYSTEM BY THE PEOPLE GOVERNED.

2. SOCIOLOGY. A RADICAL AND PERVASIVE CHANGE IN SOCIETY AND THE SOCIAL STRUCTURE ESPECIALLY ONE MADE SUDDENLY AND OFTEN ACCOMPANIED BY VIOLENCE.

3. A SUDDEN, COMPLETE OR MARKED CHANGE IN SOMETHING.

4. A PROCEDURE OR COURSE, AS IF IN A CIRCUIT, BACK TO THE STARTING POINT.

5. A SINGLE TURN OF THIS KIND

6. MECHANICS
   A. A TURNING ROUND OR ROTATING AS ON AN AXIS.
   B. A MOVING IN A CIRCULAR OR CURVING COURSE, AS ABOUT A CENTRAL POINT.
   C. A SINGLE CYCLE IN SUCH A COURSE

7. ASTRONOMY

8. A ROUND OR CYCLE OF EVENTS IN TIME OR A RECURRING PERIOD OF TIME

9. GEOLOGY A TIME OF WORLDWIDE OROGENY AND MOUNTAIN BUILDING.

BUILD A GARDEN WHERE THINGS CAN GROW.

The Public, the Police and the Rediscovery of Hate!

No-No, No Love for the Po-Po

'The police are the public and the public are the police,' said cop-founder Robert Peel in 1829. What a noble sentiment! A delightful idea! 'I know, we could get people to run themselves, it'd be great, all we have to do is split them into two groups and just make sure everyone knows they're on the same side, brilliant, yeah' ...and thus the modern police state is born, with those in uniform facing those they are supposed to still be a part of, yet somehow beating them up when they dare to do 'public'-type things, like have fun on the streets, or voice their opposition, or do anything other than scurry anxiously between school, (non-)job and the shops.

As we know, of course, the police never were the public. That much is true and it's reinforced by the way being 'a police' is often a family matter, with police streets, police towns, places where they cluster together like violent squirrels, hiding from everyone else. They were always just police.

But what has happened to the public? The public that cheered when officer Robert Culley was killed after police violently attacked a meeting organised by The National Union of the Working Classes in 1832, when the judge described it as 'justifiable homicide' and medals were anonymously sent to the jury; the public that the police never were but have spent almost a hundred years crushing, killing with impunity and now, as the recent anti-fascist action in Tower Hamlets showed, kettling, mass arresting (286 at the last count) and loading onto buses commandeered especially for the purpose... from no-longer-public transport to the jail...

The public, that living body of astute passions, has been squeezed out of existence. No more public space, only public order. This phrase has been going around my head for about a year and a half, when I think about the immense efforts put into guarding every tiny piece of land, of the private ownership of virtually everywhere you can think of, where is the public to go, what is it to do? When people chastised rioters for not going to the 'right' places to burn down Parliament, perhaps, or to attack poshos in Kensington, they missed the point: there is nowhere else to go, and attacking Parliament would have missed the mark entirely (not to mention the cops with machine guns that hide just inside). When all streets are just iterations of richer or poorer versions of themselves, what does it matter where you riot? It's the same shit everywhere, after all.

Public order is what the police in their crude way 'protect' when they beat protesters back, or cart them off to police stations all over the city, or harass black youth. But 'public order' or, really, the ordering of the public—transcends the police. It is every CCTV camera, every potential 'have you seen?' poster, every 'dob in your scrounging neighbour' leaflet posted through your door, all the bored security guards whose uniforms are indistinguishable from the cops' own. Any counter-idea of the public depends upon there being a space for that public to go—a 'realm'—but any attempt to find this magical realm, perhaps filled with communist unicorns, results in being 'moved on', incarceration or a quick baton to the head.

The public is a bad joke whose punchline is whispered in every piece of 'public art', in every attempt to 'engage the public', in every 'public consultation'. Whenever the public is desired it vanishes into thin air, and when it turns up it gets quickly turned into something else: an unruly mob, a violent crowd, a riotous assembly. But why kill off the public? If the public has been killed off, what has taken its place? What more malleable entity can you try to get people to think they are? Think of the rise of the consumer, the client, the stakeholder, the one who has a vested interest, but no rights beyond that of getting a replacement chocolate bar. This is the social being that decades of inequality wants to bring about, whether as student, employee, or unhappy individual desperately looking for remedies.

The attempt to smash the public by making the public private has its counterpart in the invasion of the private by the public. A different kind of public in this case—this is the public of enforced sociability, the sunshine ray of self-presentation, all the while the death-mask of the big other glares on (whilst not actually existing, of course). All the time you used to have that wasn't colonised by very much, perhaps a radio, perhaps a book, perhaps the TV, is now 24/7 party-central, and any room you enter you can buy something if you have your smartphone in your pocket. While the domestic ideal was also a pile of dangerous nonsense, the bright glowy public–private melange of perky group photos is just as bad, and further indicates that in order to have a real public, you need a real private to think about it.

If they've tried to kill off the public, they've nevertheless managed to create vast numbers of negative collectives—groups forced by the wrong done to them to unite around negations: the unemployed, the dispossessed, the marginalised, the excluded, those not included in the 'happy young people having a good time' photofit. Not content with creating these groups in the first place, they then force them to suffer the further indignities of being made the multiple objects of hate and derision: you're poor and crap! You can't work and we hate you! You don't have anything but I want to take it all from you anyway! Like all good fascisms, the logic of victimhood is inverted: those with everything must nevertheless have more by hating those who have less, or ever less than that. As if hating added a vinegary sauce to an otherwise tasty meal: the sour faces, the bitter spitting out of misplaced loathing.

In the name of the public sullied by decades of splitting, we need to reclaim back this hatred from those who would seek to turn it against those who instead deserve to wield it. We need to divide hate into two: the victorious, joyful hate of protesters, of those who break out of kettles, who escape arrest, who fight back against the police, of the true public who want everything taken from them back; against this, the dead-eyed suspicious hatred of the cops that treat them like they might be an alien species crossed with a whack-a-mole machine.

The police are not the public, and never were; public space, it turns out, is never ours and public order hangs like a ghostly shroud over all social life. The hate that rightfully belongs to the public must be reclaimed by force, before it kills us all... The public is dead! Long live the public!

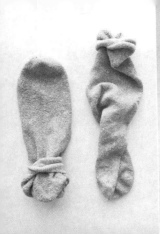

The Laziness of Prison

Being locked in a cell for 23 hours a day doesn't give you much of a chance to run in to people, let alone start up many conversations, but whenever there was the opportunity I would ask screws, in-house 'charity' workers, the Serco van drivers—whoever was around—what is the point of prison? What is it for? I asked everyone I could; what is meant to happen to me or any one of us in here as a result of spending 6 months, 6 years or even 16 years in prison?

This question became quite pressing about one week into my prison sentence when it started to become evident that somehow all of us behind those walls had travelled back in time. Somehow we were now part of an institution, a set of buildings and a way of thinking that hasn't changed for many hundreds of years and was probably redundant, and certainly intellectually corrupt, when first conceived, in any case.

Whenever we had 'association' time (free time out of the cell that would last for 30–60 minutes), I would also try to read the information pinned on the noticeboards, thinking perhaps I would find a statement about what prison was for, what would happen to me in the 2-6 months I would spend there. In three different prison wings I didn't come across anything of the sort. It was a pretty strange feeling being locked in a cell 6 by 8 feet for 23 hours a day and really having no idea why or what should happen as a result of such an endeavor.

Since leaving prison I have only been able to find statements explaining what the prison service does, such as 'holding prisoners securely' and 'providing a safe and well-ordered establishment in which we treat prisoners humanely, decently and lawfully.' What is meant to happen in, and as a result, of the secure and well-ordered establishment seems less important, or not important at all. It is this gap between machine, admin and humanity that makes spending time locked up behind a steel door, far away from loved ones, so difficult.

There are many institutions, and particularly so in Britain, that seem to exist purely as a result of historic momentum, 'tradition' and a lack of imagination. Prisons, which should have been abolished generations ago, are ballooning. The prison population has increased by 30% in the last decade and doubled in the last 20 years. In the last decade, prison sentences have increased on average by 20%. The UK is on something of a prison-building spree, and has the highest number of private prisons anywhere in Europe. Britain, Romania and Bulgaria are the only European nations to withdraw the right to vote for prisoners.

Despite not knowing what prisons are for, the corporate-state continues their mushrooming growth right across these islands. At the same time, funding is being dramatically cut to education and health services for prisoners. If you end up in prison the chances are you will be spending your time working for little or no money in corporation work camps. And, of course, if you are black or Muslim, the likelihood of you ending up in prison increases significantly. If you are Afro-Caribbean you currently have a greater chance of being criminalised and ending up in prison than entering higher education. 25% of prisoners are from ethnic minorities, who are only 10% of the general population. Black men make up the largest percentage of this group. These men are disproportionately dying at the hands of prison screws, police and G4S and Serco—over 1,000 deaths in custody in the last decade. These men are also experiencing the highest rate of the use of the Mental Health Act to detain them.

Apart from supplying readily available and highly managed slave labour, prisons do one thing particularly well and that's create and maintain the idea of a 'criminal class'. Prison creates a collection of people that all of us so quickly and often without thought deride and ridicule—and, at the same time, fear. Prisoners and ex-prisoners are at the bottom of this county's hierarchical pyramid—they're there for everyone else to kick. How often do we call for a person we dislike to be sent to prison, to 'rot in jail'?

Despite 'doing our time' prisoners come out with a criminal record, which only serves to further stigmatize, undermine and criminalise. This is particularly problematic when there is clearly institutional class and race bias in sentencing decisions. With just a little imagination and just a little bit of work, there's every possibility of criminal records and prisons being abolished. It's lazy to have prisons. They are a vestige of another time and don't have a place in any modern, progressive society.

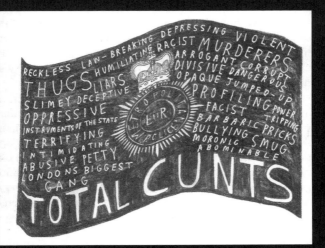

Refuse to Collaborate
An Open Letter

This is an appeal to friends, comrades and organisers of protests. In light of the mass arrest of 286 anti-fascist protestors on 7th September (as well as Fortnum and Mason, Critical Mass, BNP Whitehall etc) we appeal to all organisers of protests from all organisations to immediately cease from negotiating with the police in any form whatsoever and, for protests currently being planned, that organisers withdraw immediately from communication with the police.

The police have become the protest organisers. It is they who organise what happens on the day, who goes where, what is said and not said, how the protest acts, behaves, moves and demonstrates. We now have not only state-sanctioned but state-organised protest. Be effective and you are liable to mass-arrest; deviate from the meticulous state planning and you're liable to mass arrest. We must not get used to this!

The police have markedly stepped up their intentions against street protests and demonstrations. This is a planned strategy to suppress effective protest and is part of the Total Policing agenda of the Metropolitan police. There are those who believe that effective street protests are not just about letting off steam or performing a state-sanctioned role in the political system, but are one of the ways to begin to achieve radical changes in society. We cannot be debilitated by these new malign strategies of suppression—kettled, arrested, processed, released under threat of being hauled back into custody if we dare attend another protest in breach of bail conditions.

The state and the police cannot simply be asked to stop what they are doing, or behave more nicely towards protestors. By its nature, protest doesn't ask for permission.

It's been clear for a long time that this type of state sanctioned non-protest should end. It's no longer merely a matter of frustration at their ineffectiveness, but now also of the safety of friends and strangers who come to protest on our streets. While this type of non-protest is accepted, everyone who doesn't think it is legitimate, or who doesn't know the rules of the police's game, is liable to arrest. Negotiating with the police now means putting protestors in serious danger; negotiating with the police is complicity in the suppression of protest.

The action we must take is to encourage and pressure all organisers of protests, from all organisations, to refuse to negotiate with the police in any form. No negotiation of times, dates, rally points and routes of the march.

While this may not prevent mass arrests absolutely, they are arresting us en masse anyway, by the hundreds. Can they arrest us by the thousands? Even if they could, we would at least all be acting against the police's efforts to suppress protest, collectively.

There can be no false separation of good and bad protestors, legitimate and illegitimate protestors; that is used to weaken protest and social movements. We can't dismiss those arrested as not really part of the demo, or as hijackers causing trouble for not obeying protest restrictions. The complicity from organisers in this police practise of de-legitimising genuine protest must end. Acting collectively in this way means that we will all be illegitimate together—which makes us legitimate.

We must attempt to win back some space on the streets for protest ourselves. This is a direct appeal: do not be complicit in endangering protestors by collaborating with the police, and cease all negotiations with the police immediately.

Squatting the Frontline

It's Criminal to Criminalise the Homeless

Britain is facing the worst housing crisis since the Second World War. There are 40,000 homeless. On an average night 4,000 people sleep on the streets. The sell-off of council houses and the failure to build new homes has resulted in 1.7million households currently being on housing waiting lists. Most families in London and the South East will have a 10-year wait before being offered a council or housing association property. Overcrowding has become endemic.

With little social housing available people are forced to rent in the private sector where they are faced with high rents and the return of Rackmanite, bullying landlords charging extortionate rents for generally poor quality accommodation—often slum conditions. Increases in rents, cuts in housing benefit and the recent introduction of the Bedroom Tax mean that benefits fail to cover the rent, which in turn brings with it the threat of eviction.

Fighting for a person's housing rights and eviction is made increasingly tough with the cuts in legal aid, and the withdrawal of many solicitors' practices from legal aid work altogether. If a single person is evicted there is virtually no support available from the local council, as the person is either designated as intentionally homeless for failing to pay the rent or capable of supporting themselves and therefore not in need of assistance.

For homeless families presenting themselves as homeless at the local council offices, increasingly the assistance offered is a placement in a squalid B&B for a number of weeks, sometimes located some distance from the family's community, the children's schools and the parents' workplace.

The number of families in B&Bs has risen sharply over the last year and now stands at more than 2,000—the highest number in a decade.

Whilst this is all going on there are in an average year between 650,000 and 700,000 properties standing empty, with 300,000 properties empty on a long-term basis (that is, for at least 6 months).

Inevitably, faced with a choice of being homeless, sleeping rough and witnessing a property stand empty, some people will take what can only be described as a completely rational decision to squat an empty property. From the survey figures produced by the homelessness charity Crisis, we know that 6% of the homeless population will be squatting each night and that 40% of single homeless people have squatted at some time.

The survey demonstrates that many of the people who have squatted have real and serious needs. 90% have slept rough. 42% have physical ill-health or a disability. 41% of homeless squatters report mental health needs, with 21% self-harming. 15% have a learning disability and 47% have experienced drug dependency.

The survey confirmed that people were squatting because they had no alternative. 78% had already approached the local council for help but had been turned away.

It is a grotesque injustice and immoral that hundreds of thousands of homes stand empty whilst people are sleeping on our streets, living in squalid, overcrowded conditions, or are being ripped-off by private landlords, who make fortunes out of housing benefits. As homelessness grows and people become more and more desperate for a roof over their heads, squatting increasingly becomes an option.

True to form in representing the landlord class, the Coalition Government has appreciated this potentially growing threat and—at the behest of Tory backbench MPs, many of whom are landlords themselves—has responded to the appalling housing crisis with typical class bias by introducing new legislation to criminalise squatting with the imposition of a £5,000 fine or up to a year in prison for squatting a residential property.

Prison sentences have already been handed out and we witnessed the recent tragedy of Daniel Gauntlett, who it seems may have died after being turned away from squatting a site by the police. With the potential of a severe winter ahead of us, many predict a heightened risk of more deaths and suffering as people are deterred from squatting and, without other alternatives, put their lives at risk to avoid arrest or prison.

There are now calls from Tory backbench MPs, aided by a small number of Labour MPs, including the high-profile Chuka Umunna, for new legislation to criminalise squatting in commercial or other non residential properties.

The involvement of Labour MPs in this reactionary demand flies in the face of the history of the key role labour-movement activists played in the squatters' movement. After the war when squatting private properties became commonplace in many areas, as families waited for the Attlee government to deliver them a council house, Labour activists were at the forefront of many local squatting campaigns.

In each decade since then when people have been forced to choose squatting rather than homelessness, the labour movement has responded with understanding and compassion, not hostility and prejudice. Occupying factories and community facilities threatened with closure has also been a critical strategy used by the labour and trade union movement in our campaigns to protect jobs and public services over generations.

When the Government forced through the last legislation criminalising squatting it was faced with an amazing breadth of opposition, including the Law Society, the Magistrates Association, and the Criminal Bar Association. Even the Metropolitan Police advised Ministers that the law as it stood 'was broadly in the right place and the existing array of offences allowed them to tackle the worst cases of squatting (e.g. where squatters caused the rightful home-owner to be displaced).'

It was already the case that if someone came home and found that someone had squatted where they were living they could ask them to leave and if they refused it became a criminal offence. People's homes were already protected. There was never any evidence produced by the Government demonstrating the need for a change in the law.

The Law Society, representing the solicitors dealing with this area of the law, criticised the government for introducing the new law without any evidence of the need for it. The Society explained that the government's own consultation paper on the new proposals acknowledged that 'there are no reliable data on the nature and extent of squatting. In the absence of such evidence, we have no reason to believe that the existing law does not deal adequately with squatting.'

The Law Society was not alone in rejecting the need for the criminalisation of squatting. There were over 2,000 responses to the Coalition's consultation on its proposals and over 90% were opposed to this change. The Government ignored its own consultation and railroaded the new law through Parliament. Despite all the claims to evidence-based policymaking, when it comes to legislating on squatting it is government by bar-room anecdote and prejudice.

The Government is starting to go down the same path again in seeking to extend the criminalising of squatting even further. A few anti-squatter stories are planted in Tory-supporting papers and media. Tory backbenchers, and now unfortunately some Labour MPs, commence the clamour for more ruthless laws and penalties. The urban myths of wealthy squatters are hauled out again and again. The centuries-old divide and rule tactics are rolled out as squatters are depicted as the undeserving poor contrasted with the deserving poor image of hard-working families, who pay their rent and wait their turn on the housing waiting list.

In response to this reactionary claptrap this is the time for us all to stand up and be counted. Homelessness has been seen for too long as either at the micro level a matter for personal charitable donations or at the macro level a debate about the policy of housing supply. It is also increasingly becoming a struggle over the ownership of and right to the use of property, especially at the time of crisis. Squatting is on the frontline of that struggle.

An Anarchist Guide to...
Exchange

Sit Down Next to Me

We've always been quick to point out that the thing that unites everyone who comes to The Haircut Before The Party (THBTP), is the need for a haircut. But what else do people want from the situation, what are the prerequisites for an interesting exchange and what further potentials are there to explore? After all, the premise of offering free haircuts isn't to meet that singular need, but to recognise other needs and desires that are shared socially; to open up space for clear and intensive communication, and to recognise the cross-overs and tensions of the private and public, for example.

There's something about the quality of cutting hair that establishes an immediate rapport between barber and client. From the first mention of the word short, both of us are keen to understand one another, to make sure communication is actually happening. This is important; after all, hair is one of the biological features of our identities which is most malleable, playful, and temporary. It is also caught up in ritualistic behaviour and private psychologies. Dare we talk of resistant aesthetics yet?

Adorned in a black-and-red cape, David Graeber meets us in the mirror, drops of water running down his neck from the quick shampoo. A little combing reveals some of the previous patterns from crown to nape.

'We're all anarchist with our best friends', comes as the after-thought to the initial introduction as a self-defined anarchist academic. The root to an anarchism or anarchisms being a path that draws ever closer to, but never reaches, a destination. Something that already exists within our behaviours and daily exchanges. Perhaps a thing to practice rather than deprecate, a thing to recognise rather than dismiss.

'If I ask someone for directions, I don't expect them to say "five pounds, please."'

He further proposes that behaviours typical of anarchisms and communisms also exist within capitalist production, which takes creativity and social relations and turns them into nightmarish scenarios.

Is this what is happening with mutual aid and Big Society? In which case, what does radical mutual aid look like?

I think we know. I mean we do it all the time. It's recognising the forms of imminent communism as being values in themselves, rather than simply being valuable to maintain the platform from which people can then extract profit.

I mean what fascinates me, the haircut is a great example, is just how much even the things that we do for money, most of the time, are things which involve these intense levels of interpersonal trust and communication, in which the boundaries between our very selves flow into each other. They're all embodiments of the very principles which then this logic of exchange that we have to look at everything from tries to make disappear again. So we're constantly living one kind of life and then, for very elaborate reasons, that kind of life can't exist. It's unrealistic. It means denying the reality that's around us all the time and most of what we're doing even when we're saying it.

Is it feasible to expect all of us to become friends for the purpose of affinity and support with our personal politics and shared struggles? There's a hesitance towards implementing friendship as a program, but I can still hear John Holloway's ideas on anti-power, existing within 'relations of love, friendship, comradeship, community, cooperation'. We can ask questions of these intimate expressions, how and where they happen, and how to proliferate the material conditions of solidarities across multiple shared needs.

With circular motions, the barber warms the styling wax between palms. This promises to be the first of many meetings between the two of them, if this bond is true.

In the vicinity of the chair, the artist and architect Celine Condorelli has something to say in relation to where the radical-barber stands on matters of political support in lieu of friendship.

Support's first operational feature is its proximity. No support can take place outside a close encounter, getting entangled in a situation and becoming implicated in it. A desire emerges, an offer opens; they are expressed in different ways, emitted or projected without or before being fully formed. It is not a word but a call, a longing; it cannot rely on intellectual awareness or abstract information, but requires a proximity and intimacy.

The scissors' blades make their interval snips, punctuating what is said, taking it onboard with a certain movement of its own. Quoting Derrida she recalls, 'the specific political distinction, to which political actions and notions can be reduced, is the distinction between friend and enemy.'

The implication of support is that of the politics of friendship, for to give or receive support is an allegiance, and establishes who and what one can count on.

The barber shifts from one foot to the other, trying to take a measure of what was said. A supportive exchange is attainable from where they stand; they find themselves privy to all kinds of expressions, anecdotal, hypothetical, analogical. This barber listens for the tune of affinity, patterns of resistance, matching and combing through the aesthetics of the hair within their social contexts. The particularities of the individual's identity and expression, whether it be in relation to gender, class, race, profession, personal experience and forms of communication, with their many intersections and contradictions, have to be acknowledged and met. 'We want to cut your hair, not give you a haircut' was one of the guiding statements to come out of a recent gathering of radical hairdressers in Edinburgh. This point gets to the heart of where the radical hair practitioner starts from: does it finish with the haircut?

What is in-common is a popular point of discussion in the salon these days; the idea of a relationship with and to private property, historically and presently, the common as an asset, a relation, or a process of 'commoning'.

A woman with short curled hair sits in the adjacent chair, almost lost in the cutting cape. She swings her legs to find a particular tilt. Her hands are calmly clasped in lap, but her eyes shimmer with an urgent clarity. Silvia Federici, she is neither a regular at the salon, nor a stranger.

'Let me tell you as concrete as possible, what I know about reproduction and commons...'

Ears prick up.

'On the one side, there has been the demise of the statist model of revolution, that for decades has sapped the efforts of radical movements to build an alternative to capitalism. On the other, the neoliberal attempt to sub-ordinate every form of life and knowledge to the logic of the market has heightened our awareness of the danger of living in a world in which we no longer have access to seas, trees, animals, or our fellow beings, except through the cash-nexus.'

Magazine pages ruffle and eyebrows raise.

'The new enclosures ironically demonstrated that not only have commons not vanished, but new forms of social cooperation are constantly being produced, also in areas of life where none previously existed.'

The haircut that is about to happen no longer feels separate from any political gesture or activity that existed before it. It is the same gesture as anyone who has behaved uneconomically—anyone who goes beyond what is expected of them—or sought to identify their individual struggle as inherently social and potentially collective. The hair clippings on the tiled floor softly take their place in the path well-trodden, in moments of creativity and struggle, that feels like it's heading somewhere.

TXT: NIALL MCDEVITT

The Proletarianization of the Bourgeoisie

Regularly, in the newspeak of the class-ridden state,
we're informed of an all-encompassing sociological theory:
'The Bourgeoisification of the Proletariat'
i.e. how the galley-slaves these days are happy as Larry,
weighed down with loot, Marx-free, nay, at long last
'indistinguishable' from their middle-class betters
and how all we have to worry about's the underclass
of crims, sluts, schizos, beggars, junkies, poets etc.

Yet all I see's the proletarianization of the bourgeois,
media-brainwashed and work-programmed bootlicks
into computer games, suntans, tracksuits, soap operas,
office parties with strippergrams, cakes like chocolate dicks.
Codes of ettiquette are those of the 'tough' not the 'toff'
and stats show they increasingly resort to violence:
headbutting, glassing, biting people's earlobes off.
They too are being successfully schooled in the new science.

TXT: PETER KENNARD

Private First Class

Claw over the parapet
Voice raised
Is voice gagged.
The world as in fact it is,
Isn't. In a Democracy of liars
Is a lock-up for facts.

Three blows of a whistle:
One in hiding, embassy, London
One in hiding, transit building, Moscow
One in prison, U.S.A, somewhere

The stars and striping
Are bruises and lashes
This is the land of the free—
Where the fee for whistling
Is 36 years.

Chelsea Manning is born free and is everywhere in chains.

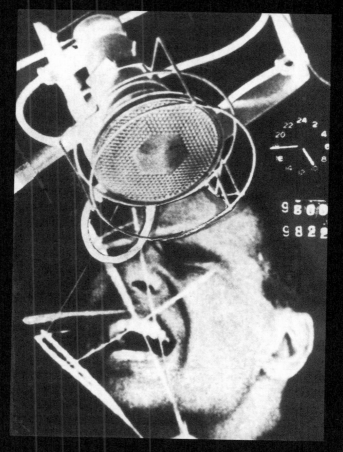

HIGHGATE

A Paddy Mortsworth Story

BY ANNA TRENCH

As Paddy Mortsworth climbed Swain's Lane he cursed the world and all the injustice in it.

* ?! * £ / : (

Stupid market bully...

Stupid SUVs...

Stupid private property with big stupid gates keeping out poor little proles like me...

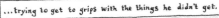

Recently he'd been reading more...

...trying to get to grips with the things he didn't get.

But it was difficult.

There was so much to untangle.

And what was the point, anyway?

WORKERS OF ALL LANDS UNITE

...addy Mortsworth felt very small.

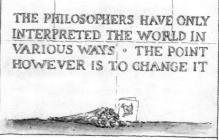

THE PHILOSOPHERS HAVE ONLY INTERPRETED THE WORLD IN VARIOUS WAYS · THE POINT HOWEVER IS TO CHANGE IT

But perhaps not completely useless.

Anna French   P.2.

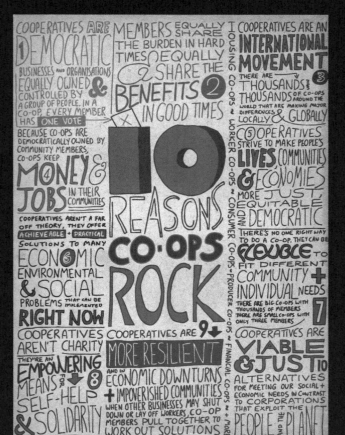

ADVERTISING
IS
LEGALISED
LYING

INJUSTICE

vimeo.com/34633260

RIOTS REFRAMED
DOCUMENTARY
VOICE OVER

SAVING PRIVATE ENTERPRISE

the
Radical
Media
forum

zero books

YOU MIGHT WATCH ME
BUT I WATCH YOU TOO
– AIN'T A THING YOU
CAN DO TO STOP ME

www.strikemag.org

THE
COMMON
House

ANARCHIST BOOKFAIR 2013

HOUSMANS

NO DASH
for
GAS

GRASP THE
NETTLE

PEOPLE SCATTERED
LIKE RAIN
ACROSS THE LAND
SCAPE OF AMERICA
ARE SO SEPARATE
FROM EACH OTHER
AND LOST, THEY WILL
TURN TO ANYTHING
THEY CAN RECOG-
NISE FOR SOLACE,
LIKE FAST FOOD
DRIVE-INS WITH
THEIR SIGNS LIT UP
SO PRETTY IN THE
NIGHT OR MOVIE
STARS OR WAR

ISSUE___5

Hollaback

When Did You Know that You Were a Woman?

That's the question a workshop facilitator posed to a group that included Tina Fey, who then related the following in her book, *Bossypants*:

The group of women was racially and economically diverse, but the answers had a very similar theme. Almost everyone first realised they were becoming a grown woman when some dude did something nasty to them. 'I was walking home from ballet and a guy in a car yelled, "Lick me!"' 'I was babysitting my younger cousins when a guy drove by and yelled, "Nice ass."' There were pretty much zero examples like 'I first knew I was a woman when my mother and father took me out to dinner to celebrate my success on the debate team.' It was mostly men yelling shit from cars.

Sound familiar? If you're like 70–99% of women, it probably does.

When I was 18, I moved from suburban Richmond, Virginia to New York City. The first time someone greeted me on the street, he said: 'Hello, baby.' Hmmm, I thought, maybe this is the New York way of saying hello. Eager to fit in, I said 'Hello.' His response? 'I want to fuck the shit out of you.'

I thought it must be a fluke. Who says that? So I pretended it didn't happen. But two, three, sometimes four times a day a range of lewd, sexual comments were directed at me. 'Hey baby, I want to hit that.' Or 'Girl, I want to be your pony.' Or 'Smile.'

I ignored them, kept going, pretended like it didn't hurt—thinking that if I let myself cry and feel the hurt, it meant

I wasn't strong. What I and countless others experienced was street harassment, and it started slowly chipping away at my right to be me. I felt like if I wore what I wanted to wear, walked how I wanted to walk, when I wanted to walk there, that it meant that I was 'asking for it', and with every degrading comment I felt more and more put in my place.

Like Tina Fey, I felt like a woman. And not in the cute new dress kind of way.

Since co-founding Hollaback, a global movement to end street harassment, I have learned that with each identity—being young, being queer, or being a person of colour—comes an exponentially greater likelihood of experiencing street harassment. And the more you experience it, the more it chips away at you.

It's a vicious cycle, further complicated by the fact that street harassment is really tricky to build a movement around. First off, when it came to addressing workplace harassment they sued the corporations. But with street harassment, you can't sue the sidewalks. The larger system that you need to change is called culture, and it's big. And secondly, street harassment is totally unpredictable. In the civil rights era, African American organisers had a pretty good idea what was going to happen when they sat down at a 'whites only' lunch counter. But with street harassment, you never know when it will happen, you never know where it's going to happen, and you're almost always alone.

The explosion of technology has given us an unprecedented opportunity to end street harassment—and, with it, the opportunity to take on one of the final new frontiers for women's rights around the world. By collecting stories from women—lesbian, bisexual, and transgender individuals—in a safe and share-able way, platforms like Hollaback!, Blank Noise Project in India, or Harassmap in Egypt are thriving.

As organisers, we're mapping these stories along district lines so that we can show legislators: 'Here is what is happening in your district. Here is the experience of over 50% of your constituents. What are you going to do about it?' And we're using these stories for research: employing content-analysis to identify the role of bystanders and the long-term impacts of street harassment, including anxiety, depression, and post-traumatic stress disorder.

Digital storytelling is good for movements, but it's also good for you. Activist researcher Jill Dimond studied Hollaback and critically asked, 'does online storytelling matter?' What she found is that it does this really cool thing called 'reframing', which is key to social-movement building. Reframing is when your understanding of an experience shifts as you re-examine it in a different context.

For example, in the world we live in now, most people experience street harassment and think to themselves, 'well that was CRAPPY!' But once someone has been through a reframing process they might think: 'Street harassment is a societal issue. This isn't about me, even though it's directed at me right now and that feels crappy. This is about the messed up world we live in!' And that's a game-changer.

But stories alone cannot build a movement. That's why we've trained over 300 young people to launch Hollaback! sites in 71 cities and 24 countries. We pair digital story-telling with on-the-ground action that leads to sustainable change. The demand is staggering, our waiting list has people from over 60 cities eager to bring Hollaback! to their communities.

The power of this movement rests in the global network of leaders championing it day-in and day-out. There are those that think eventually we'll come to accept street harassment as a fact of life—they're wrong. There are others who think they can silence us with threats on our lives and to our safety—they can't. The power of decentralised leadership is that the harder they attack, the stronger we become.

Each of us can only represent our own experiences of being harassed: together, we tell the story of a global epidemic. We're fierce. We're loving. And we're coming to a town near you.

Here's what what we want you to know:

—You deserve to walk home, alone, without being told that you're 'asking for it.'
—You deserve to have short hair without being asked if you are a girl or a boy.
—You deserve to ride the train without fear of being groped.

Because none of us are as simple as a list of physical attributes. We have a right to be who we are, not who we are told to be. We have a right to define ourselves on our terms when we walk out the door, whatever that means that day. That hour. That minute.

I want to be able to walk out my front door and strike up a conversation with the guy down the block about his flower beds without thinking twice about it. I want to tell the guy I see running every morning that he's gotten a lot faster lately without worrying he'll 'get the wrong message' and see it as an opening for a conversation about my body. I want to live in a world where street harassment is so rare that when it does happen people are shocked because everyone knows it's not OK and they have my back, they know how to respond.

But to get from here to there, we need to change the narrative. We need to make visible every foul and unfathomable detail of our harassment to the cynics who say 'street harassment doesn't matter', or that it will 'never be changed'. We need to put into high relief what is wrong, if we want people to see what is possible.

So what are we waiting for? It's time to go big, go public and reclaim the spaces that have been owned for too long by street harassment. It's time to tell your story...

How the Other Half Live

Why are We Waiting?

One of the most telling statements I've ever heard about feminism came from one of its grande dames, Sheila Rowbotham, who said at the launch of her brilliant book *Dreamers of the New Day*: 'In the Seventies we assumed once you made a gain it would stay there.' I was only a child in the Seventies, but I can remember a time in my youth when I thought that feminism should have a list of goals that you could tick off one by one, collecting one advance and then moving on to the next.

Those were the days, you might say. Such confidence today is thin on the ground.

Some advances have proved relatively stable. Access for women on equal terms to most jobs, at least at entry level, has been broadly secured. You might get the occasional old consultant complaining about the number of women at medical school, but, in general, girls and young women do have access to courses on equal terms that their grandmothers could only dream of. About 40% of young women finish their initial run of education with a degree today, compared to 30% of men.

And the expectation that women will build a career, rather than just filling in time between finishing their education and marriage—the way my grandmother worked in the post-room of a department store and rose to be the boss of the 'girls' because she was the oldest one left, and practically 'on the shelf'—is now entirely the norm.

Lip-service, at least, to full employment opportunities is also now de rigeur. With the exception of headline-seeking dinosaurs like Nigel Farage, few will claim that women have less to contribute to the workplace than men, and disclaimers along the lines of 'we're seeking to be an equal opportunity employer' scatter across the jobs pages.

Yet it's not an accident that it's in areas in which they contribute to the economic model of growth, consumerism and the god of 'the economy' that feminists have found it easiest to make and hold ground. That two wages for most of the lifecycle are essential for all but the richest to achieve a basic decent lifestyle was not what was being sought.

When it comes to changing the model of work—making the workplace appropriate for women (and men) with caring responsibilities, allowing for different life-paths and experiences—there's been little real progress. And where we saw the most progress was in the public sector—the jobs that are now being privatised, with slashed pay and conditions, at a great rate.

The welfare state that in past decades, however imperfectly, acknowledged that there were different forms of contribution to the present and future of society—in caring for the young, the old, those who couldn't find an economic place—is under severe and sustained attack, little-defended by even those you'd expect to be standing up for it. Who can forget Rachel Reeves, Shadow Work and Pensions Secretary, promising that the Labour Party, if elected, would be tougher on benefits than the Tories?

When on average one-fifth of an average woman's income comes from benefits (the figure for men being one-tenth), the likely impact is obvious. The bedroom tax, the cuts to council tax benefit, the welfare benefit cap, the slashing of legal aid—all of the attempts to make the poor pay for the crisis created by the (overwhelmingly male) bankers—are falling significantly more heavily on women. Single pensioners, predominantly women, have lost more than 10% of their income, while single parents (92% female) have lost 15.6%. And the loss of services means women as carers, as community stalwarts, as the final backup, are facing an even heavier load.

So, economically, it's clear that women are going backwards. The news at the end of last year that the gender pay gap, which was creaking slowly under 10% for full-time workers (nearly double for part-timers), has grown again, is no surprise.

Then there's the question of women's access to power. The painful, halting struggle to get more MPs into the Commons is awful to watch, as the largest parties wriggle and twist, often with push from the leadership and pushback from local selectors, only to see many women MPs find the boarding school atmosphere and general blokeishness more than they want to tolerate, leaving after a term or two. Britain ranks equal 53rd in the global ranking of percentage of women in parliament.

I'm proud of the fact that when I took over from Caroline Lucas in 2012 as leader of the Green Party of England and Wales, it was the first time one woman leader of a parliamentary party had handed over to another in British political history. But that it took until 2012 to get to that point is telling.

Women make huge contributions in terms of citizenship: when I go to local community meetings the norm is to see a female-dominated audience of citizens, women who've squeezed time out of child care, elder care and long working hours, unpaid of course, facing a line of suits, officials paid for their work of consulting the experts—the local residents. Yet in local government too, they're hugely under-represented.

Then there's business and the question of female leadership. Norway has shown the way with its 40% quota for women on major companies' boards; many other European states are following. Yet here in the UK, the City and its allies are kicking and screaming about the impossibility of it all— just as they are at restrictions on bankers' bonuses and on making multinational companies pay their taxes.

Women's institutions still struggle to maintain funding and hold out for the long term. The Fawcett Society (declaration of interest, I'm a trustee) is a rare example of a long-term women's political institution, with a continuous history dating back to 1866, but the wonderful, purpose-built, lottery-funded Women's Library lasted a scant decade before it was abandoned by its former sponsor.

And all of these levels of disadvantage for women are multiplied for those who suffer discrimination in other ways, through their membership of an ethnic minority, through disabilities, through class.

These deficits of cash, resources and power play into the issue of violence against women. There's little doubt that financial pressures, unjust immigration laws and cuts will force more women to stay in dangerous relationships, that the services that might have helped them escape are struggling to survive, let alone to provide all of the assistance and support that is needed.

As a politician, I quote lots of statistics, and have to regularly check they're still up-to-date, but sadly the figure that two women a week are killed in Britain by a partner or ex-partner just goes on and on.

I've focused here on women in Britain—but of course on balance overall the situation of women in Britain looks positively rosy compared to the global situation. Three statistics are all that is needed to paint the picture: women do around two-thirds of the world's work, grow about half of its food, and own 1% of the world's assets. As we approach the centenary of significant numbers of women getting a vote in Britain, you have to think that our great grandmothers would have expected we'd have made a great deal more progress by now.

So what to do? We can, and must, keep battling on over all of these issues and others (I fear that the need to defend access to abortion and contraception will be back in the news soon.)

But there's a huge looming positive opportunity. It's very clear that our current economic model is broken (not to mention our political model). There will be massive change in the short to medium term: a society in which 20% of workers earn less than a living wage, with somewhere between

1 and 4 million workers on zero-hours contracts, one in 10 working fewer hours than they'd like, where food banks are one of the few boom industries, and which uses each year on average more than three times the sustainable resources available to it will not continue.

New ideas are gaining ground: a living wage for all would be a start, a citizens' or basic income a more revolutionary step forward; making multinational corporations and rich individuals pay their taxes is something that even David Cameron pays lip-service to, even if the practice is the reverse of the rhetoric; a land-value tax that might eventually significantly rebalance wealth is on the table and ground-up democratic initiatives and community groups are establishing themselves, sometimes in unlikely places.

The world is going to change. And for women, that's good news. What we have to do is make sure the new world works for all of the human race, not just a small percentage of the male half of it.

Feminist Wit

Dare To Be Devastating

There is a type of corporate feminism that never seems to go away. Here there is an image of the world in which the world itself is exactly as it should be, only there aren't enough women in it. The remedy for this imbalance is a simple numerical one: stock the world with women CEOs, MPs, judges and senior police officers, and everything will be just and equal. The idea that there might be something wrong with capitalism, parliamentary politics, the criminal justice system or the police force is buried in a pile of aspirational exhortations, empowerment workshops and a hard-work, competitive ethos: 'come on, women, pull yourselves together!' Not wanting to compete on these terms is seen as a kind of character weakness, a betrayal of the gains of feminism: but you have a proper education now! You don't have to be a wife and mother! You can make (almost) as much money as men do!

Being basically a Tory-flavoured individualism with a kind of feminine sheen, this brand of feminism has no analysis of larger structures, and subsequently no critique of them either: the world is all that is the case. But not wanting to play the game, and not believing that feminism is over, job done, hands dusted, means that other strategies are required, other techniques, other analyses. Not wanting to compete, let alone win, is a tactic in itself: a refusal to validate the system, and the world as it is, drawing attention to the holes and cracks in an otherwise supposedly seamless picture. When someone points out 'why are there no women here?' at a political meeting or workshop or conference, a gap is opened up: why are there no women here? Are women not interested? Are they too busy? Or do they actively oppose the structure and format of the event at which their absence has become a problem? Refusal is an option, but perhaps there are already too many hermetically-sealed bubbles of self-reinforcement: how to take a pin to them without getting sucked inside?

Nobody wants to be a token, because being a token means your attributes (or at least those attributes attributed to you, which may not be the same as the ones you think are important to you) are being isolated and treated as a means to an end by someone else. Late requests to join all-male panels are transparent in their breathlessness—'we really think you'd be the perfect person for this topic!'—you can just picture the meeting just a few weeks before the event when someone suddenly goes 'shit...no women! Er, ask, er...oh who's that one, you know, er, wrote about such and such...the one that always speaks...oh her...yeah suppose we'd better.' One can certainly gleefully participate in such events, and maybe even enjoy them, but the perpetuation of the same old crap is ultimately unsatisfactory for all con-cerned—and being a token gets boring, fast.

One, perhaps slightly different, strategy that has long interested me is one that could be described as 'feminist wit'. Here the idea is to cut across both the structural pat-terns and the attributed attributes, where you are neither upholding the structure, nor exactly an individual. Partly this is a matter of necessity: you get used to people not wanting to let you speak, who talk over you, who cut you off, who look sceptically at you so that your words trail off, confirming the sceptic's point (a situation so irritating you want to stab them in the eye). Your time is short because the court is not yours to hold. But you can see the structure of the court—the security guards, the judge, the box, and also the exit; the judge cannot see what is behind him, and he can only demand that you do not turn your back to him. Your role is that of someone who runs into court, flicks the wig off, smashes the box with a baseball bat and pulls the fire alarm before running out into the sunshine (or rain, more likely.)

Wit can be funny but it can also hurt: to say something that undermines the entire premise of an argument, and say it briefly and curtly is to treat one set of words like jelly and the other like a sword. Because women are not supposed to be funny, their wit has all the more power: 'ha ouch ha ouch ha ouch'—the laughter all the more painful because men are not supposed to be amused by anything women say, unless it falls between the bounds of the legitimately 'cute'.

When forced to choose between humour production and humour appreciation in potential partners, women valued humour production, whereas men valued receptivity to their own humour.

Said Dr Martin, a psychologist at the University of Western Ontario, in a study that asked men and women in their twenties to adjudicate on the question of humour between the sexes. According to a report in the Independent, when asked if they found a sense of humour to be attractive in women, most men said 'yes'. However, when they were asked if they would want to be with a woman who cracked jokes herself, the answer was 'a resounding no'. Feminist wit would surely laugh hard at the entire premise for the research: of course straight men are going to say they hate funny women, because funny women remind them of the foundationless void that is their very existence. Ha ha ha sukerz!

The witty woman, and there are many throughout history, occupy a role that is hard to pin down. They take nothing seriously because they can see through structures and mock the image of individuality that would see ego and arrogance take centre-stage. That is not to say that what work their wit does reveals nothing of importance— on the contrary, it highlights everything in a flash, which is precisely why it is so unsettling. Wit doesn't want to be a CEO, or a cop. On the contrary, it wants to destroy the world that makes CEOs and cops possible. Feminist wit is the strategy to end all strategies because it speaks from the vanishing point that is exactly midway between the individual and the collective, the structure and the specific situation. You will laugh, but you will also feel wounded, and it is from such wounds that the real work of politics begins.

I don't even kno wot feminism is ??

There r bare ppl who don't even kno wot feminism is. The way how when girls get the talk about blood + hair, it is read as a warning - like this wil happen to you soon - you wil have to get a bra just to stoppid staring at ur nipples and pay ur luxury tax on tampons - whereas getting hair growing out of your face isn't traumatic at all   There are some girls who won't leave the house, ever, to go to the cornershop, without high heels and full slap on, who live in dread of the day when a pair of white hotpants will sell them out, who aren't bothered by arranged marriages + kinky boots, who dutch LV bags, boiling, bubbling, full of trouble + strife, tissues + issues - who wil marry men for the bank account + do the washing up despite not having had an orgasm. Ever. Groupies + high class hookers. Wombs rotten by late-night cocaine sessions with rock'n'rollers who wear skinny jeans, write shit tunes + whose dad was - what did he do again? True-blue slave-tracing   trust fund twats - if, on the other   hand all you are after a smack   in the mouth, you will find Your Mum jokes to be globally insulting Not merely, as wikipedia states, playing on vague notions of filial piety (cos then there would be ur dad jokes 2), but revealing the way (some) boys think about sex - how they wouldn't want anyone to think about the pill-popping mothers the way they think about girls they bang.   In remote mountain villages, and in the desert to girls have to cover up - protection as much from the pervy town elders as the elements. In the cities they wear cover up to hide the lines. Have a daughter, so African preachers occupying pirate airwaves screeching the perils of shaving legs to all midnight sinners can freak u out. Do not let your ppl children sit on any uncle's top! Only, girls like to be objectified - don't they? U want a boy to think u r fit so if daddy didn't love u enuff, every l else is gonna have 2.

Women call themselves girls, and boys call themselves men. Of these aspiring persons, there still r more male CEOs, more members of parliament, more first born sons inheriting the lot - more men with more money, more power and less time on their hands. It's changed a bit, in places like Engerland at least, where shave their heads and throw themselves under horses.   It's bin said that women should not go up, more that as much as men should comedown. The who fem-dom-less-bi-freak-fucked debate is less pro-grrl. + more anti-macho. No one's looking for a quickie, and ladette culture is hashtag unbearable. Recall that well worn-point, that we all suffer from prejudice, whether we practise it or not. It is not only those who publish manifestos dedicated to those who had to lie, and those who told the truth but weren't believed anyway [sic]. Lester Lloyd is a rapist - he fucks girls while they're sleeping. Has a good go at ruining ppl's lives, then disses them behind they're back - calling bitches crazy. What is a rape fantasy anyway - do grls dream of gang bangs? Or do they prefer silent coercion? Go on bbz, u kno u want it.   There once was a queer boy, from Houston who made glitter paintings and played with computers. the   end of the story saw him skinny and pale, repeating the words over + over l'd rather be beautiful than be male. Almost all hetero-men freak at the idea of getting bummed. What does it mean to have a dick in your mouth + like it? Armed Love means the Future has No Future. All fellas should have dildos of thr dicks made, and sit on em once a month; 2 realise it's tough 2 take it. Is it different 4 girls?   Women (+ their magic vaginas) have learnt to find satisfaction in seeming disadvantage. Altogether, there is more precision to their territorial pissings. But 4 all the fucking bullshit women have a nicer time of it, in the end. There are bitches + ugly vanilla types who make crotchless parties + call it fashion but even so, bleeding every month is a great leveller reminding you on the regs that stuff happens 2 you, not 4 you that urbody is not under ur jurisdiction. In behaviour doesn't change so drastically as when there are only boys on the firm. Banging strippers en masse seem crass whereas floobly boobs and tattored stomaches out on parade without scorn or revolt seems alrite 2 me. In the end its the same old choice - fear or love - take ur pick - whether u want to climb back inside a punaani or get down on ur knees in front of one. :)

THAT'S WHY YOUR MUM WENT TO

Iceland

TXT: RHIAN E. JONES

Sisterhood at the Intersection

Solidarity at the Crossroads of Struggle

I grew up a feminist as well as a socialist, with both of these identities rooted in class. Feminism and socialism seemed to go hand-in-hand when I considered, for instance, the legacy of the 1984–5 Miners' Strike and the support groups formed by miners' wives, partners and other women in communities like my own. Although such groups were primarily established to distribute food and cash donations to the families of strikers, as the strike progressed their female members increasingly found themselves taking more explicitly political roles as part of fundraising and outreach work, and becoming public figures and community leaders in what had traditionally been a male-dominated political sphere. Through these networks of mutual support and solidarity, working-class women, while on the one hand defending what might be seen as a macho and patriarchal industrial culture, on the other hand gradually challenged the chauvinism in which this culture could be steeped.

Similarly, factory work, despite its immediate associations with industrial masculinity, has historically also been a potential hub of female working-class solidarity. This unfashionable species of feminism was commodified in the 2010 film Made in Dagenham, a dramatisation of the 1968 strike by sewing machinists at Ford's Dagenham car plant. The strike saw female workers take on their male bosses over sexual discrimination and the right to equal pay, with several becoming radicalised in the process, and its success eventually resulted in the 1970 Equal Pay Act. Awareness of this history also helps to break down overly essentialist and unhelpfully narrow ideas of class identity, present on the left as well as the right, which tend to characterise 'the working class', or even just its politically organised sections, as composed only of men—or, more specifically, of white, male, urban industrial workers. The decreasing relevance of this concept of class is frequently used in the denial of 'working-class' as a viable contemporary political identity, despite the continued existence of class inequality. Over the past thirty years, deindustrialisation, structural unemployment, and the loss of skilled factory jobs have not only destroyed a former source of masculine status and self-respect, but also weakened what could be a source of political and social empowerment and consciousness-raising for women.

All this is desperately unsexy stuff, of course. Today, the face of mainstream feminism is likely to be turned away from the bleak financial and employment futures facing women under austerity and towards symbolically financial issues such as the campaign to put Jane Austen on a banknote, or the low number of women attending this year's World Economic Forum. It is instructive to compare the attention given to these issues—or to even more peripheral concerns, such as the representational value of Lena Dunham's Girls—and the lack of attention given to, for instance, the current campaign by single mothers in East London to draw attention to their impending eviction following Newham Council's austerity-driven decision to reduce single-parent housing.

The mainstream media's preoccupation with 'lifestyle' or 'Lean In' feminism does little to engage with the material pressures experienced by a growing majority of women, or to draw meaningfully on the traditions of working-class feminism. The closest we seem to have come to attempts to alter this has been the recent self-conscious debate on the need to 'rebrand' feminism as more inclusive, particularly of women who fall outside of its supposed white and middle-class power-base. This has been, in some ways, even more frustrating, as attempts to explain why feminism should be relevant to the working class have invariably focused less on content than on form, on the need to make feminism 'accessible' to 'ordinary people'. What this apparently meant was that feminists, when attempting to bring the gospel to the working class, should be careful to use words of less than two syllables—you know, lest their proletarian interlocutors become discombobulated to an irretrievable degree.

It's fine to argue against a feminism that you see as too theoretical, remote and academic to gain mass appeal. The idea of a divide between academic and populist ways of promoting progressive politics is not unique to feminism; a similar debate periodically engulfs much of the left. How can 'ordinary women', or indeed 'ordinary people', be appealed to in language that will resonate with their everyday concerns, and not alienate them by using long words and abstract concepts? The trouble with this question is that the first half of it doesn't automatically imply the second. Being 'ordinary' doesn't mean being stupid. Too often, in debates within feminism—often well-meaning, valid and necessary debates—over how best to engage working-class women, these women are implicitly othered, there to be appealed to and won over by more enlightened middle-class feminists rather than considered capable of engaging in the debate on their own terms and by themselves. This idea of an absolute binary of 'high theory' middle-class feminist activists and disenfranchised, politically unconscious working-class women involves buying into narratives that see working-class parents, schools and communities as intrinsically unable to impart education or instil political consciousness in the same way as their middle-class counterparts, and which present working-class girls in particular as the helpless inhabitants of some kind of neo-Victorian netherworld. Whereas, as we have seen, working-class communities, notwithstanding their lack of access to resources, have historically been capable of responding to their circumstances with resilience, solidarity and innovation.

Advocating that feminism be 'rebranded' in simple words, however well-intentioned the argument, can entail false and counterproductive assumptions about the ability of 'ordinary women' to understand, for instance, theoretical ideas like 'intersectionality'. A term coined by Kimberlé Crenshaw in 1989, the concept of intersectionality has a long history, and has informed the political work of women of colour from Sojourner Truth in 1851 to Selma James's 1975 pamphlet *Sex, Race and Class*. Crenshaw's use of the term emphasised how women of colour experience multiple systems of oppression—most obviously including, but not limited to, those based on race, gender and class—and how their experiences and voices are frequently marginalised or erased, even within feminist or anti-racist discourses that aim at justice or liberation. Intersectionality has been the subject of much recent discussion within feminism, some of which has dismissed the concept on grounds of its supposed academic obscurity and irrelevance to 'ordinary' people—but, in fact, the lives of working-class women offer many practical examples of intersecting oppressions.

Under austerity, much of the burden of analysing and opposing the impact on women of rising unemployment and the erosion of the welfare state is being shouldered by women whose identities mean they are under attack from several intersecting angles: not simply as women, but as women of colour, as mothers, as carers, as low earners or unemployed—very often, all of these at once. These identities are mutually reinforcing and cumulative, not zero-sum. The problems of the 'ordinary' working class are inherently intersectional: material disadvantage amplifies, and is amplified by, racism, sexism, homophobia, and ageism, all experienced as real and immediate issues enforced by existing structures of power. Women's grassroots organisations and actions, from the Ford Dagenham machinists to Women Against Pit Closures to Southall Black Sisters to Focus E15 Mothers, are informed by awareness of how gender and race impacts on class, and how class impacts on race and gender. This is intersectionality experienced and practiced as a day-to-day reality—not intersectionality as it is often caricatured, as a distant and alien theory into which one chooses to opt. The past and present experience of working-class women offers a real-life, intuitive and logical application of the ideas and concepts that are apparently considered too complex for the likes of them.

There is a difference between wishing feminism to concentrate on material matters relevant to 'ordinary' women—the driving down of wages, living standards and working conditions; closures and funding cuts to women's refuges and childcare services; the sale of council housing and removal of housing, child, and disability benefit—and assuming that the people affected by these concerns cannot recognise, analyse and talk about them for themselves, in language which can be sophisticated as well as rudimentary. I believe that a lot of working-class awareness of disadvantage and oppression is already informed by a feminist impulse, even if the women in question wouldn't necessarily call themselves feminists. The type of feminism visible in the mainstream media has, unsurprisingly, been dominated by women whose race and class allows them greater access to the channels of mass communication, but this does not reflect the variety of women to whom feminism can be relevant. In this debate, as in so many others, liberal condescension, which pays lip-service to issues of race and class, is less meaningful than attempts to address both structural inequality and the many failings in cultural and political representation that make it difficult for non-privileged voices to be heard on their own terms.

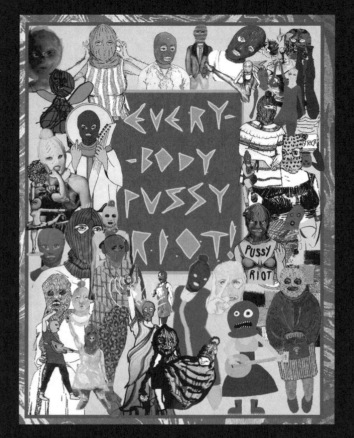

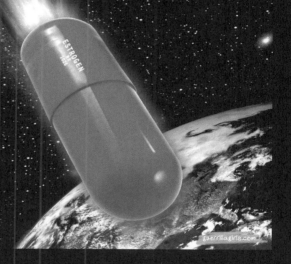

The world needs
a new weapon:
The Estrogen Bomb

Drop it on the superpowers and
the guys in charge will throw down
their big guns, hug each other,
apologize, and start to work on
human rights, education, health care
and an end to income inequality.

Send estrogen pills to presidents,
prime ministers, generals, oligarchs,
and CEOs everywhere.

guerrillagirls.com

The Colour of My Struggle

Black Feminism and Double Jeopardy in a World of Whiteness

I am a Black Feminist. I mean I recognize that my power as well as my primary oppressions come as a result of my blackness as well as my womaness, and therefore my struggles on both of these fronts are inseparable.

Audre Lorde

I, like Lorde, hooks, Walker, Hill Collins, Davis, Morrison, Malveaux, Beal, and countless other women before me—declare fearlessly, unapologetically, and relentlessly that I am a Black Feminist. I am a woman. I am a member of the working class. I am a person of colour. I am a working class woman of colour and I wish to be accepted in my entirety. And it is only through acknowledging every facet of my complex identity that you will be able to understand my liberations, my incarcerations, my struggles, and my stance.

As Lorde also said, '...what is important to me must be spoken, made verbal, and shared, even at the risk of having it bruised or misunderstood.' Amongst many things, it was this call to face adversity and have those difficult conversations that first encouraged me, the reluctant feminist, to wear the title for all to see. Having become radicalised at university after one too many 'you're pretty for a black girl' comments—and certainly countless occasions when it was argued my gender was more important than my race when it came to 'the fight'—I was compelled to supersede the former and take on the label of Black Feminist. I have learnt that there is no such thing as a single-issue struggle because 'we do not live single-issue lives' and oppression works across several axes at any one time.

Having been told I am an 'angry black woman' (a very damaging and reductive caricature of a black woman who understands, what is more often than not, her difficult position in society) because I am outspoken, present, and resistant to patriarchy, I know very well the importance of refusing to be silent when people are uncomfortable with your truth. Let's face it, women, in particular women of colour and working class women, have much to be angry about. When Frances Beal wrote of the 'double jeopardy' of being both black and female, and offered her powerful analysis of the relationship between capitalism and racism, she spoke of how both were intertwined in denying the humanity of all people, especially the humanity of black people.

When Friedan spoke of 'the problem that has no name', she was not talking about the plight of women who were not like her—white, middle-class, well-educated housewives of privilege. She spoke for a select group of women who were bored with leisure, with the home, with children, and with cleaning the house. For some women, this was the 'problem that has no name' and the cure for said problem was a career and independence. For most others, being given equal access with white men to the professions would not solve their problems. These women without men, without children, without homes, without time for leisure, non-white women and poor white women did not feature in Friedan's brave new world. Significantly, the one-dimensional perspective on women's reality presented in *The Feminist Mystique* became (and remains) a marked feature of the contemporary Feminist Movement. As bell hooks observes in her *Feminist Theory: From Margin to Centre*, like Friedan before them 'white women who dominate feminist discourse today rarely question whether or not their perspective on women's reality is true to the lived experiences of women as a collective group.' Arguably it may be impossible to ever speak of the 'lived experiences' of women as a collective group, as we are not homogeneous and nor should we be. I cannot assume that the lived experience of a woman like me—a child of a Sierra Leonian single mother, raised in a council flat in South East London, who went on to study History at the University of Cambridge—will be the same as the lived experiences of my female friends, black or otherwise. And I do not ever wish to speak for all women like me, despite sometimes feeling as though those that do not understand but wish to understand expect me to. I think therefore I am? I speak therefore I speak for all?

And it is this frustrating pigeon-holing of my experiences, particularly at university, that drove me to seek refuge in a movement that argues that sexism, class oppressions, and racism are inextricably bound together, with their relationship being called 'intersectionality', a concept often used in critical theories to describe the ways in which oppressive isms (racism, sexism, homophobia, transphobia, ableism, xenophobia, classism, and so on) are interconnected and cannot be examined separately from one another. In the past, I and many other black feminists have been accused of trivialising the experiences of white women because I stand by Walker's claim, and one of the theories that evolved out of the Black Feminist Movement—Womanism—that black women experience a different, more subversive, and more intense kind of oppression from that of white women. The added axis of oppression—race—combined with factors of marginalisation such as class, gender, and sexuality amplifies the consequences of oppression more intensely.

Mainstream white feminist theory has neither comprehensively accounted for the economic, racial, and gender exigencies of black female experiences, nor in many cases tried to. And although in recent times white women have been called to 'check their privilege', from my own experience, it is something that many find difficult to do. It's tough for the majority to put themselves in the position of the minority—not least because of fear and guilt of seeing what you may have knowingly or unknowingly been complicit in.

And as is often the case when the minority finally have their five minutes in the spotlight, the majority takes offence. I've been in conversations with white women who claim that 'check your privilege' is a tool to exclude them from the feminist discourse and silence them. I find such claims deeply troubling and ironic.

In December 2013, my friend and comrade at London Black Feminists, Lola Okolosie wrote in the *Guardian*:

Within the media, and indeed the movement, there has been much celebration of our feminist resurgence. Yet our success is being marred by infighting. White, middle-class and young women are often seen as the ones spearheading this new wave of activity. Their high-profile campaigns—to have women on banknotes, challenge online misogyny and banish Page 3, for example—though necessary and praiseworthy, do not reflect the most pressing needs of the majority of women, black and minority-ethnic women included. The problem is not that these campaigns exist, but that they are given a focus and attention that overshadows other work feminists are engaged with.

No matter how well-meaning prominent feminists are, many have put their foot it in it at some point and dismissed intersectionality as an unnecessary consideration in Feminist theory. Intersectionality may be an academic term that has spilled into common usage among many feminists, but that does not mean that the concept it refers to isn't real and worthy of discussion.

When Lorde wrote, 'The failure of academic feminists to recognize difference as a crucial strength is a failure to reach beyond the first patriarchal lesson. In our world, divide and conquer must become define and empower.' is as true now as it was then. She goes on to say, 'We welcome all women who can meet us, face to face, beyond objectification and beyond guilt.' Black Feminism does not exist to divide. It exists because there is no room in the mainstream currently for the voices of women of colour. It exists because white privilege is real and it is only through accepting this, and endeavouring to rid oneself of such privileges, that we will be able to struggle together as sisters who accept that we are not homogeneous.

I spoke at a conference to celebrate International Women's Day recently and Baroness Flather closed her speech by claiming 'Women do not support women.' She is right. Constant infighting between different groups within the movement will only serve to keep us fractured. The ultimate aim is a united sisterhood, which will nurture a movement that is part of a greater struggle and more noble cause: The struggle for equality for all.

'It is not our differences that divide us. It is our inability to recognize, accept, and celebrate those differences.'

EMMELINE PANKHURST
SUFFRAGETTE

EMMA GOLDMAN
ANARCHIST

MALALA YOUSAFZAI

MAYA ANGELOU
AUTHOR, I KNOW WHY THE CAGED BIRD SINGS

SILVIA FEDERICI
AUTHOR&CAMPAIGNER, WAGES FOR HOUSEWORK

JUDITH BUTLER

LAURIE PENNY
JOURNALIST

SIMONE DE BEAUVOIR
AUTHOR, THE SECOND SEX

bell hooks

ROSA LUXEMBURG

AUTHOR, AIN'T I A WOMAN?

MARXIST MARTYR

MARY WOLLSTONECROFT

SYLVIA PANKHURST

ION ACTIVIST

AUTHOR, A VINDICATION OF THE RIGHTS OF WOMEN

SUFFRAGETTE

NINA POWER

LUCY ANNE HOLMES

GENDER TROUBLE

AUTHOR, ONE DIMENSIONAL WOMAN

CAMPAIGNER, NO MORE PAGE 3

The Left Needs Feminism

Putting Down the Pony

Every now and again, one catches an article by a sweet-natured, well-meaning, often gaunt and gentle-looking beta-male, explaining why men need feminism. And they are so, so precious. Be a feminist so that you can cry, so that you can be compassionate, so that you can be into cooking, and watch *My Little Pony* without embarrassment. If this doesn't make you want to vomit into your own mouth, then I question your integrity and that of your parents.

Perhaps this is unkind. These articles also call one to a basic level of self-reflexivity, which is always a desideratum, and their demand that you 'check your privilege' can be useful. Shorn of the pleas to emote, and let emote, the desire to examine and take a share of responsibility for the micro-politics of gender can only be positive. Not only that but, as bell hooks suggested, the success of feminism depends on winning over men; if only women could be convinced of feminist analysis, it would stand little chance of succeeding politically, and could be comfortably ignored rather than provoking a backlash.

The problem is that the macro-politics can be lost in what usually turns out to be an individualised analysis in where the male desire to be an 'ally' or (Jesus fucking Christ) a 'male feminist' is both ratified by individual behaviour, and ultimately explained in terms of individual conscience and suffering. Not only that, but it leaves expediently nebulous the status of the term 'feminism'. Hugo Schwyzer much?

I propose to re-pivot this whole question onto a different axis, and ask: can the Left get anywhere without feminism? And how should male activists respond to the answer?

By now it is clear enough that we are amid a fourth wave of feminism. In the anglophone countries, this is driven by a particular demographic: 18–29 year old women, usually social media adepts. It has its own particular concerns, some of which are inherited from the third wave: media representations, the micro-politics of #everydaysexism, and the delicate politics of difference (class, racial, national, sexual) among women. Emblematising the latter concern, the term 'intersectionality' is at the fulcrum of contemporary feminist debates, and the attempts particularly by black feminists and women from the global south not to be squeezed out of the emerging debates.

The question of what to do about this is not merely a tactical question prompted by the conjuncture. The fact of the global women's insurgency is of huge significance, but it presents no surety of the future salience of feminism; the fact is that women, and women's bodies, have actually been central to the dominant political narratives of the last decade or so, and are disproportionately leaned on in the context of austerity politics.

In the 'war on terror', women were used to provide what Zillah Eisenstein calls a 'sexual decoy', conscripted to war narratives in order to obscure the fundamentally masculinist nature of the imperialist drive under Bush the Younger, as well as to provide a vaguely progressive-sounding rationale for racist, Islamophobic repression. This purloined 'feminism' was always rather thin. Neither Malalai Joya nor Malala Youzafszai could be comfortably assimilated into such imperialist narratives; and in the imperialist countries themselves, women's groups were generally in the antiwar camp. Nonetheless, the gender-conservative thrust of such war fables should be spelled out. The argument, then as now, has been that women in 'the West' have essentially 'made it'.

They have reached, through their achievement of the vote and the ability of a few of their number to scale the summits of industry and politics, the zenith of civilization. Everything else is downhill. The only thing to do, in this context, would be to defend what has already been gained (against Muslims, chiefly), and rally to the Pentagon and the State Department as the sanctified defenders of women's liberation.

The global recession has since changed the context and valence of such appeals. When the recession hit, it was women who suffered first and most. When the austerity solution was pioneered, it was clear that the effects—since a central component of it is an assault on the social wage, which covers the invisible labour of reproduction still disproportionately carried out by women—would fall harder on women. Increasingly, state occupants such as David Cameron fall back on the idea that 'the family' (meaning the unacknowledged labour of women) can replace the welfare state. This is not a plea to go back to the 'male breadwinner' model in any simple way: the idea is that women continue to participate in the labour market, and indeed should do so more eagerly given the penury of living on welfare. In essence, women should work more for less; thus, some of the costs of the recession can be allocated according to a moral economy in which women are deemed most blameful, and least deserving. In this context, the fusion of Islamophobia and nationalism takes on a new role, allowing the problem of women's servitude to be represented as a pathology of foreign dogma, rather than a structural feature of advanced, neoliberal capitalism.

This is merely to mention a couple of the ways in which gendered politics has been essential to the forms of political domination, to repression, imperialism and exploitation, in the last decade or so. It is merely to gesture at the fact that politics can hardly be done without confronting the huge, invidious fact of women's oppression; merely to hint at the material circumstances from which the fourth wave has emerged. So, how well has the Left acquitted itself in this context?

'Manarchists', or 'brocialists': does it matter what we call them? The fact is that there is something particularly incongruous about men of the Left, whether they are George

Galloway, or 'Comrade Delta', or their many apologists and acolytes, or (in the case of Delta) the institutional forms that defend them, who betray their ostensibly egalitarian ideals with sexist behaviour. And in fact, the cited cases are merely the prominent tips of the chauvinist iceberg. From the horizontal networks of Occupy, to the more traditionally hierarchical organisations of the far left, case after case of sexist abuse has come up in which ingrained assumptions or institutional pressures led to perpetrators being protected.

To be absolutely clear: this is not more serious than the problem of sexism in the wider society; it is probably far less prevalent on the Left than on the Right. It is simply that the Left does not exist in splendid isolation from the oppressive society in which it seeks to operate. It is immersed in the world and is susceptible to its pressures. Sexism is not peculiar to the Left, but it is a problem for the Left, relative to its normative aspirations, and its aspiration to grow and assemble an alliance of forces capable of challenging capitalism.

The fact is that the discourse of a section of the Left around recent controversies about sexism is at its best strikingly conservative. In its most ostensibly serious form, this involves claiming that the focus on feminism and intersectionality is just identity politics, and a distraction from the real issue of class. This totally ignores the fact that, as feminists such as Silvia Federici, Selma James and Avtar Brah, or more recently Abbie Bakan and Brenna Bhandar, have shown, our understanding of class, labour and surplus value is totally transformed once the realities of gender (and race, and so on) are assimilated. This is hardly irrelevant to the age of austerity and the attacks on the social wage. What those talking about class in the unreconstructed sense want is not to defend class politics, but to conserve class as a kind of identity politics for a specific layer of white men.

This is an inherently minoritarian approach: white men, no matter what the television says, are not the majority of people on the planet by a considerable distance. They may in general hold more power and influence than others, but they cannot by themselves assemble the movement necessary to challenge capitalism. They are not necessarily even the most politically militant sections of the working class. Gramsci's point about building hegemonic alliances holds. No authentic alliance is possible in which oppressed groups are expected to hold their tongue, and submerge their own interests and demands—indeed, using the language of intersectionality, this is exactly the problem that fourth-wave feminists have been confronting.

The Left needs feminism, then, because it urgently needs to update its epistemological assumptions in order to analyse the situation in which it finds itself, and because it needs to be able to fuse together the interests of all the oppressed and exploited in order to be adequate to the political circumstance. But to get to grips with this challenge, it needs to combat its most retrograde elements, those who in fact represent at worst a pungent form of rape culture, or who are at best the left representatives of the backlash culture.

Either that or you can weep over *My Little Pony*. Your call.

Occupy Feminism

Voices From the Women's Library Occupation

Last year, on 8th March, feminists gathered at two locations in London, ready to mark International Women's Day
by taking direct action against the austerity regime. They
didn't know where they would be going, or what the action
would entail, but had been persuaded by a 'call to action'
circulated online, through leafleting and by word of mouth,
coordinated by a coalition of feminists and anti-cuts activists.
The call-out invited people 'tired of watching helpless while
the government destroys people's lives and creates a world
we don't want to live in' to use International Women's Day
to take action against the cuts and their gendered impact.

The focus for the action was The Women's Library in
Whitechapel, London. Activists from two East and South
London meeting-points arrived to find that it had been
occupied by a small group of feminists minutes before. What
followed was a two-day occupation of the historic building
in London's East End; an act of protest not only against the
library's imminent closure, but also in opposition to the
austerity regime—highlighting how cuts exacerbate existing
inequalities along lines of gender, race, class and disability.

Over two hundred of us came in the days that the building was occupied, of all ages and genders; we discussed
together, planned together, and lived together. At the time,
there was a sense that something a bit different was happening. The occupation was mixed-gender but women-led and
explicitly feminist, and this affected the way people organised being in the space and how we related to one another.
It was also a protest defined by joy as well as rage—with

music, dancing, new friendships, and a drawing of strength from the history of earlier feminist struggle documented in the Library's world-renowned archive. And for many of us, it was the first time we had been in a political space where an 'intersectional' approach to feminist politics (the idea that any struggle for gender liberation also needs to encompass struggles against racism and class exploitation) was a consensus from which we started, rather than something we had to argue for.

The occupation was just a tiny part of wider (if fragmented and sporadic) resistance against the destructive impact of austerity on people's daily lives. And yet, despite the small-scale of the action, a number of us from the coalition that organised the occupation felt it was important that the occupation was not lost to memory. For us, it had been a significant event in our political lives and we wanted to find out more about other people's experiences of it, and what political reflections it might have provided. We have therefore embarked on a project to record the voices of The Women's Library occupiers. What follows are some of those voices, collected during one semi-structured group interview conducted in January 2014. We hope that this will form the basis of an ongoing oral history project in which we will not only seek to add to a revolutionary memory, but also reflect upon and critique our own participation in the occupation. We want to think about how memories and histories of political struggle are created and how they inform subsequent struggles. Such a project will, we hope, be an appropriate contribution to The Women's Library archive itself, and help to ensure that it remains a library that can play an active role in day-to-day struggles against oppression, rather than just becoming an academic resource.

'The interesting thing is that it's the university (London Met) with the highest percentage of working-class and ethnic minority students in the country.'

The occupation took place on the day that the Women's Library's exhibition *The Long Road to Equality* was due to be closed, pending the building's permanent closure. London Metropolitan University, who had held the library's world-renowned collection since 1977, announced the previous spring that it wanted to rid itself of the library, claiming that too much of its use now came from outside of the university. Such outside use of the library and visits to its exhibition space included local schoolchildren, women's groups, adult education students and local families. The occupation challenged the decision to close the doors of the historic building in a predominantly working-class area of London's East End, and move the collection to the fourth floor of the academic library of the elite London School of Economics.

A sense of anger against the closure of a building that was a community as well as an academic resource was expressed by lots of the interviewees, many of them reflecting on their own experiences of using the library. However, the impetus behind the occupation was much broader. As one interviewee, who had been involved in the organization of the occupation explained: 'The idea was to have a thing that was about cuts to women's services and the gendered impact of austerity.'

Much of the Women's Library collection is a history of women's struggles, and the occupation explicitly drew on this history as an act of protest against the government's austerity regime. An interviewee recalled a fellow occupier's creativity in extending the timeline in the exhibition space detailing milestones in women's fight for equality in Britain to include the occupation. This occupation set out to be explicitly a feminist occupation and this was important to the organising group, as previous experiences of student occupations and also the Occupy movement had highlighted gender inequalities within the Left. One person said of her experience at a student occupation: 'No one really spoke to you, no one welcomed you. I found it hard to find out about anything. I did sleep there, but it felt very unsafe.' By contrast, The Women's Library occupation was explicitly feminist:

'From the beginning we had quite an explicit understanding that we wanted this to be a feminist occupation, and partly what that meant was a response to cases of sexual violence within what were incredibly exciting new political spaces that were emerging.'

Yet the occupiers were also clear from the start that the kind of feminism they thought to practice was not to be limited only to questions of 'sex' or 'gender'. Rather, the occupation represented an attempt to put into practice the now famous quotation from the Latina feminist blogger Flavia Dzodan: 'my feminism will be intersectional or it will be bullshit.' This message was emblazoned in 2 foot high letters in the front window of the occupied library. It informed the occupiers' decision to focus not only on the imminent closure of the women's library, but to situate this in the context of an austerity regime that worked upon intensifying inequalities of class and race as well as those of gender. The challenges of putting 'intersectional' feminism into practice was the theme of one of the workshops at the occupation. Occupiers subsequently agreed that the political lessons drawn from there were one of the most important legacies of the occupation.

'It came a year after all those student occupations and the UK Uncut action...definitely I think things changed in those few years in terms of political strategies and confidence about things...'

Interviewees recalled the diversity of groups involved in the planning of the occupation, which included: Disabled People Against the Cuts, Fem Cells, Feminist Fightback, Occupy, Solidarity Federation and UK Uncut. They felt this diversity and the coalition-building process was an important part of the action: 'I felt it promoted some interesting coalitions.' Another, involved in Feminist Fightback, recalled how working together during The Women's Library Occupation had led to more joint working on other actions in the months that followed:

'The links we built in the planning and during the occupation, and I think the trust that was necessary for that, has led to us doing other joint actions since then. In Feminist Fightback a couple of us went and helped with the UK Uncut action [against welfare cuts] outside Lord Freud's house, and we have also done some pickets of shops who take staff on the workfare programme with SolFed. It really helped to get to know people in other groups personally—I think it helps to create a basis for working together, in a political scene that is very often pretty fragmented.'

This occupation built from the momentum that had been ignited by the student occupations the previous year, yet differed from them in seeking to widen participation beyond students, to include a cross-section of people trying to highlight the effects of the cuts. This form of direct action seems to have been particularly inspiring to participants frustrated with more traditional methods of political protest:

It provided a tiny glimpse into possible ways of living differently. People kept commenting on how good the atmosphere was, how well people were treating each other, how it was possible to bring children. In meetings it felt like people were very genuinely trying to think about how we best organise the occupation and what our strategy should be, and were listening to each other. The Friday night where [the feminist band] Moby Clit played is a very happy memory. And while we were waiting for the eviction and someone put on the sound system and we started dancing.

An Anarchist Guide To... Feminism

The Emma Goldman Angle

Emma Goldman finds a desk in utopia. Jazz is playing on the radio. She liked jazz: it worked to different rules and you couldn't pin it down. She flicks furtively through Proudhon's *What is Property?*. The man she thought of as the great French anarchist was now remembered as a misogynist and anti-feminist, she realised. She hovers over the famous dialogue:

'But,' as some of my younger readers may protest, *'you are a republican.'*

Republican, yes, but that word specifies nothing. Res publica; that is, the public thing. Now, whoever is interested with public affairs, under whatever form of government, may call himself a republican. Even kings are republicans.

'Well, then, you are a democrat?'

No.

'What! You are a monarchist?'

No.

'A constitutionalist?'

God forbid.

'Then you are an aristocrat?'

Not at all.

'You want a mixed form of government?'

Even less.

'So then what are you?'

I am an anarchist.

There was a lot in this small extract that still appealed

to her but she wanted to pinpoint where she and Proudhon diverged. Needing to concentrate on the text, she turned the radio off.

Proudhon was right about republicanism, she thought. Of course, he knew that politics couldn't be reduced to 'public affairs', an independent realm of justice—not even where people were blessed by the leadership of a benevolent ruler. Nor, either, could it be moulded into a sphere of liberty, equality and fraternity. Power might be seized from hereditary elites by virtuous citizens, but it was impossible to resist the corruptions of power by means of participation and eternal vigilance. The public realm was based on slavery and Proudhon's genius was to recognise that property—'robbery without risk and danger to the robber'—underpinned it. No matter how the government was constituted, property was its master. Property meant that politics had become 'the reflex of the business and industrial world', exploiting workers and inventing programmes of work that were not only exhausting, but stupefying.

What niggled? Poor dear Proudhon was too much of a home man to push this insight. He failed to see that property worked in complex ways and that for women there was a double enslavement. Like men, women experienced the effects of property in sweated workshops and domestic drudgery. However, woman was also, uniquely, 'a sex commodity', and marriage, the institution 'that stands for the sovereignty of the man over the woman, of her complete submission to his whims and commands,' was the chief medium of exchange. Proudhon's blindness made her shudder. Emma wrote:

The institution of marriage makes a parasite of woman, an absolute dependent. It incapacitates her for life's struggle, annihilates her social consciousness, paralyses her imagination, and then imposes its gracious protection, which is in reality a snare, a travesty on human character.

On a Post-it she scribbled 'send Proudhon my copies of Ibsen,' before turning to the question of democracy.

As far as representative systems were concerned, Proudhon was right to dismiss it.

What does the history of parliamentarism show? Nothing but failure and defeat: a process of 'wire-pulling, intriguing, flattering, lying, cheating... chicanery of every description.'

Emma thought about all those women that she'd argued with about formal emancipation, vote fetishism, the demand for rights—mere inclusion as citizens to realise an equality of oppression with men. What a waste. The struggle was for freedom. Stirner had taught a valuable lesson when he said that, 'man has as much liberty as he is willing to take.' Women must likewise take theirs and overcome the passivity and pettiness that sex commodification had bred in them. To Reclus's thrilling exhortations—Ouvrier, Prends la Machine! Prends Ta Terre, Paysan!—Emma added a third: Femme, Prends Ta Corps! Refuse to manufacture children either for industrial production or war. Learn about contraception and safe abortion—not in the name of choice, 'race purity' or overpopulation, but to refuse the duty that government, religion and the economy impose. Revolutionary transformation comes from flouting convention and the discovery of genuine 'free choice, of love, of ecstasy, of defiant passion.'

Back to democracy: the important point that Proudhon overlooked was that there was power in the mass-resistance campaigns that had forced rulers to grant limited rights of participation. Would-be citizens had wrongly confused democracy with a single process and a set of matching institutions. It really meant direct action, resistance, illegalism and the exercise of 'integrity, self-reliance, and courage.' In my day, she thought, the syndicalists embraced this democratic idea, combating authority, servility and elitism through education, mutual aid, sabotage and strike. And although she was sad and frustrated by her confinement in utopia, she was comforted to know that these democratic principles survived, and immensely cheered to see so many women involved. If I was on earth again, she thought, I'd go with Sasha to join the Indignados, the Greek comrades, the friends in Gezi park. I am the 'Spirit of Wall Street.'

'Hey Sailor Girl!' a familiar voice called. Alexander Berkman broke the spell of her imagining. 'Am I a MANarchist?' he asked, looking anxious.

'You can be a bit of a puritan, dearest, but of course you know that I don't think that. Isn't that funny, though, I was just thinking about how things have changed in the movement since we were active. Were we naive to treat our love as a model for anarchism?'

'It's true that not everyone thinks about relationships the same way we did,' Sasha replied, 'but whichever way you cut free love, the problem you identified all those years ago—'how to be one's self and yet in oneness with others, to feel deeply with all human beings and still retain one's own characteristic qualities'—still holds, I think. With you it was never philosophy, but love that provided the resolution.' He continued, 'You told me once that you always wanted to give me more than you expected in return. Isn't that Kropotkin's anarchist principle, giving without expectation of reward?'

'Yes Sasha. It is. And because of you, I also knew that anarchism was the freest possible expression of my latent powers.'

'It is! You never said that the love you had in mind was only for straights, or that it was constrained by nature—motherhood, witchery, nurturing. Only that love was natural and that human nature, driven by defiant passion, is fluid, plastic, responsive to new conditions and that it can be changed.'

'That's true.' But Emma only rallied momentarily. 'I don't understand why some anarchist women hate men and want to escape patriarchy by living apart. I never wanted estrangement. I wanted to break down the walls of superstition, custom and habit—just as Edward Carpenter did.'

'It's a bit late for you to get downhearted by disagreement', Sasha said softly. 'You have to cling to your ideals.

That means believing that people are capable of finding the love within themselves and using it to extend anarchist values and practices.'

Sasha left, leaving Emma to mull over some of the bitter disappointments of their lives. She re-read a letter she had written to him in 1931:

The still voice in me will not be silenced, the voice which wants to cry out against the wretchedness and injustice in the world... I know there is no place where I can or will gain a footing and once more throw in my lot with our people who continue the struggle of liberation.

More than seventy years since she'd arrived in utopia, she couldn't see much progress on earth. But loss was part of the struggle and she could see that thousands of women felt the same as she had done, and lived life as passionate revolutionaries, with partners of their choice, resisting commodification, the pressures to conform to markets and imposed morality; organising safe spaces for each other and each other's children, fighting FGM, working in no-border campaigns, against sex-trafficking; all this resonated with her. Emma picked up the pen and re-wrote Proudhon's exchange:

'But,' as some of my younger readers may protest, *'you are a republican.'*
Republican, yes, but that word specifies nothing. Res publica; that is, the public thing. Now, whoever is interested with public affairs, under whatever form of government, may call ~~himself~~ herself *a republican. Even* ~~kings~~ queens *are republicans.*
'Well, then, you are a democrat?'
~~No.~~ Yes, but not a parliamentarian.
'What! You are a monarchist?'
No.
'A constitutionalist?'

~~God forbid.~~ _That's madness._
'_Then you are an aristocrat?_'
~~Not at all.~~ _No. A Dionysian, perhaps._
'_You want a mixed form of government?_'
Even less.
'_You want no government?_'
Yes!
'_So then what are you? An anarchist?_'
Not that alone!
'_What are you then?_'
I am an anarchist, feminist.

EDITH MARGARET GARRUD

'THE SUFFRAGETTE WHO KNEW JIU-JITSU'

Edith Margaret Garrud (1872–1971) was among the first female professional martial arts instructors in the Western world. She is remembered for having trained the Bodyguard unit of the Women's Social and Political Union (WSPU) in jiu-jitsu self-defence techniques.

In 1913, as a response to the so-called Cat and Mouse Act whereby Suffragette leaders on hunger strikes could legally be released from jail and then re-arrested, the WSPU established a thirty-member, all-woman protection unit referred to as "the Bodyguard".

Edith Garrud became the trainer of the Bodyguard and taught them jiu-jitsu and the use of Indian clubs as defensive weapons. Their lessons took place in a succession of secret locations to avoid the attention of the police.

VOO-OOOM!

The Bodyguard fought a number of well-publicised hand-to-hand combats with police officers who were attempting to arrest their leaders.

Jiu-Jitsu as a Husband-Tamer.

On several occasions they were also able to stage successful escapes and rescues, making use of tactics such as disguise and the use of decoys to confuse the police.

LOOK! a harmless member of the public going about their day!

POW!!

SAFE FROM ATTACK

WHEN YOU KNOW JIU-JITSU

"We have not yet made ourselves a match for the police, and we have got to do it. The police know jiu-jitsu. I advise you to learn jiu-jitsu. Women should practise it as well as men."

See Red Women's Workshop

1973–1990

See Red Women's Workshop was founded by three ex-art students in 1973. We met through an ad placed in *Red Rag*—a radical feminist magazine—asking for women interested in forming a group to look at and combat the negative images of women in advertising and the media. See Red grew out of that meeting and a collective was formed producing silk-screened posters for the women's liberation movement, as well as for community groups and others on request.

Working collectively was central to the ethos of See Red, as was sharing skills and knowledge. Members belonged to women's consciousness-raising groups and were active in various radical and alternative organisations. In the early days the posters were mainly produced about our personal experiences as women, about the oppression of housework, childcare and the negative images of women. An idea for a poster would be discussed, a member would work on a design, bring it back for comment, someone else might make changes and so on until the collective were satisfied with the end result; no one individual took the credit. This was a concept many in the art world found hard to accept: 'Who holds the pencil? Someone must hold the pencil!' Quality was important and many hours would be spent on ensuring that only posters that were well-printed and -produced left the workshop.

Our first premises were a squat in Camden Town, but after a brick was thrown through the window See Red moved to

South London and eventually to premises off the Walworth Road, which we shared with Women In Print. The premises were derelict and all the renovations were carried out by the collective or by women in the building trades. The workshop was attacked on several occasions by the National Front—from stickers to smashed doors, ink poured over the machinery, phone lines cut and the mail pissed over.

The collective on average consisted of about 6 women at any one time, but in all over 35 women passed through the workshop. Some came to produce posters around issues that were important to them, some were on apprenticeship schemes for a few months and some just wanted to join the Collective. Until we received grants, first from Southwark Council and then the GLC in 1983, funding for the workshop came through the sale of the posters, printing for community and other groups and from donations. We all had part-time jobs as well, and some had child care commitments. Equipment, inks, paper etc. were acquired from firms closing down or through donations.

The workshop changed in 1983 to focussing on service printing and although the original posters for the women's movement continued to be printed, no new designs were produced.

See Red members have recently met up again due to increased interest in our work, and we are working on the See Red Women's Workshop website, with archivists, women's groups and galleries, as well as on other plans for the future.

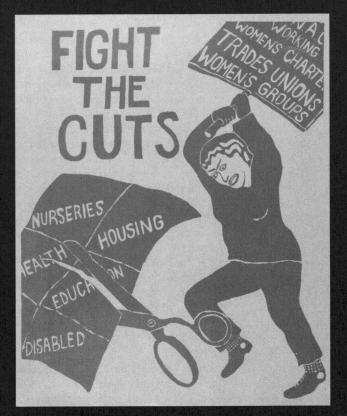

IT'S DONE!"

ARTHUR SCHOPENHAUER
MARY WOLLSTENCRAFT
& FRIEDRICH NIETZSCHE

It wasn't as piratey as she'd hoped, but it wasn't as bad as she feared.

The eye doctor said if she
it every day, especially
looking closely at stuff,
left one would get stro

JULY:

AUGUST:

'98 by Anna Trench

re
en
r.

Fingers crossed, they said,
it'd be off by September.

SEPTEMBER:

Girls, netball with me,
Boys, football with Mr. Smith.

Ruins

We will continue with whoever survives.
Female activist, Syria, 2013

now I see we don't survive it—
not like that, at least.

when you said no gets out alive,
you meant no one gets out alive, but also:
no one gets out intact.

suheir hammad wrote:
'if a body can carry through you follow'
but sometimes the you that follows
looks a lot like something else.

well, we build from pieces, don't we?
we build from the ground up, didn't someone say:
we aren't afraid of ruins, not even
the ruins of ourselves?
                                        Oh, she looked not like
the ruins of her youth but like the ruins of those ruins --
those ruins where we live where we breathe where we
break bread and break heart and break through.

I am not in the least afraid of ruins:
we build up from beneath debris, yes,
we build the wall with the bricks that are available, yes,

we will continue with whoever survives.

Us, Black Women

Us, Black women
Like samples at a grocery store
Set out to be picked over and never fully paid for

Us, Black women
With vaginas that still smell like unwanted mixed babies
Blood
And four hundred years of forced entries

And this nigga ask you
Can he hit it
As if it hasn't already been beaten

Outkast goes to court with Rosa Parks
Ludacris makes a diss record about Oprah
And rooms full of upstanding black men say, hell, we don't know
what happened in that car
Rihanna may have given Chris Brown a REASON to beat her down

I take it you don't have little sisters
and there must be shrapnel in your back to replace the spine that
once made you a man, see
I'm not mad at you for your opinion
I'm just hoping
that we are never two pop stars alone in a car and you get mad at
me for mine

I can still hear the cries of all the babies that had to get left behind
by their own mothers
I've got the tongue of Harriet Tubman I can still taste the blood of all
the wounds she licked to get us here

And we are constantly trying to get back there
Then you say that she don't like her own people
Because she built a school in AFRICA
Nigga, you must have forgotten your roots
Do you think that we only exist here?

I've never seen you leave a penny in a gas station
You couldn't imagine the pain of raising a Black Panther, only to hear
your son calling you bitches and hoes on the radio
You are no Afeni Shakur

Your jaw couldn't walk a Miles Davis inside the mouth of Cicely
Tyson
And you question the charity of a black woman
While this man asks
can he hit it
As if it hasn't already been beaten

We have been running this world since it started
Have yet to receive a day off of our feet
There are no holidays dedicated to us
Just a bunch of poems used to undress everything but our minds
Millions of songs played to make us feel like we were born to be
called everything but our names
And cemeteries, dressed up like videos, burying our images every
other T.V. station

We get one Michelle every 44 years
We get one African American teen pregnancy every 44 minutes
And little Wayne says that he wants to fuck every girl in the world
Sarah Goodes takes part in inventing beds
Trey Songz says we gone think he invented sex
How disconnected we are
Yet hanging from the same umbilical cords we clipped you from
Stop asking 'can you hit it'
Take your mother flowers for no reason
Stop making excuses for you putting your hands on us

Stop
Putting your hands on us
Stop
Running out on us
Stop
Running over us
Stop treating us like samples at a grocery store

Do not touch us
If you have no plans on making this home.

TXT: MARÍA MARÍA ACHA-KUTSCHER

Indignadas

Indignadas (Outraged Women) consists of a visual record of the role of women in recent public protests around the World. The first stage focused on Spain with the movement of *Indignados* in 2011, while the second stage, which began in 2013, expands the project globally, including movements like Occupy Wall Street and feminist groups like Pussy Riot, Slutwalk and Alfombra Roja (Red Carpet, Peru.)

Acha-Kutscher turns photographs from press and witnesses into drawings that she shares on the internet and prints into large-format tarps for exhibitions in public spaces.

The aim of the *Indignadas* series is to make visible and place the woman at the centre of this social struggle. A memory-register that reminds future generations that social changes throughout history were made by women and men together.

The drawings record a popular aesthetic, where the woman's body is not offered as support for the eyes of men, but as support for the political message. Transforming photographs into drawings, they are set in the supposed 'timelessness' of art. This is another way to connect with society, spread the protest and preserve the memory of the women.

we have to

FREE
HALF

OF THE PEOPLE

★ THE WOMEN ★

SO THEY CAN HELP

FREE

THE OTHER

HALF

emmeline pankhurst

JUL—AUG

2014

ISSUE__6

JCDecaux

Escape from Cameron Island

Trapped in a Neoliberal Nightmare

In 2012, two years into David Cameron's premiership, and one year after his famous speech attacking multiculturalism, the BBC ran an article with the following headline: 'Illegal Immigrants Desperate to Escape the Squalor of Britain'. One could easily work out from the title that this was not the sort of story that would neatly fit the current cultural climate. It was too irreconcilable with the prevailing fantasy of Britain as an idyllic island, an island that the poor global multitude will do almost anything to enter. Unsurprisingly, the story passed unnoticed.

The most striking detail of this article was related to what is known as voluntary deportation. In 2005, 330 illegal immigrants gave themselves up to the authorities to be sent back to their homeland. Seven years later, in 2012, that number had grown to 23,148 (an increase, statisticians would not fail to note, of almost 7,000%). These people had left behind a life of hardship and poverty, only to find themselves in the same misery once again. As the report discovered, they typically lived a silent underground life, away from the authorities, in overpriced makeshift shelters, littered with rotting rubbish and hungry rats. Only occasionally would they find work, and then slave-like work that would barely cover the rent. For them, Britain has become another hellish place from which they want to escape.

What is worse is that many of these people are trapped in the country. They cannot get out since they followed the traffickers' instructions and destroyed their papers on their arrival. After all, illegal immigrants risk their lives for a purpose. They arrive with the hope of settling down properly, and in the event of getting caught, they have no reason to aid the authorities' task of deporting them. In retrospect, perhaps they should've ignored the traffickers. Had they known that deportation was going to be what they most desired just a few years down the line, they surely would have weighed their options more carefully.

Perhaps the traffickers took this possibility into account, with the advice to destroy all papers part of a cunning business idea. Because, without the appropriate documents, illegal immigrants are left with no other option than to return to the traffickers—this time to get out of Britain; in early 2013 one British tabloid reported that foreign nationals are indeed now smuggled out of the country. They are transported in the back of lorries across the English Channel to France. The cost is still relatively modest—according to their sources, a mere £1,500.

Escape has become a shared desire for many of those trapped in this neoliberal nightmare. Britain, as its character has morphed into that of David Cameron's (making its appearance unapologetic, twisted and menacing), has become an island from which not just foreign nationals but practically everyone wants to exit.

This has given rise to an emerging genre of escape fantasies. They take different forms, mainly determined by class. Many in the upper classes have already integrated moments of escape into their daily lives, with houses in France, apartments in Saudi Arabia and frequent visits to Bali and South Africa. The middle-classes, although intermittently going abroad, spend most of their time dreaming about alternative lives: making detailed and elaborate plans about next year's holidays; talking endlessly about moving abroad, or to the countryside, where they could live peacefully, with a garden to cultivate, neighbouring an authentic local farm from where they could buy fresh duck eggs, those wonderful brown ones with real freckles.

What makes the middle-class fantasy of escape so distinct is the way in which it is articulated in relation to work. While unemployment is a haunting nightmare, in many ways the worst thing that could happen to them, both symbolically and economically, they nevertheless romanticize life after work, telling themselves: 'if only I could escape work—make a proper exit—I could finally do all of those things I currently have no time or energy for.'

This culture of exit is especially prominent in the public sector, where workers are predominantly middle-class. A recent employee-engagement survey of the UK police force revealed a striking level of disillusionment. According to one police officer, 'morale is the lowest I have ever known... I wish I could leave tomorrow.' Another example is the UK Border Agency, which was forced to recruit new staff, since 'more people than expected wanted to leave'. Even university lecturers, who supposedly enjoy one of the last, few 'good jobs', are aching to leave. In a recent interview following his retirement, Terry Eagleton was asked what was different about academia today compared to when he started. His response: 'Most people I know in academia want to get out. Which is a pretty new situation. I've never encountered that before'.

If not completely new, this sentiment has reached unprecedented heights. The desire to escape is deeply human, true, but you cannot deny that some places are more likely to prompt this desire than others. And Britain, after years of nihilistic neoliberal experimentation, appears to have become such a place.

This is a remarkable transformation if one considers the elevated place that Britain has always had in the imagination of the outside world, not least among young children. For them, as for many others, Britain has been more of an image than a physical place, a land shaped by Mary Poppins and Charles Dickens and the red miniature double-decker buses displayed in local toyshops around the world. It is the world one finds on postcards picturing Big Ben and Buckingham

Palace and the solemn guards in bearskin hats. It is an image of an island where people are eccentric, sport the latest fashion, and talk rapidly and wittily. In this image, even the rain appears different, somehow softer and lighter, especially in the late evenings, as in *The Singing Detective* or *Tinker Taylor Soldier Spy*, where you could see it shimmering in the city lights, as elongated shadows deftly disappear down narrow lanes, lending the city-night a particular mystique. All is cosy and snug. There is nothing to fear. Even Jack the Ripper is harmless. His story being so deeply entrenched in this romantic image of the city that his killings appear trivial in comparison.

Today, however, this image is largely dead. True, the political right wants us to hold onto it, but it belongs to a different era. And we know it. Even the children growing up far away from Britain know it. Something that became painfully apparent during the opening and closing ceremony of the 2012 Olympics in London, where Danny Boyle presented a nostalgic array of scenes involving Shakespeare and James Bond, and, most bizarrely, a scene saluting The National Health Service—which, no doubt, was meant as an obituary. Run-down public services, neglected regional planning and inflated cost of living has made this island ever-more inhospitable. The wish to escape, then, appears to be the only logical response.

One of the most significant features of capitalist culture in the UK today—and this is a point that very rarely gets addressed—is the way in which this idea of escape, an imagined escape from the cold realities of a neoliberal wasteland, has itself become an industry. Just flick through *The Sunday Times* property pages and you will see that there is now a whole business sector that seeks to accommodate this most desperate urge. And this industry appears to flourish in times of social turmoil, such as during the 2010 London riots, when a well-known commuter tabloid asked its readers: 'Want To Escape?' But no place is more devoted to these escape fantasies than television, and especially daytime television, when you're bound to find one of the variations of the Channel 4 hit show, *A Place in the Sun*, where middle-class Britons are escorted through medieval villages in Tuscany or old Portuguese fishing villages, all the while eliciting long 'oohs' and 'oh-my-gods'. If these dreams of a new life in a foreign country only appear far-fetched and mocking, too disconnected from your immediate reality, you will always have Ryanair and daily flights to Ibiza, Rhodes or Bari.

We suggest there is something significant here, a shift in capitalist ideology, a strange continuation of what Adorno and Horkheimer called 'the culture industry'. For them, corporate ideology had thoroughly permeated everyday life, mainly via the organs of mass consumption and media. What was most perverse about the culture industry, they maintained, was not that it reconciled the masses to an inherently barbaric system, but that it hijacked and exploited a range of democratic sentiments: especially the yearning to be included and recognised as an equal member of the community.

But the sentiment that we find today, especially in Britain, is different to what Adorno and Horkheimer described. It is no longer inclusion that is desired. Rather we find a desire to escape. To exit the scene of power. Or even disappear. While politicians delusionally believe that the prevailing cultural imaginary is still galvanized around inclusion, business strategists have known for quite a while that the dominant desire today is that of withdrawal—mentally, phantasmagorically, and physically. What we see emerging, then, is a new industry—not the culture industry, which promises inclusion—but the escape industry, which promises another form of salvation, namely exit. This industry already exists. Corporations have discovered this widely shared desire to escape, and are now selling various forms of escape products. In so doing, they wed us even more profoundly to that from which we seek to escape—for the possibility of true exit is no more remote than deep inside the escape industrial complex.

Fuck Your Hard Work

Where's Our 3 Day Week?

Recently, I interviewed a dozen of my former classmates, now aged in their late thirties and early forties, to see how their lives differed from those of their working-class parents. Was it true that Britain was becoming classless, and people more individualised? Had this generation embraced the 'flexibility' apparently offered by the global labour market? Or did they yearn for a return to the certainties of a job for life?

I quickly discovered that the answer to all three of those questions is no. Superficially, my classmates appeared to have climbed the social ladder. They had to wear suits for work, not overalls, and they had fancy-sounding job titles: they were all 'analysts', 'consultants' or 'managers'. But in reality, their lives were little different from those of their parents, most of whom had worked in the factories and shipyards of 1980s Tyneside, or (in the case of their mothers), in shops or as office cleaners. What bound them to their parents was the experience of really hard work:'they worked hard for us'; 'I work very hard' were phrases I heard repeatedly. Their supposedly middle-class lifestyles were built on credit and debt, and on the insecurity of zero-hour, or temporary, or part-time contract work. 'Flexibility' did not inspire them; strangely enough, most of them wanted to work close to home, and close to family and friends, and didn't like having to move jobs at the whim of their employers.

Perhaps more surprisingly, none of them exactly relished returning to the alleged certainties of the past. That's the postwar past, the 1950s and 1960s, often mythologised by politicians as a time of job security, affluence and upward social mobility. In reality, Britain never experienced entirely full employment, working-class 'affluence' relied on the expansion of credit agreements; and only a tiny minority of people travelled from a manual working-class home into a profession. These were years when working-class people had greater bargaining power than ever before, because of demand for their labour and the progressive reforms introduced by the 1945 Labour government. But there has never been a time when capitalism existed without the exploitation of most people, most of the time.

My classmates weren't necessarily aware of this historical detail, but they were aware that working for a living was unlikely to bring them what they want and need. They didn't aspire to greater job security because their aspirations didn't focus on work. They were tentative about admitting this at first. That's understandable, in a country where politicians of all hues claim that being a member of a 'hardworking family' is a criterion of citizenship. Yet as my classmates slowly began to admit, most people don't see hard work as a virtue. Their aspirations focus on getting more leisure: time to spend with family and friends, doing things they consider worthwhile. That might be childcare, but it might equally be creative or craft work. In a study of 1990s Basildon, the social scientists Alan Hudson and Dennis Hayes found that 'Basildon man' and woman—the supposedly arch-working-class Tories—felt disenchanted with a society that offered them meaningless work. Asked about their aspirations, most of this group of manual workers put 'making a scientific or medical discovery that could benefit the human race' top of their list. Similar sentiments were evoked by their children's generation when I interviewed them. They dreamed of winning the lottery—and concurred that they'd use the money to leave work, spend more time with family, and ensure their children didn't have to work for a living.

This is a sensible attitude. Hard work causes stress, poor health and early death—above all, it has never solved poverty. We work longer hours now than we've done for fifty years, yet the gap between the rich and poor has never been wider. Working hard cannot solve an economic crisis. The fact we are all expected to work so hard is in fact a result of economic crisis: a crisis that did not appear in 2008, but has been with us far longer. This is the crisis at the heart of capitalism: a tension between the 1% who control the economy, and want to continually increase their wealth, and the rest of us, who are expected to work ever harder, in order to generate profit and to keep us from occupying our time in meaningful ways like questioning or challenging the status quo.

Yet throughout the last century, that strategy has never been completely successful. The history of the working class is often told as a constant struggle for work. But in fact working-class people have constantly strived to reduce the amount of time and effort spent working for 'them'. For men that meant trying to get into reserved factory work during the Second World War because fighting in 1914 had brought no benefits for ordinary people. For women, it meant leaving domestic service, which was Britain's largest single occupation until 1939. Thousands of servants simply deserted their posts in the weeks after war was declared, in the knowledge that factories and offices would require their labour. They weren't enamored of working on an assembly line or behind a desk, but they were aware that clerks and factory hands had regulated hours of work, basic pay rates and in some cases a holiday entitlement. Domestic servants, by contrast, were expected to work six and a half days a week for a pittance: it was by depending on such labour that the professional middle class reproduced itself in the 19th and early 20th centuries.

After the war, the real gains of the 1950s and 1960s were achieved by ordinary people themselves. The Labour victory in the 1945 General Election delivered a welfare state and near-full employment, but more interesting is how ordinary working people chose to exploit these improvements. Factory and, increasingly, office workers mobilised to improve working conditions and, importantly, reduce the amount of time they spent at work. That's why so many of the disputes in the 1960s and 1970s were over the basic rate of pay, and who distributed overtime. If you're paid a decent basic wage, then you don't have to spend evenings and weekends at work, or take on evening or night shifts in order to pay for your mortgage, car or holiday.

Why, then, have people voted for the Tories, the party championing hard workers and entrepreneurialism? Precisely because the Conservatives seemed to offer an answer to many people who wanted to stop working for 'the man'. The Tories have only ever offered individualistic solutions: home ownership or the chance to start your own business. These promises of social mobility and self preservation have always failed, because only a few can ever possess the wealth and opportunity in a capitalist country. Bankruptcies rose in the 1980s, following Margaret Thatcher's scheme to fund business start-ups, and owner-occupiers suffered record levels of repossession in the 1990s. Today, those who 'own' their homes are in reality in hock to banks, burdened with huge, unsustainable debts.

Solidarity, on the other hand, has delivered important victories, and could offer a real alternative to austerity. Look at the tremendous achievements that collective struggle made over the last century: better working conditions, shorter working hours, an expanded public sector that gave us better jobs and care, democratically controlled housing and free education. The working class has declined as a collective political force, but the desire to help each other out has not—it's just that its only outlet is now in worrying about children's and grandchildren's uncertain futures. By showing that collective effort can bring huge gains for all of us the Left could justify the redistribution of income and property, which is the only way to create a truly classless society. The political establishment scoff that this is ludicrous: but they have yet to reveal the logic behind their own incredible notion that 'hardworking families' can overcome the inequality perpetrated by a powerful elite determined to hang onto their privilege.

'Everything I see about me is sowing the seeds of a revolution that is inevitable, though I shall not have the pleasure of seeing it. The lightning is so close at hand that it will strike at the first chance, and then there will be a pretty uproar.'

Voltaire

The Promise of Revolutionary Humanism

From time immemorial there have been human beings who have believed that they could construct, individually or collectively, a better world for themselves than that which they had inherited. Quite a lot of them also came to believe that in the course of so doing it might be possible to remake themselves as different if not better people. I count myself among those who believe in both these propositions.

The belief that we can through conscious thought and action change both the world we live in and ourselves for the better defines a humanist tradition. The secular version of this tradition overlaps with and has often been inspired by religious teachings on dignity, tolerance, compassion, love and respect for others. Humanism, both religious and secular, is a world view that measures its achievements in terms of the liberation of human potentialities, capacities and powers. It subscribes to the Aristotelian vision of the uninhibited flourishing of individuals and the construction of 'the good life'.

There are plenty of contemporary signs that the enlightened humanist tradition is alive and well, perhaps even staging a comeback. This is the spirit that clearly animates the hordes of people employed around the world in NGOs and other charitable institutions whose mission is to improve the life chances and prospects of the less fortunate. There are even vain attempts to dress up capital itself in the humanist garb of what some corporate leaders like to call Conscious Capitalism, a species of entrepreneurial ethics that looks suspiciously like conscience laundering along with sensible proposals to improve worker efficiency by seeming to be nice to them. All the nasty things that happen are absorbed as unintentional collateral damage in an economic system motivated by the best of ethical intentions.

There are two well-known undersides to all of this. The first is that, however noble the universal sentiments expressed at the outset, it has time and again proved hard to stop the universality of humanist claims being perverted for the benefit of particular interests, factions and classes. This is the problem that has bedevilled the doctrines of human rights enshrined in a UN declaration that privileges the individual rights and private property of liberal theory at the expense of collective relations and cultural claims. This is what turns the ideals and practices of freedom into a tool of governmentality for the reproduction and perpetuation of capitalist class affluence and power.

The second problem is that the enforcement of any particular system of beliefs and rights always involves some disciplinary power, usually exercised by the state or some other institutionalised authority backed by force. The UN declaration implies state enforcement of individual human rights when the state so often is first in line violating those rights.

The difficulty with the humanist tradition in short is that it does not internalise a good understanding of its own inescapable internal contradictions, most clearly captured in the contradiction between freedom and domination. The result is that humanist leanings and sentiments often get presented these days in a somewhat off-hand and embarrassed way, except when their position is safely backed by religious doctrine and authority. The result is what Frantz Fanon characterised as 'insipid humanitarianism'.

There is plenty of evidence of that manifest in its recent revival. The bourgeois and liberal tradition of secular humanism forms a mushy ethical base for largely ineffective moralising about the sad state of the world and the mounting of equally ineffective campaigns against the plights of chronic poverty and environmental degradation. The growth of the charitable industrial complex mainly reflects the need to increase 'conscience laundering' for a world's oligarchy that is doubling its wealth and power every few years in the midst of economic stagnation. Their work has done little or nothing in aggregate to deal with human degradation and dispossession or proliferating environmental degradation. This is structurally so because anti-poverty organisations are required to do their work without ever interfering in the further accumulation of the wealth from which they derive their sustenance. If everyone who worked in an anti-poverty organisation converted overnight to an anti-wealth politics we would soon find ourselves living in a very different world.

There is, I believe, a crying need to articulate a secular revolutionary humanism that can ally with those religious-based humanisms to counter alienation in its many forms and to radically change the world from its capitalist ways. There is a strong and powerful—albeit problematic—tradition of secular revolutionary humanism with respect to both theory and political practice. It is very different from bourgeois liberal humanism. It clearly recognises that the prospects for a happy future for most are invariably marred by the inevitability of dictating the unhappiness of some others. A dispossessed financial oligarchy which cannot any more partake of caviar and champagne lunches on their yachts moored off the Bahamas will doubtless complain at their diminished fates and fortunes in a more egalitarian world. We may, as good liberal humanists, even feel a bit sorry for them. Revolutionary humanists steel themselves against that thought.

Consider, as one example, the revolutionary humanism of someone like Frantz Fanon. Fanon was a psychiatrist working in hospitals in the midst of a bitter and violent anti-colonial war in Algeria. Fanon wrote in depth about the struggle for freedom and liberty on the part of colonised peoples against the colonisers. His analysis, though specific to the Algerian case, illustrates the sorts of issues that arise in any liberation struggle, including those between capital and labour. It incorporates the additional dimensions of racial, cultural and colonial oppressions and degradations giving rise to an ultra-violent revolutionary situation from which no peaceful exit seems possible.

The foundational question for Fanon is how to recover a sense of humanity on the basis of the dehumanising practices and experiences of colonial domination. 'As soon as you and your fellow men are cut down like dogs,' he writes in *The Wretched of the Earth*, 'there is no other solution but to use every means available to re-establish your weight as a human being. You must therefore weigh as heavily as possible on your torturer's body so that his wits, which have wandered off somewhere, can at last be restored to their human dimension'. Revolution, for Fanon, was not simply about the transfer of power from one segment of society to another. It entailed the reconstruction of humanity.

Fanon, of course, shocks many liberal humanists with his embrace of a necessary violence and his rejection of compromise. In a divided world, where the colonial power defines the colonised as subhuman and evil by nature, compromise is impossible. The theory of the 'absolute evil of the colonist' is in response to the theory of the 'absolute evil of the native'. Lacking a dialectical relation between the two, the only way to break down the difference is through violence. There is nothing mushy about such a programme. As Fanon saw clearly: at the individual level, violence is a cleansing force. It rids the colonised of their inferiority complex, of their passive and despairing attitude. It emboldens them and restores their self-confidence.

I do not raise the question of violence here, any more than did Fanon, because I am or he was in favour of it. He highlighted it because the logic of human situations so often deteriorates to a point where there is no other option. Even Gandhi acknowledged that. But the option has potentially dangerous consequences. Revolutionary humanism has to offer some kind of philosophical answer to this difficulty, some solace in the face of incipient tragedies. While the ultimate humanist task may be, as Aeschylus put it 2,500 years ago, 'to tame the savageness of man and make gentle the life of this world', this cannot be done without confronting and dealing with the immense violence that underpins the colonial and neo-colonial order.

But is the social order of capital any different in essence from its colonial manifestations? That order has certainly sought to distance itself at home from the callous calculus of colonial violence. It had to disguise at home the far-too-blatant inhumanity it demonstrated abroad. 'Over there' things could be put out of sight and hearing. Only now, for example, is the vicious violence of the British suppression of the Mau Mau movement in Kenya in the 1960s being acknowledged in full. When capital drifts close to such inhumanity at home it typically elicits a similar response to that of the colonised. To the degree that it embraced racialised violence at home, as it did in the United States, it produced movements like the Black Panthers and the Nation of Islam along with leaders like Malcolm X.

But what Marx makes so clear in *Capital* is the daily violence constituted in the domination of capital over labour in the marketplace and in the act of production as well as on the terrain of daily life. How easy it is to take descriptions of contemporary labour conditions in, for example, the electronics factories of Shenzhen, the clothing factories of Bangladesh or the sweatshops of Los Angeles and insert them into Marx's classic chapter on 'the working day' in Capital and not notice the difference.

Oligarchic capitalist class privilege and power are taking the world in a similar direction almost everywhere. Political power backed by intensifying surveillance, policing and militarised violence is being used to attack the well-being of whole populations deemed expendable and disposable. We are daily witnessing the systematic dehumanisation of disposable people. Ruthless oligarchic power is now being exercised through a totalitarian democracy directed to immediately disrupt, fragment and suppress any coherent anti-wealth political movement (such as Occupy). The arrogance and disdain with which the affluent now view those less fortunate than themselves, even when (particularly when) vying with each other behind closed doors to prove who can be the most charitable of them all, are notable facts of our present condition.

The 'empathy gap' between the oligarchy and the rest is immense and increasing. The oligarchs mistake superior income for superior human worth and their economic success as evidence of their superior knowledge of the world (rather than their superior command over accounting tricks and legal niceties). They do not know how to listen to the plight of the world because they cannot and wilfully will not confront their role in the construction of that plight. They do not and cannot see their own contradictions. The billionaire Koch brothers give charitably to a university like MIT even to the point of building a beautiful day-care centre for the deserving faculty there while simultaneously lavishing untold millions in financial support for a political movement (headed by the Tea Party) that denies welfare, nutritional supplements and day-care for millions living in or close to absolute poverty.

It is in a political climate such as this that the violent and unpredictable eruptions that are occurring all around the world on an episodic basis (from Turkey and Egypt to Brazil and Sweden in 2013 alone) look more and more like the prior tremors for a coming earthquake that will make the post-colonial revolutionary struggles of the 1960s look like child's play. If there is an end to capital, then this is surely from where it will come, and its immediate consequences are unlikely to prove happy for anyone. This is what Fanon so clearly teaches.

The only hope is that the mass of humanity will see the danger before the rot goes too far and the human and environmental damage becomes too great to repair. In the face of what Pope Francis rightly dubs 'the globalisation of indifference', the global masses must, as Fanon so neatly puts it, 'first decide to wake up, put on their thinking caps and stop playing the irresponsible game of Sleeping Beauty'. If Sleeping Beauty awakes in time, then we might be in for a more fairytale-like ending.

How We Might House Ourselves

A View From 100 Years Hence

You can, if you are lucky, talk to people who were around almost a century ago. Talk to them and they will tell you about how different life was back then; about how people were far less wasteful; about how similar everyone's clothes were and how life appeared to be so predictable; about what they thought would happen next and just how differently everything turned out.

In 1914 the British could look back to 1814, to before almost any mills or factories had been built, to before the construction of the great warehouses that came to dominate cities, to before the steam-powered lift was even dreamed of. The first in London in 1823 was called an 'ascending room'. Look back a century, or two, and it helps you see how much possibility there is for change. We are very unlikely, for instance, to still house ourselves as we do today. But we can also now look back on people who looked forward to see just how little we can know.

In 1930 John Keynes looked forward to 2030. He said we were in a 'temporary phase of maladjustment [...and that the] love of money as a possession—as distinguished from the love of money as a means to the enjoyments and realities of life—will be recognised for what it is, a somewhat disgusting morbidity, one of those semi-criminal, semi-pathological propensities which one hands over with a shudder to the specialists in mental disease'. 2030 is still far away. There is time in which to establish that the love of money purely for itself is a disgusting disease, to determine what are the causes and consequences of that disease, and to act on those findings.

Any one individual can be born unable to empathise, or share, and with a thirst to accumulate. It could be that a few simply cannot help themselves and are so greedy that they have to be helped by others not to make the world a misery for so many. We need to know if this is the case—if the rich need to be better controlled—if we are to better house ourselves. Researchers have studied rats in mazes and found that many will care for other rats they are unrelated to, freeing them from traps, but they have to learn to do that. Rats help,

...trapped strangers only if they are familiar with that type of rat...exposure to and interaction with different types of individuals motivates them to act well toward others that may or may not look like them...these results have a lot to say about human society...

There is so much we do not know about ourselves and other mammals, and so much we have learnt in just the last century. However, the sad fact that we still trap rats to try to better understand ourselves does not offer great hope for what we might be capable of.

Presuming we can accurately guess might happen even fifteen years from now is foolhardy. Trying to look ahead with confidence one hundred years, to 2114, is plainly impossible. There is one exercise that can be undertaken and which has proved to be useful in the past—ask yourself how people in the future might look back on your own times and what may appear most odd about what we do now. This can be done for any issue, but I think it makes sense to start with something mundane which affects us all—housing.

Everyone needs a home, we all need somewhere to sleep at night, we all need to feel safe where we sleep, many of us live in families and most of us have places we need to get to during the day that are not too far from our home. People have been housing themselves for almost as long as we became people. Just how hard can it now be? To see what is strange about just one aspect of life in Britain today—how might someone in 2114 look back at how we are housed today?

The first thing that is strange about housing in Britain (and much of the rest of the rich world) is how incredibly expensive it is. Rents can often consume a majority of a person's earnings, certainly in London, and house prices are astronomically high today—higher than they have ever been when expressed as a ratio of average earnings. In Oxford, where I now live, the average house now costs eleven times the average salary. For the vast majority of young people the idea of ever owning their home appears to be an impossible dream.

But if you bought a house in 2014 what were you actually paying for? Your descendants might ask you when you are old, when you try to explain to them just how much of what you were paid went on paying for the privilege of being housed. If the price was high, was the house you bought of much better quality than it had been when it was newly built? Or if you were renting in 2014 was your landlord working very hard to improve the quality of your flat in return for all the rent he charged you? You campaigned for a living wage but had no living rent? Explain all this to them and your grand-children might look up at you a little sadly. If in the future it is normal to rent and not be ripped-off then you'll have to explain why being ripped-off was normal. You'll also have to explain why so many people dreamt of the possibility of being responsible for the upkeep of their own guttering, or as they called it in 2014: home ownership.

Of course, we know that most of the money we spend on housing is not spent on its upkeep. Instead it goes to the very rich and makes them richer—we just try not to think about it too much because it makes us feel such dupes. Only 2% of people in the UK are landlords and most landlords are aged at least 50. In just the last five years this small group saw their total wealth rise by £245billion. This was because they bought so much more property with money from the rising rents they can now charge. Many landlords qualify as being within the richest 1% of all Britons. Thus, although not all landlords are doing well, on average this group is making a killing.

Looking back from 2114, how will we understand that people had to give up so much of their income purely to pay the rent? It may be hard for people in the future to understand how, in 2014, London homeowners thought that somehow their flats could carry on increasing in value, despite there being no-one even richer than them coming through the system to buy their properties in the near future. But given the sky-high rents and appalling insecure tenancy agreements, worse than anywhere else in Europe, our descendants will hopefully at least understand why people did try to buy homes in increasing numbers as prices rose and rose at the start of 2014.

When you are old you might well have to explain that people bought houses by borrowing huge sums of money from a few very rich people and then had to pay back twice the sum borrowed—but only twice when 'interest' rates were low: much more than twice when they rose. Originally this borrowing had been to build houses and the money came from what were then—with good reason—called 'building societies'; societies (social organisations) which did not make a profit and were very common in 1914. Back then London was still full of rookeries. The slum landlord was king. So much has changed in one century we should expect just as much change in the next.

We can have no way of knowing what will happen by 2114, but we know what cannot happen. Short of aliens arriving from outer-space with bars of platinum to buy London housing or pay the escalating rent, the current bubble will at some point burst. At least in time for the one hundred year anniversary of economist Keynes fortune telling (2030), if not a little earlier—say by the 2023 centennial anniversary of scientist John Haldane's predictions for the future. In all likelihood it will pop early, but pop later and the bang will echo for a long time to come.

Just under a century ago Haldane was prescient when he wrote that the hills of England would be lined with wind-mills, as coal and oil became exhausted, that we would mass-produce sugar and starch, and that test-tube babies would soon come to be born in large numbers. But he also said that '...In the next war, no one will be behind the front line'. What people like Haldane did not foresee is the mess we would make of many of our social arrangements in the century to come, although famously he did write that 'My own suspicion is that the universe is not only queerer than we suppose, but queerer than we can suppose'.

In response to Haldane, in 1924 the philosopher Bertrand Russell wrote that:

At present, science does harm by increasing the power of rulers. Science is no substitute for virtue; the heart is as necessary for a good life as the head...By the 'heart' I mean, for the moment, the sum-total of kindly impulses. Where they exist, science helps them to be effective; where they are absent, science only makes men more cleverly diabolic.

However, just because a few men are currently driven by diabolical greed is no guarantee that such amassing will con-tinue. Such greed tends to bring about its own destruction.

This year is the anniversary of another man's writing, a man not drawn from the 'stock' of Keynes, Haldane or Russell. Robert Noonan was a labourer who decorated houses. In 1914 his book *The Ragged-Trousered Philanthropists* was published posthumously. It ends with a prophecy of the cost of living crisis of 2014 and rising gas prices. Its last words were: '...but although it cost the Gas Works a lot of money for coal dues, the Company in its turn got its own back by increasing the price of gas they sold to the inhabitants of the town...' After housing costs, it is fuel, and then food, that badly taxes most household budgets today.

The future is always different. Not everything gets better. How we come to house ourselves in future will have as much to do with escaping our current phase of maladjustment, and with controlling the very rich, as it will be determined by the minutiae of policy progress. Like other mammals, should we have exposure to and interaction with more different types of individuals in future then we may well behave better than if we polarise more and become more isolated and mutually suspicious. As the 1% get richer and richer, and the rest are all in-it-together more, the scope for greater interaction grows, the scope for empathy and solidarity grows; as too does the scope for disaster.

THE HOUSE THAT

Paddy was looking for a house. But after some simple arithmatic, he realised, like a bulldozer to his gut, he couldn't even afford the rent on a shoebox.

It didn't make sense. 710,000 homes in the UK l 800,000 people are on hou 740 uninhabited properti 6,400 people slept rough

But Paddy wasn't a politic

... then set out ~~acquiring~~ borrowing and relocating. Well, why not? If no one used this stuff, no one would miss it.

ADDY BUILT.

by Anna Trench

June '14

pty.
waiting lists.
ondon are worth over £5m.
ndon streets last year.

just wanted a nice yard.

It so happened that Paddy's potential housemates were an architect, a kleptomaniac and a man with a van. Together, they compiled a list of desirables...

They created a beautiful house. Then, after a year, they gave it all back and moved on. And no one even knew anything had ever gone.

TXT: PAVAN AMARA

My Body Back

Recently, I started a project I wish had existed when I needed it most. It didn't, so I started it myself.

In March, I started *My Body Back Project*, a project that explores the way survivors of sexual violence feel about their bodies, sex, and sexual health.

There's no easy way to describe why I started it. Rape left me hating my body. It's not fashionable to admit this in our society—because apparently women should 'get over it'.

But I didn't get over it, and I don't believe I ever will. Years on, it no longer controls me, but it still has the power to disrupt everything. To this day, the way it left me feeling about my body can dictate the clothes I choose to wear, the relationships I have and don't have, feeling desperately vulnerable when I walk through a room full of people if my clothes aren't loose, and even if I go to the doctor. That's not because I am weak, that is the truth.

I am not alone. Since starting the project hundreds of female survivors have written in about how they feel about their bodies and about sex after rape. One woman wrote she developed anorexia because she 'wanted her body to disappear'; another woman wrote about self-harming genitally after being raped to 'scrape away every bit of him'; another opted for a caesarean rather than a vaginal delivery when giving birth to her son—because she couldn't bear the flashbacks that came with doctors and nurses touching her during labour.

Soon, the project will be beginning monthly workshops for survivors of sexual violence at Sh! Women's Emporium, which is the UK's first and only women's sex shop. These will be for women to explore their sexuality again in a safe environment. We will be discussing masturbation, sex with a partner, and orgasm—things that can be terrifying after experiencing violence. But these workshops will be about supporting women who are ready to connect with their body and sexuality again.

Two weeks after starting the project, I began speaking to survivors about their experience of healthcare. I was overwhelmed at the response. A significant number of women spoke of experiencing flashbacks during labour and had experienced incredibly insensitive attitudes from staff when they told them this. Another woman was told she was 'lucky' as a nurse examined her the day after she was raped—apparently the nurse had seen 'far worse injuries on other women'. Another woman had a nurse shout she was 'wasting staff time' when she burst into tears during a gynaecological exam. Nearly every woman I spoke to had her story to tell.

For all these reasons, the project is now campaigning for a compulsory module on working with survivors of sexual violence in all healthcare degrees. As these women's stories reveal, there are too many doctors, nurses, and midwives who don't have a clue about working with survivors sensitively. We're in the early stages and I know it will be an uphill battle, but it needs to be done. Statistically, every hospital ward and GP practice in this country will work with dozens of survivors of sexual violence every day. According to the Ministry of Justice's figures, 1 in 5 women has experienced some form of sexual violence since the age of 16. These figures do not include the women too scared to speak about it, or those sexually abused in childhood.

Later, I interviewed around 30 female survivors about their experiences of smear tests. I did this because I have never had the courage to have one. I have attempted to several times, and each time had to deal with terrifying flashbacks of rape. It may sound strange, but the thought of someone being in control of my body again was an impossible one. As I began speaking to other survivors, again, I discovered I was not alone. One woman told me she would 'rather get cervical cancer than go for a smear test, because it's like being raped again'; another said 'the worry of a smear test and the flashbacks happening was worse than the worry of getting cervical cancer'; others said well-meaning phrases used by health professionals unintentionally echoed the words of their rapists. One woman was repeatedly told to 'relax' while the nurse tried to insert the speculum during the smear test—something the rapist told her throughout the rape. She could not go ahead with the test, and has avoided them since.

Nearly all the women said they wanted cervical screening for their own peace of mind, but simply couldn't go through with it given the time constraints of a conventional nurse's appointment. Women spoke of an ideal place they could have screening that was specifically for survivors of sexual violence, where they would not have to explain their history, it would be explained by their presence. They spoke of wanting to control the environment they had their test in—being able to play soothing music in the background, wanting comforting pictures on the walls to focus on, being able to burn relaxing oils in the room. They wanted a room to ground themselves in before and after the test 'because it was an emotional experience, not just a medical one'. One woman, who has not had a smear test in over two decades, said she would go ahead with it if she could book a series of appointments. One to insert the speculum halfway, another to insert it fully, and another for the test.

I am working with two fantastic nurses at the moment, and we want to set up a clinic like this for survivors of sexual violence, where their needs come first. We are now looking for a venue with smear-testing equipment, which would allow us to use their facilities once a month. One monthly clinic won't have the capacity to see many women, but we need to make this a reality. It may save a life, it may not, but it would give survivors what they need—the sensitivity, care, and peace of mind their bodies deserve. And that is why I started *My Body Back Project*.

STRIKE!

presents:

WE DO NOT CONSENT!

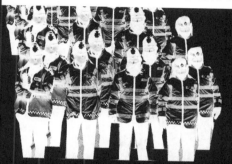

<u>A discussion and critique of the</u>
<u>British police force.</u>

The police are not the public and never
have been. From rampant corruption
to institutional racism and the
riots, their entire barrel is rotten.
Have the police ever had any moral
authority -or merely the best weaponry?

Join us as we ask: what it would take to
move towards a world without them?

Houses of Parliament
7pm - Tuesday
July 8th 2014

#WEDONOTCONSENT

Chair: David Graeber
Speakers: Hannah Dee, Fahim Alam
& Richard Garside

LEFT–RIGHT: RON ENGLISH, PRINCESS HIJAB, HUTCH,
PETER KENNARD, CLEON PETERSON, PAUL INSECT, GOLD PEG

Power To The People

We have experienced the most serious economic crisis of the capitalist system since the great crash of 1929 and yet mainstream politics has sunk to a philistine level of political debate, best characterised by the recent spoof B-film party political broadcast made by the Labour Party and the succession of UKIP candidates spouting racist, homophobic bile.

How could we have let our politics become so degraded?

Three centuries ago the Enlightenment led us to believe that the exercise of reason would lead to a linear progression of how we understand the world and the society we live in. Many were convinced that this intellectual evolution would inform the political decisions taken on how best to organise our society.

Still within this tradition, Marx then introduced us to the dialectical process of history and thought. Thesis and antithesis would lead to a progressive synthesis.

In our recent period, far from securing progress we seem to have gone back into the darkness. Popular political discussion, as witnessed in our mainstream media outlets, is a pretty bleak, barren wasteland. Newspapers print the sensationalist lies determined by their oligarch owners. The liberal *Guardian* very rarely strays beyond its acceptable establishment comfort-zone.

What masquerades as political debate on radio and television on programmes such as *Any Questions* and *Question Time* is largely a parade of posturing political hacks with barely a cigarette paper between the politics of the supposed political opponents who appear on the shows.

This intellectual vacuum has led to a situation best depicted by Stan Jameson in which for most it is easier to imagine the end of the world than the end of capitalism.

Politics doesn't have to be like this and we can't let this continue.

We have a responsibility to promote a real political discussion and debate about the lives we lead, the society we live in and the alternatives there are.

It is these sentiments that lead me to launch the idea of the People's Parliament.

Back in the 1980s I was elected as a GLC (Greater London Council) councillor and became Ken Livingstone's deputy. Despite all the rhetoric about the Labour GLC being a golden age of radicalism, the reality is that initially the GLC-controlling Labour group was fairly traditional social democratic.

Physically opening up County Hall as a building to a wide ranging array of groups and individuals, those campaigning or promoting ideas to be implemented by the GLC, radicalised the Livingstone administration.

County Hall buzzed, with its meeting rooms packed with activists thrashing out their ideas on how to transform the lives of Londoners. Everything from fares policy to LGBT rights and securing the capital's creative and manufacturing sectors was up for grabs.

This open democratic engagement created the radical GLC that is still remembered for its exciting creativity. It implemented policies that were seen as extreme at the time but have subsequently been accepted as mainstream common sense.

Just like County Hall, Parliament has a supply of halls and meeting rooms specifically designed for discussion and debate. The building is paid for and owned by the people and so I thought why not open up the building to the people and encourage anyone who has an idea to discuss, a policy to promote or an argument to be heard, to come along and use the building's meeting rooms to democratic effect.

You never know, by inviting MPs and Lords to these discussions and debates we might even infect some of the debates taking place in the main Commons Chamber.

From January, a group of us have organised a series of meetings in Parliament's committee rooms, discussing a vast range of issues suggested by people who have heard about this initiative. The only bar so far is that fascists are not invited.

The mainstream media has largely ignored us but that is par for the course, and with social media we don't really need them. The occasional plug in the *Guardian* doesn't do any harm, but if we rely on this country's press to stimulate a creative political debate we will wait forever.

Running with two sessions a week, the meetings have been packed. Having been around for quite a while I can usually recognise most of the faces in radical political meetings.

Not with the People's Parliament.

The meetings are packing in people, especially young people, activists and campaigners who have a genuine interest in engaging with the issue being discussed and are looking for change.

The discussion of ideas and theory is important but is only really effective if it informs our political practice. Hence the concept of praxis, the combination of theory and practice, underlines the People's Parliament sessions.

So far the discussions have addressed questions of what sort of democracy we need, who is watching whom in our surveillance society, and what is really needed to tackle our environmental crisis.

Specialists and expert practitioners have wanted to explain what is happening in their fields of activity. Lawyers have come along to expose the undermining of access to justice, tax experts have joined us to reveal the continuing scale of tax avoidance and evasion, and housing groups have explained the grotesque failures of housing policy that have led to our worst housing crisis since the Second World War.

People have brought along some of their ideas for solutions to problems. Citizens income to overcome poverty, how to reclaim the media by confronting its ownership by the rich and powerful, and constructing a sustainable economy by rejecting concepts of all-consuming growth.

Campaigners have come to seek support for their struggles. This has included campaigns against the latest wave of racism, the fight to end the Coalition's privatisation plans to finally kill off the NHS, and the campaign to hold back legislation criminalising sex workers.

People have posed and tried to answer questions that have troubled us all. The radical publishing house Zero Books went to the heart of our search by addressing the question that underlies a large part of the People's Parliament initiative: how has capitalism got away with the financial crisis and why is politics scared of political ideas?

The next stage of the People's Parliament discussions is looking at how we learn from the resistance to the capitalist crisis so far, to enable us to move beyond capitalism.

Each of our sessions has been introduced by experts and campaigners within their particular policy area but the discussion is dominated by the participants who turn up. Most of the debates have led to agreements on further action.

A thread running through the sequence of the People's Parliament sessions has been that words are not enough. The elite who still dine at the Ritz, shop at Fortnum and Masons and who populate the company boards in the City of London will remain content while our talk remains only talk.

They will only be fearful when our talk moves on to action and they know that our direct action only becomes effective when it is armed with an understanding of our society and its potential alternatives.

The People's Parliament attempts to make its contribution to arming that resistance. Come along.

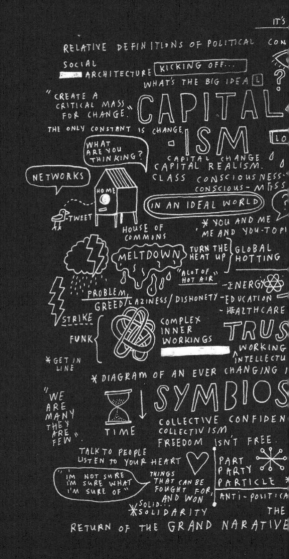

IDEA...

"ᴿ ROOF OVER YOUR HEAD"

TURKEY'S DONT VOTE FOR XMAS

RA$H 'N' BURN

MOTIVATE A
RECONNECTION
RE COMPOSITION

CHALLENGE
THE SYSTEM

◊ MIXED BAG
* FUNDAMENTAL
RELATIONSHIPS
SPARK

"ITS ABOUT
COORDINATION"
WHAT WAS THE QUESTION?

◊ ◊
TALK - BUT LISTEN
1 MOUTH - 2 EARS

ALL EARS
SPIN-OFF

HOW TO
GATHER
POPULAR
DESIRE

OFF
ON

ZERO
BOOKS

?

HALF FULL

SCREAM OF CONSCIOUSNESS

?! X 💀 ☺ ♁ E ‡

HISTORY
REPEATING

SPEEEECH

DOUBLE TALK
DOUBLE DUTCH
THINK TWICE

35%

HALF EMPTY

TURE

"❝ IM NOT A
FORTUNE
TELLER ❞"

AND OTHER
IMPORTANT
STATISTICS.

SPEAK INTO
THE MICROPHONE
BE HEARD.

LEFT ⇄ RIGHT

PERSONAL
POLITICS.
PROBLEM
SOLVING
SOLUTIONS.

THE
KEY

POLITICAL EXPRESSION

GET READY FOR A CRASH

"IT WAS ACCEPTABLE IN THE 80's"

WHAT SHOULD A JUSTICE SYSTEM
LOOK LIKE?

(YOU DONT HAVE TO AGREE)

* COMPASSIONATE REVOLUTION.

FOR
THE
PEOPLE
BY THE
PEOPLE

ENDA

EW:

PLE
KES

E
O ?
AT ?
HOW ?

IAN THE SUM OF ITS PARTS.

S. POLITICS OF POPULAR IDENTITY.

ARE REVOLTING

... WE NEED SOMETHING TO BELIEVE IN.

Co-Operate or Die

Options for the Alternative Generation

Two years ago I graduated from university and found myself in a reality that I was totally unprepared for. I had what I considered a strong CV: a first-class degree from the University of Leeds, a range of part-time jobs and a list of different volunteer roles and projects I had been involved in. I was ready to get a good job and start living the London dream.

As I competed against other graduates for unpaid internships, volunteer placements and took up a part-time job waitressing, I felt my confidence plummet, aspirations lower, financial situation worsen and a slight existential crisis kicking in. I started to question where my life was going, what I was doing with my time and whether it was just me that felt this way? As I looked around me I began to realise that nobody I knew was getting paid to do a job they loved: friends were running abroad to teach English and escape the crisis here, settling for jobs they hated or taking up low-paid, part-time jobs to support them while they followed their real passions.

One afternoon, after an interview for an unpaid internship that 150 others had applied for, I had a moment of clarity: as long as we all fight for the scraps of work at the bottom of the economy that is all we will get—we will remain powerless and without influence. We will remain the generation without a future. And guess what? We are not the problem. We have ideas, skills, knowledge, energy and talent but the economy we are entering into no longer knows how to utilise our creativity for the common good.

Our role as the next generation should be to change it, to create something better. To create an economy that allows us to earn a living, do what we love and contribute towards nurturing people and our environment rather than destroying it. Ok, yes, in an ideal world I thought, but how in reality am I going to make that happen?

First I decided to gain a better understanding of the context and learn from what's already happening across Europe. So I embarked upon a three-month research project across Portugal and Spain, where youth unemployment is as high as 50%. My question was: what new ways of living and working are young people creating in response to this crisis?

Youth in Lisbon were setting up social movements to campaign for basic citizens' income and free transport for the unemployed; in Granada creative hubs to support youth in industries such as art and music; in Madrid social centres offering affordable food, consultation on how to resist housing evictions and free classes in media, web development and dance. Around Barcelona young people had gone back to the land, reclaimed old buildings, begun to grow their own food and sell bread, preserves and furniture. My research showed me that all across the Iberian peninsular youth were creating new ways of working and living. The alternative that most inspired me, however, was worker's co-operatives. I found food co-ops, bike co-ops, co-operative bookshops, web development co-ops, co-operative schools and in one example a 'co-operative integral' to provide for all basic needs, such as housing, transport, education, health and childcare, co-operatively.

Now it's true that co-ops aren't particularly new, emerging in the UK with the Rochdale Pioneers in 1844. However, as people are increasingly struggling to meet their basic needs, co-ops seem to be having a resurgence—because they seem to offer solutions to many of the problems my generation faces.

Firstly, they allow us to reclaim control over our work. Co-operatives are a specific form of social enterprise where workers own the business, profit is distributed fairly and equally between the workers rather than distant shareholders, and decisions are made democratically by all members rather than one person at the top. In an economy where wealth is unequally distributed and youth lack decision-making power and agency, this gives us control over a key area of our life and allows us to make decisions about who we want to work with, how much we want to work and for what purpose.

Secondly, they enable our generation to stop competing and start collaborating. On our own we are powerless. Together we are more powerful than we could begin to imagine. In contrast to what our education system teaches us, collaboration is key for creativity, for innovation, for finding solutions to all the problems our world faces. In contrast to the idea of the individual entrepreneur making it out there on their own, co-ops offer a more supportive model for young people, who may be afraid of taking a big step outside the standard work options currently offered. One where we can share risk, build confidence, learn together and allow a larger number of young people to get involved with social enterprise—let's face it, not all of us have the character to make it on *Dragons' Den*.

Finally, the seven co-operative principles provide guidelines for an ethical approach to business, both internally and externally. Through the principle of concern for the community, the social and environmental impact a co-operative enterprise has on the world is taken into account. Through the principles of democratic member control and economic participation, the structure of a co-operative reflects the kind of change they want to see in the world, something many other social enterprises and charities could learn from.

Taking on board the insight and inspiration gained from my research I returned to London and set up *AltGen*. Standing for *Alternative Generation*, *AltGen* supports 18-25 year-olds to set up worker co-operatives as an empowering and collaborative solution to youth unemployment. It aims to empower our generation to take control over our future by creating an economy in which we feel fulfilled and in which we are solving social and environmental problems rather than creating them.

AltGen is now a registered co-op with three co-founders. In its first year it will achieve its aims through: sharing young peoples' stories so we can begin to realise we are not alone; running practical workshops to empower and inspire young people to set up co-ops; connecting those that are interesting in creating an alternative economy through an online hub space; running courses on how to set up co-operatives; providing start up grants; and by giving legal and business advice. In the following years we hope to develop and grow a network of young co-operatives across the UK and Europe, trading with one another and sharing knowledge, ideas and resources to create a more fulfilling, equal and sustainable economy. An economy that we are in control of.

As we move forward it is important to acknowledge that the co-operative movement in this country is currently in crisis. The Co-operative Bank and its parent, the Co-operative Group, have been in the news over the last year—and for all the wrong reasons. It's been the subject of countless press stories: a record trading loss, the Paul Flowers scandal, CEO Euan Sutherland's abrupt resignation and fines for unethical business behaviour. The Bank and the wider Group's troubles have been variously attributed to bad business acquisitions, expensive and abandoned IT projects, hubristic management, weak board oversight—even the very fact that it was a co-operative, owned and controlled by millions of people like you and me, and therefore ungovernable.

As someone recently inspired by the alternative economic future co-operatives can offer young people this left me confused and doubting the whole co-operative model. But as I investigated further I realised it couldn't be further from the truth. In fact, the problems stemmed not from the group's egalitarian and ethical principles, but from a straying away from them towards the mainstream model and values of banking and consumerism in this country. From decisions being made by outside 'experts' and unaccountable managers, not by members and customers, to organisational structures becoming more top-down and bureaucratic rather than more horizontal and participatory.

Therefore the solution to the co-operative crisis in this country lies not in a rejection of the co-operative model and principles, but by using this crisis as an opportunity to bring the co-operative movement back to its roots of promoting and enacting democracy, equality and transparency. And who better to lead the way than a new generation of young co-operators, supported by the wisdom and history of a movement that is hundreds of years old, but bringing in new ideas for how co-operatives can provide solutions to zero-hours contracts and the rise of the freelancer, can move into new industries at the forefront of innovation, or can use technology to make co-operation and collaboration even easier.

The work of *AltGen* is just beginning, but already I have experienced its potential and power, from the stories young people are sending in to our blog, to the look of excitement I see on a normally apolitical friend's face when I talk about new ways of working and living. Our generation is waking up and there are numerous ideas being shared for how we can make our life and economy more sustainable, more equal and more fulfilling. I hope that *AltGen* and the power of co-operatives will play a big role in making it a reality.

An Anarchist Guide To...
Distribution

When one gets to a certain age it becomes really easy to bore the fuck out of your mates by repeating your latest fave anecdote over and over without realising. I am in danger of this with my decidedly self-congratulatory tale of last month's excess. 'April was mad, I broke my own record: I did a different anarchist bookfair every weekend, each in a different country'. This fact does, though, illustrate various themes I have been asked to pontificate upon, having been described recently as an expert on Anarchist Bookfairs, DIY and not-for-profit.

There was an LP released many years ago by a bunch of ageing radical rockers called *Where Do We Draw The Line?* The music was not noisey and the lyrics were concerned with the dilemmas and compromises that artist activists trying to be true to their ideals come up against. The DIY scene that I have operated in for the last quarter of a century is nothing to do with flat pack furniture or elementary plumbing, but is the spirit of how and why many punx and revolutionaries try to operate. One early slogan of the anarcho-punk movement says much rather succinctly: 'DIY NOT EMI!' The Buzzcocks famously set up their own record label rather than sign up with an established one in order to have complete control over what they could do. This idea was developed further by anarcho-punk labels like CRASS, who added the concept of being actively against the music business, refusing to play the media's games, releasing their records as cheaply as possible and, along with many other bands, notably Chumbawamba, attacking

EMI and other major labels for being part of corporations with investments in the arms trade etc.

Where one draws the line of radical DIY purity versus capitalist compromise is a never-ending argument. Never-ending, one might say, because idealist young bands almost always get old and tired and greedy, and end up seeing the bottom-line of financial security as more important than a less-remunerative hard core political stance. I remember reading a statement of Chumba's when they left the independent label Southern for the larger One Little Indian (originally an anarcho-punk label), who had recently done deals with major labels to secure 'better' distribution. The crux of their argument was that all capitalism is capitalism whether it's small or large, so they saw no merit in staying with a small label when they wanted to get their message out there. A form of 'the ends justify the means' argument, with the unstated side-benefits of wealth and fame.

This concept smacks at the whole problem with an alternative culture that tries to survive and support radicals within capitalism. Can it be done with any sincerity? Is it credible? Does business-success mean it is no longer anti-capitalist?

These questions were very live in the punk and H/C (hardcore) scene when I started Active back in 1988. There were distros and fanzine writers who would get apoplectic about 'sell outs' who charged people for postage costs rather than soaping their stamps. We were pretty dedicated to the concept of non-profit and that is how I have stayed.

The most obvious direct comparison between DIY distribution models within the anarcho-punk scene is AK Press and Active Distribution. Both started with the same concept: to distribute radical, primarily anarchist, literature. The methods were and are similar: we both do stalls at events, produce catalogues, run a mail-order service, supply others at wholesale rates, blah blah.

Ramsay, who started AK, and I would meet at Freedom and Housmans bookshop (back in the day when hippy Malcolm ran its basement like an Aladdin's cave of anarchy). But even our chosen transport methods showed the difference between the two distros: Ramsay would take the train down from Stirling and I would hitchhike from Swansea. Where AK sold books at full price, I'd knock them out as cheaply as I could afford. Subsequently, AK became an international book publisher with offices and warehouses in both Edinburgh and California—Active stayed within the scope of my spare bedroom. As a workers' co-op, AK employs and pays a bunch of people; it does not seek to make the workers rich, but it does pay them a living wage. Active will cover the cost of food from Veggies food stall when people work at a bookfair and that's about it.

AK has also succeeded in publishing and distributing many wonderful books and I hope they continue to do so. In order to do enough business to do this and to spread the word as widely as possible, AK has crossed many lines—so that many would say it has become another capitalist business.

Active decided it did not want to grow up or do-it-properly, and continued to hitch-hike our way through life, begging and borrowing, stealing and scamming, and ultimately putting in a lot of effort 'for the sake of it'. We don't worry about costs or bills as AK and other 'real' businesses do: we add a small margin to cover costs but we don't worry if that doesn't always happen. Margins and profit lines are what business is all about.

The problem with capitalism is that ultimately businesses are only interested in their profit margins. When a publisher prices a book, it will mark the cover price anything from 3 to 7 times the cost price of producing the book. Distributors of books get between 50 and 60% of the cover price of a book, so they can supply shops who take 30-40% of the cover price. Active ignores these rules and adds the smallest percentage possible to keep us going. We specialise in supplying other distributors and infoshops with stock cheaply. What money we do make goes into our publishing projects (The Bottled Wasp etc.), and to cover for the costs of stock that never sold.

I started my radical journey as a pacifist heavily steeped in the ideal that we should act in the manner that we want the revolution to be. I think Ghandi put it better—and I like the irony that the anarcho-insurrectionists have a similar view about life and revolution, despite being on the other side of the anarchist milieu to Ghandi.

So last month's record-breaking (and carbon huge-boot-print inducing) bookfair attendance by Active was done not by the larger and more famous distributer/publisher AK Press but by the two-bit, part timer Active. How come? Well, Active didn't need to judge the bookfairs by their likelihood of being 'financially viable', which any profit-orientated business needs to do. AK might attend quiet, non-money-making events and consider them good publicity, or even 'acts of solidarity' but they can only do this on a limited scale. Active stalls get to bookfairs using 'punk-post' and maximizing airline baggage allowances; the travel costs are paid by the individuals who see the events not as work but as an act of support (and maybe a holiday too). This isn't so difficult when you consider that the first three bookfairs in April were Zagreb, Gent and Prague (and I am a self confessed vegan tourist always happy to try out new cruelty-free food outlets). But our book stall probably had the biggest selection of books at all four bookfairs.

Don't get me wrong, I'm not knocking AK or PM or any of the other 'big' anarchist publishers; Active has a good comradely working relationship with them all. And although we have different priorities, sometimes these differences work to our mutual benefit. For instance, when a new punk squat bookshop suddenly appears asking for books on credit, AK groans inwardly with the weight of a history of unpaid and unrecoverable debts. Active, being (relatively) unworried about cash up front or 30-days credit limits, is able to supply places that others would find uneconomical (it must be said we are owed a fortune in unpaid book sales.)

At bookfairs abroad, Active specialises in leaving all unsold stock with the local bookshop or anarchist distro with the promise to settle up at next years bookfair. If Active were under pressure to pay the rent or justify the expenditure of leaving books in Barcelona for a year after we have already paid for them, without a guarantee that they will indeed sell, this attitude would be unfeasible. But this non-commercial attitude is an essential element for me. I don't want to run a business, I want to propagate anarchist ideas and culture. I don't want to profit from the words, deeds, writings or ideas of anarchists who have fought in battles far worse than I have ever seen. I don't want to sully the beauty of the ideas of the likes Emma Goldman or Kropotkin with the percentages of mercantile profit motivations. No, I want to give this stuff away, I want it to be as free as the ideal itself. When I hit the reality of printing costs, postage and fuel costs I make as small an addition to the cost price as I can and hope that the bargain price will inspire people to buy a book rather than just a badge. Even better, they might get two books and pass one on to someone else. And I have profited over the years by doing Active: it has brought me many friends, some lovers, quite a few books and CD's, but most of all it has helped keep my belief in an alternative, non-profit-based, way of dealing with other people alive.

It was reading the likes of Malatesta, the Freedom Paper, Poison Girls and CRASS lyrics that helped me find my voice and set me free, and that is why I have a passion to continue the work of distributing such ideas. I bought those texts from a long-gone radical bookshop; nowadays, the internet allows us to find such literature wherever we are but I don't want people to have to compromise themselves by giving profit to the likes of Amazon. So please: support your local radical literature outlet.

TXT: CATHERINE FLOOD
& GAVIN GRINDON

Disobedient Objects

How do we think about and reflect upon social movements? The magazine you're holding continues the legacy of one of the first ways movements were able to speak for and to each other—through print and publishing. In the early twentieth century experimental workers' photography collectives became a new way to reflect and represent, and activism filmmaking and online indymedia have followed more recently. Beside movement media, some people have tried to open institutional spaces to amplify these discussions, mindful of their limits but hopeful for the possibilities. Radical academics have opened spaces in academic publishing for reflection, just as some professional filmmakers have tried to produce radical documentaries within mainstream circuits of film and TV distribution. An upcoming exhibition called *Disobedient Objects* takes the rare opportunity to try and open a gallery space in a public museum as another such means of reflection and discussion. It is the first exhibition to focus on the objects of movements and brings together for the first time many objects made in the global cycles of struggles from the late 1970s to the present, from revolutionary barricades; to giant puppets; and DIY drones. It offers a chance to reflect on how the things we make are bound up with making radical social change.

Just inside the grand entrance to the museum, on a balcony looking down over the space, there is a sculpture of Hercules. It is one of many images of him in the museum—he appears not only in Greek and Roman sculptures and pottery, but resurfaces in eighteenth-century oil paintings, ceramics and statues. In their history of the revolutionary Atlantic, Peter Linebaugh and Marcus Rediker observe that for the classically educated architects of the

Atlantic economy, Hercules represented power and order. They saw in his mythical labours their own epic imperial ambition and aggressive economic enclosure of the world. He is often pictured during his second labour, slaying the Hydra of Lena. Here, leaders of state and industry saw an antithetical figure of resistance and 'disorder'. It was an unruly monster, part-whirlwind, part-woman, part-snake. When Hercules sliced off one of its heads, two more sprang up in its place. Eventually he killed it and, dipping arrows into the slain beast's gall, harnessed its power for himself and his future triumphs. For Linebaugh and Rediker, the Hydra suggests, in silhouette, the lost history of the multi-ethnic classes essential to the making of the modern world. Historians like them have tried to look at history from below, instead of from the perspective of 'great men' and the agency of state and capital. History is a matter of selective inclusion. This is especially true of the objects of art and design history, whose collection is most often shaped by a market of wealthy collectors, while history's disobedient objects go undocumented and unkept. In that inevitable taking of sides, our project turns to objects that disclose hidden moments in which, even if only in brief flashes, we find the world is also made from below. This exhibition is one for the Hydra.

The exhibition was developed through a series of workshops in which groups lending objects and other movement participants helped set its terms, the questions it asks and even its physical design. It approaches the institution of the museum as Stefano Harney and Fred Moten recently described radical thought's place in universities—'to abuse its hospitality, to spite its mission, to be in but not of.' It takes the museum at its word to be a space for debate and public thought. Before the exhibition, some of these object sat mouldering in private lofts of social-centre basements, but now they are returned to public visibility. Others are from unfinished struggles, and after their visit to the museum, they will return to the streets. We are co-curating the exhibition, and we spoke with two Syrian artist-activists, who for the exhibition have recreated graffiti stencils they used on the walls in Syria.

Catherine:

The stencils use x-ray sheets—an ideal material for intricate stencil work and one which escapes inspection at checkpoints because it is enclosed in an official medical envelope. Why did stencils become popular, where there isn't a tradition of graffiti in Syria?

Ibrahim:

It was the only way because the regime answered demonstrations with bullets. So all you could do was hide your face, go spray something on the wall. It was the only way of expressing your anger. When it started it was people saying 'We don't want the Regime,' 'we will not be humiliated,' 'We would rather die before we get humiliated.' It started escalating when they stared shooting at us. We were not going to take that. At a certain point people decided that we just want a new thing and started to write slogans like 'We are coming for you [President Basar al-Assad], we're going to take you down, I'm coming for you.' The killing started becoming an every-hour thing and the graffiti stared taking other forms—tributes to the martyrs. People created beautifully made stencils to pay their respect to those people who had fallen. It started with 30—40 deaths a day and then reached 300 a day. There were terrible days like the chemical massacre when 1,500 died in a few hours. Numbers—that's all people know about them, numbers, numbers. So the stencils they gave them faces to say that they are not just numbers. No, these numbers have got faces; they are Syrians; they are activists; these 'numbers' did something for the revolution.

Catherine:

What are the challenges of transferring something from the street to an exhibition?

Ibrahim:

Space was our man problem, we wanted to include stencils of as many people as possible, but unfortunately we can't. So we had to decide, whom shall we put? The people who died first? It's rather confusing. So we tried to get somebody from every phase of the revolution, you know try to represent everybody as much as possible.

Zaher:

I think that in terms of creating this art piece, the greatest challenge we faced was how can we deliver the message to such a free society as the British one that doing graffiti could mean you die—under torture sometimes. So in the short film we've made [that will be shown in the exhibition alongside the stencil work] we showed people chanting in the streets, shots of people escaping from the regime forces, or actually doing the stencils quickly and under cover—which is the main point of disobedient graffiti objects in Syria.

Gavin:

Some people have this idea that objects 'die' in a museum, even though it's a public space, or that they inevitably become fixed in a dominant narrative. How do you feel about having your objects displayed here?

Zaher:

We are talking about the most rightwing museum in London! So having this kind of exhibition, not just the Syrian piece, it's really a big challenge for the space itself and it's a really good thing. To focus on people's interests—not just bourgeois art. In terms of spreading the word, we would like always to insist on one point, after three years of this revolution, about the terms itself—revolution and uprising. Most of the western media have started using the terms war, civil war, conflict to describe what is happening in Syria. But we think, and we believe actually, that the revolution is still going on. There are different layers. There is the conflict, there are the weapons and the armed revolution. But there is still the revolution. Even after all these months of people being killed in Syria, the civil society activism, the peaceful activism is still going on.

To be honest during the last two years in Syria we've felt that we are alone, that no one cares about the people killed. In Syria we used to fly the flags of other revolutionary movements or social movements—the Bahraini movement, the green movement in Iran, and Ukraine and other movements, to say we are not alone. But here in the exhibition these objects from other movements are around us, and we feel that there is solidarity around the world. The exhibition gives us this feeling. That we are not alone.

CLANDESTINE SYRIAN STENCIL

Paper Bag method: Cut out the bottom of a paper bag, leaving enough of the bottom intact to act as a frame. Tape the stencil to the bottom of the bag with clear packing tape to prevent paint bleeding through.

GHAITH MATTAR

Ghaith Mattar was a Syrian activist from Daraya much admired for his inspired ideas about non-violent protest. He was arrested in Damascus in September 2011 and died under torture. This stencil designed by Hasan Khzam is one of hundreds commemorating Syrian martyrs that are shared online and sprayed on walls in Syria and beyond.

BUCKET PAMPHLET BOMB

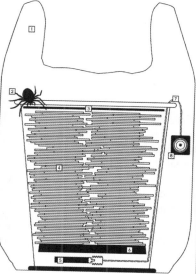

1. Carrier bag
2. Toy spider to deter inquisitive people
3. Warning notice
4. Pamphlets
5. Small explosive charge
6. Wooden platform
7. Pair of wires
8. Time switch

Port Elizabeth EVENING NEWS, Friday, August 14, 1970

LEAFLET BOMBS WARN VORSTER: END IS NEAR

From DOUGLAS ALEXANDER

JOHANNESBURG.

TWO BOMBS exploded in Johannesburg today scattering hundreds of leaflets attacking South Africa's government.

From 1969, pamphlet bombs were used across South Africa to circumvent apartheid censorship. They harmed no one, but distributed hundreds of pamphlets high into the air. Pamphlet bombs were mostly set by young non-South Africans voluntarily working for the ANC and SACP. The devices were invented and tested by ANC exiles in Britain. Several Latin American leftist guerrilla groups also used them from 1980 onwards.

Disobedient Objects

Based on drawings by Ken Keable

TXT: NIALL MCDEVITT

The Bourgeois

(after Dostoyevsky in London)

money matters are a

    baal

we no longer believe in really
panes we peer through
to a nakedness, to a nothingness
beyond the silk chicanery
though we've seen nothing in years
nor have newspapers revealed
much but morning's traumas
or evening's Russian schemas
the numbers and sacred geometrical forms
hold up
when reexamined in test-tube intellects
by heads grey as centurions

    'branson...'

moneyed, thankfully, loving technology (as we do)
it is disturbing to think
how much our modernity
is dated and arcane, rotten through
foolproof... burgomasters... for real
we will endow our scions
with what we have amassed—grey squirrels -
a fiscal nervous system

'bitcoin...'

looking out from portraits by Holbein
at the pret-a-manger crowds
with distaste as they inspect us
in this and other mirrors
(as if they'd like to eat us!)
moneyed, thankfully, never enough
for our bursaries of water light heat
gentrifying, as we lap, wild troughs
ogling with the eyes of forty thieves

'mmm...'

materially safe, not slunk to foxholes,
but fodder for the perceptive
with virtuous manners and vicious maths
cocooned in Burberry, dry
raw material for novelists (how dull)
who infiltrate as agents
suffocating us with their ears
as we drool on them from sleeping mouths

'interesting...'

a rain a rain of butterflies
swimming in butterfly strokes
the black-and-white of our patterns
blending into the substratum

TXT: SAM BERKSON

First they Came for... (Keep Calm)

First they came for the disability benefits...
Keep calm and carry on!
Or was that first?
First, didn't we have unprecedented levels of stress:
media highs hyped up to fever pitch
raging in run-down towns with closed down pits?
Then they took away support for the victims:
adults on the Prozac, children on the Ritalin...
Keep calm and carry on!

Then they came for the housing benefit,
but not before they sold off the public housing stock
propped up the prices,
mopped up the squatters,
dropped the mansion tax,
cropped the random acts of welfare
and then they left rows of boarded up, bricked-up
homes-for-the-rats till the market picks up...
Keep calm and carry on!

They finally came for the concrete estate
whose balconies looked down on your back garden gate.
There'll be temporary disturbance of drilling
while they put up the blocks of contemporary urban living,
but at least the noisy neighbours left.
They exposed the brick in the old launderette,
where they do flat whites and a retro chef.

Renters need 6 weeks upfront for that room with a view
in the warehouse redeveloped into flats for the few
but segregation is nothing new,
rising resentment in the urban banlieues,
who's going to be there when they come for you?
Keep calm and carry on!

The choice is yours on the Reality Show fake-up,
hashtag Twitter-beef, Facebook face-off;
we'll fight them in the pubs and fight them on the x-box;
credit crisis but consuming can't end,
make do, payday-loan and spend;
careless talk keeps capitalism alive,
write a poem, win a prize.
It's Topshop florals and tweeds as fashion thing,
they want the '50s without the rationing...
Keep calm and carry on!

TXT: DECCA MULDOWNEY

All We Ever Wanted Was Everything

no demands no how can you formulate
a demand around a feeling that everything
must be dissolved cannot be resolved into
a single whole everything must go all
we ever wanted was everything everything

all I ever wanted was a new world entire
our world has not yet cannot yet speak itself
into being burn those magic books speak
words aloud cast off that cloak that keeps
you safe and sound from harm this will hurt

I'll take everything dark I'll take everything
you're offering and cast it aside asunder let
no man tell me what one way is the way if
he won't walk on those brokenheart paths and
prove that we all share one blood in many bodies

say you're a comrade so treat me like a comrade
if we can't hold each other nothing will
we can take the dark but it's that neon light
will break you down in police cell station hold
better learn that shadow is in you not of you

we were promised lives lived not spent in
debt work shift shit dead end brain shed
never shirked work no I'll work for a cause
so it better be worth it we better take home
everything everything leave nothing to waste

The Interview

Describe yourself
In five words:
Irritable
Depressed
Loner
Daydreamer
Wanderer

And what attracted you
To this job?
Well,
I haven't quite resigned myself
To the idea
Of sleeping rough,
And drinking Special Brew
For a living

But I'M WORKING ON IT.

TXT: MARK BEECHILL

Another Brick in the Face

Getting smashed in the face
With a brick
Is okay, after a while

At first,
It's a shock
A surprise
But then you get used to it
You go numb,
Forget things,
And wait for the next brick
To arrive

Sometimes,
The man swinging the brick
Has a break,
Switches arms, catches his breath,
And for a moment
You remember
What it was like
Without the brick
And how it might be
If you never saw
Another single brick
For as long as you lived

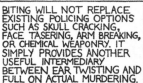

ENGLAND IS THE FIRST LIE. ENGLAND IS A LIE. ENGLAND INVADING KINGS TOLD YOU TO TAKE YOUR ACTUAL LAND FROM YOU. THIS LAND IS YOUR LAND FROM THE FLAT NORFOLK NIGHT TO THE BLUE CORNISH MORNING. JUST A WILD PAGAN LAND WITH NO NAME AND NO FLAG. JUST THIS COLD BEACH THAT NOURISHES YOU/ JUST THE WIND ON THIS GRASSLAND THAT NOURISHES YOU/ JUST THIS RAIN ON YOUR FACE IN THE MORNING IN THIS BLANK SPRINGTIME THAT NOURISHES YOU

ISSUE___7

WHEN WE ARE
SLEEPING,
        AEROPLANES
CARRY MEMORIES
OF THE HORRORS
WE HAVE GIVEN
OUR SILENT
CONSENT TO
INTO THE
        NIGHT SKY
OF OUR CITIES, AND
LEAVE THEM THERE
TO GATHER LIKE
CLOUDS AND
CONDENSE INTO
OUR DREAMS
BEFORE MORNING

Direct Action
Because We're Worth It

A young man at one of the countless meetings I've attended over the last few years told me his theory of change, during a lull in proceedings. He said,

Two things have to happen in the public's mind. One, they have to find out for themselves that the deal between them and the state is, and always has been, one sided; and two, they have to recognise they are worth more—then they begin to demand more.

As an activist, I am constantly having these kinds of conversations. What do we need to do? How do we connect with the public? When will people wake up? But this statement was a bit more interesting. It didn't mention campaigns, messages, direct actions or the media: it was all about people's own experiences bringing them into confrontation with policy makers.

Working hard, paying your taxes, living within the law, obeying the rules: that was meant to be our end of the bargain; a democratic voice, accountability, equality of opportunity, services and infrastructure, building a better future for those coming up behind us: that was what we expected in return. Fat fucking chance. Instead, those we select to represent us took our votes and our money, and duck ponds, moats and heated stables were their priority. The order of the day was serving themselves, answering the call of the corporate masters and avoiding, evading and/or laughing in the face of the general public. As punters we've voted and we've paid, so now our job is to go away until we are called upon again, and leave the important business of running shit to our representatives.

'Whoa tiger!' I can hear you say, 'We are 4 paragraphs in and you still haven't mentioned the DPAC Westminster action—get to it quickly please.' Well to understand this action, you have to understand why it came about, and some of the people that made it happen. How those people found themselves confronting the state, the church, the police. How we use wheelchairs as weapons of protest instead of mobility aids. How people who need support to eat, wash, get out of bed and get dressed, found themselves planning for bedding down in (accessible) tents opposite the 'mother of all parliaments', in the same grounds as the eternal resting place for kings and legends.

The Independent Living Fund (ILF) is a support funding-stream provided by central government and managed by the Department for Work and Pensions (DWP). This is a bit of an anomaly, as most 'care' (or support) funding is normally provided and managed by local councils. The fund was set up by the Tories (I know, I wouldn't have thought so either) in 1988 to provide extra support for people with the highest support needs. The fund is also an anomaly in another way. Local council care is based on the 'deficit' model—what are your 'needs'? What support do you need to do the things you can't do? The ILF process is based on an aspirational model—what do you want to do with your life? What are your interests/skills/priorities, and how can the ILF make that happen? A model of support for the 21st century, one would have thought.

There are about 17,500–18,000 users of the ILF at the moment. On average, the ILF costs just over £330 per person, per week. There are ILF users who are artists, actors, performers, writers, musicians and CEO's of disabled peoples organisations. The whole idea of ILF is that people are supported to be all of these things, and live independent lives, contributing to and benefiting from society on equal terms.

Without the ILF, many councils couldn't even begin to provide this kind of support, and many users would face being put into residential homes—who operate on the 'stack 'em deep, feed 'em cheap' format of care provision. Many ILF users already came from the 'care homes' we are talking about, where dignity and humanity were cast aside like dirty boots upon entry. Where people didn't even own their own toothbrush or underwear. Where, staggeringly, BUPA recently discovered that up to 45% of older and disabled people die within 12 months of coming through the door. Remember, these are residential homes—where people go to live—not nursing homes where people go to die. To many, the ILF literally means the difference between life and death.

With that kind of past, and that kind of future laid out, no wonder people place such a high value on the ILF.

But not the Coalition. You see the ILF was closed to new applicants in 2010. This was soon followed by the announcement (on the UN International Day of Disabled People 2012—you couldn't make this shit up) that the fund would close altogether the next year. Naturally, users were a bit miffed, to say the least. Many a letter was written in ire, to MP's, Lords and the media. Social media was blitzed, as social media usually is, with protest actions, meetings, short films, briefings in Parliament to politicos and articles published hither and yon to follow.

ILF users reached out to those organisations who had positioned themselves as vital to the lives of disabled people—the disability 'charities'—little realising that these same organisations had fattened themselves gorging on government millions doled out to 'support' disabled people, and weren't interested in the forced dieting that challenging government decisions would inevitably bring. These organisations value their 'inside the tent pissing out' status more than anything, certainly more than helping the voices of disabled people to be heard, or empowering people to find out what was going on.

Crucially, a legal challenge was also mounted by a group of users. In November 2013, the Upper Tribunal Court of Appeal decided that, in essence, the government's argument was a crock of shit. That the Government hadn't considered the implications of closing the fund. That it was unlawful, and breached the United Nations Convention on the Rights of People with Disabilities (UNCRPD), which the UK had signed up to.

'Ah, right,' said the Coalition, 'give us a moment to pause and reflect would you please?' Fast-forward to March this year, when the pausing and reflecting was done, and the new announcement came: 'We couldn't give a flying fuck what the courts think,' they said, 'Nor two fucks could we give about the users we now acknowledge might end up in prison—sorry, homes. We are going to close it anyway.'

Having exhausted all 'legitimate' forms of protest and resisting this decision, users found themselves back in the same position with no more avenues open to them. Unless they were prepared to raise the stakes, unless they were prepared to create the kind of space which is undeniable. The kind of space which cannot be swept away by government rhetoric, or swamped by a barrage of incorrect, misleading or simply made-up statistics. To do this, users linked up with those who have been fighting this fight where it matters—on the streets.

Through DPAC (Disabled People Against Cuts), disabled people have carried on the form of protest that disabled people have been doing since the 19th century—direct action. DPAC have shut down city centres through road blockings, occupied government departments such as the DWP and Department for Education. We have pitched up at Cabinet Ministers' homes (including the homes of Iain Ducan Smith and Nick Clegg) with UK Uncut. DPAC have been central in the campaign to drive Atos out of welfare reform. We have also been instrumental in the Save ILF Campaign since the beginning, and were keen to find new ways of challenging this government. The idea for a time-limited, accessible protest camp was discussed, and together with the frontline activist groups Occupy and UK Uncut, plans were laid to build the camp under the noses of the parliamentarians—across the road from the Houses of Parliament at Westminster Abbey.

The plan took months to prepare. Weekly meetings in sweaty rooms, working groups, sourcing funding, borrowing infrastructure, rehearsals, the whole nine yards. It was ambitious. But the fight to defend disabled people's rights and position within society won't be won through petitions and marches. If you think it will, there are plenty of opportunities for people to take that kind of action—check your local People's Assembly or TUC website for listings. But DPAC are about disabled people taking collective action on our own terms. And about supporting, and being supported by, the broader anti-cuts and anti-austerity movement.

In the end, this action managed to get over 100 people, plus 7.5 tonnes of infrastructure, to within 100 yards of 'the mother of all Parliaments'. And we only missed by a hair's breath of achieving our primary goal—setting up a camp. Only the efforts of over 250 Met Police, combined with the ignorance and callous disregard of the Dean of Westminster, thwarted our plans. But lessons have been learned and we will be better, bigger and bolder the next time.

The challenge has been set.

The challenge for government (of any colour): to reject corporate lobbying, and create societies that are inclusive for all citizens. They should do this by engaging and responding to its citizens; they must stop perpetuating myths and untruths about groups like disabled people, immigrants and claimants, in a bid to progress neoliberal, profit-driven agendas.

The challenge for society: to figure out at what point we stop talking about the 'economies' we live in, and start talking about our communities and relationships again. And what our role is in empowering people to take their part in building stronger communities and relationships.

The challenge for activists: to step up their action. To see the marches and demos for what they are: merely part of the solution, not the solution in themselves. To look at ways of building alternative structures, such as occupations, workers councils, communities reclaiming their streets and assets. All of these give people a chance to see for themselves first-hand how society is created by us, not for us.

And the challenge for the public is simple: look at the deal you have with the state, and ask yourself if you are worth more.

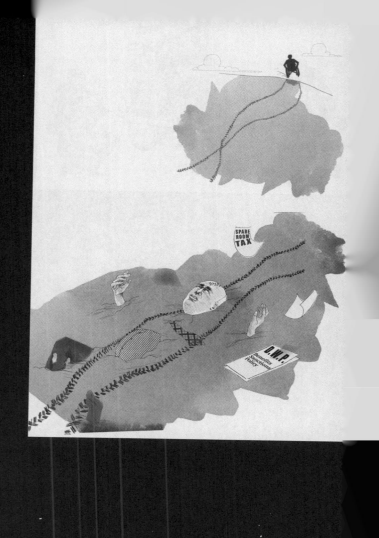

TXT: RICHARD SEYMOUR

The State of Austerity

Ceci n'est pas un etat

Anyone with weak nerves or a heart condition should look away now. For here is an exciting fact. In the fiscal year 2017–18, government spending will dip slightly below 40%.

This isn't actually very exciting. Slightly below 40% of GDP is within the normal range of public spending in Britain. Surely, with initial planned cuts of 19% across all departments and more following, the state should be shrinking a lot faster than it is. But even with brutal cuts in welfare, the relative cost of social security has increased.

Why? To answer that, we have to debunk the austerity myths. But we have to go much deeper. We have to rethink the state from the bottom up.

Not about the 'small state'

The Prime Minister promised us a lean state. His reasoning was that for Britain to be competitive in the global economy, it had to relieve the private sector of the burden of taxation and free more private capital to invest.

The neoliberal state says it is down-sizing, constantly eviscerating itself, slashing its own wrists, trying to get out of people's way since it was a cheeky glint in Hayek's eye. Of course, the second there is any serious contest, any major conflict of interests, the state appears, settling matters with sudden, maniacal violence. Ninja-like, it conceals itself in the sinks, recesses, dark corners and perimeters, emerging for swift bouts of exemplary force, only to retreat from view just as quickly.

This is not how it really works. The fables about getting the 'nanny state' off our backs are for the chumps. A core tenet of neoliberal doctrine has always been that the character, not the volume, of state activity is what must change. Throughout the neoliberal period, the size of the British state has not shrunk at all. Two things have happened instead.

First, the institutions of the state have been re-formatted in order to make them more like 'the market'. There is no such thing as 'the market', but the basic principles of competition, pricing and cost-capping have been implemented throughout the public sector. The technical discourse underpinning these changes is known as 'public choice economics', and key theorists of this ilk such as William Niskanen were forced upon the civil service bureaucracy as part of reforming the the state. One effect of this, intended by neoliberals, was to reduce the democratic capacity of the state by shifting more of its functions away from democratic control to oversight by private-sector officials, quangos and private companies. In the Seventies, it was said, a 'crisis of democracy' had taken place. The state had been overloaded with demands from too many active and mobilised constituencies, thus losing its ability to govern. This was the neoliberal answer.

Second, state apparatuses have been redeployed to incentivise 'entrepreneurial' action and discipline collectivism and non-market transactions. This of course required the expansion of repressive institutions, initially to control strikes and protests (police), and later to punish a wider range of behaviour considered harmful to viable entrepreneurial communities (ASBOs, anti-terror laws, and prison building). But it also included a more subtle reorganisation of other forms of spending. Consider workfare. This costly bureaucracy exists to keep the recipients of welfare in the habit of working. It thus, according to neoliberal orthodoxy, bolsters their human capital and their viability as future employees.

So this is the first lesson. Neoliberalism isn't about a small state. It is about the competition state. Cuts are a weapon not the goal. In every austerity project implemented since

Chile and New York in the mid-1970s, the end result is not a smaller state, but weaker labour, less democracy, more authoritarianism and a hard-nosed culture of competition.

Fiscal crisis is built into modern states

If spending cuts are not the objective, is the fiscal crisis an illusion? Not exactly. True, there is no 'overspend': we have endured decades of the neoliberal straitjacket. Labour did nothing to reverse this and was in fact more absurdly punctilious about securing a 'balanced budget' than previous administrations. Still, there is more to this than myth.

Over decades, successive governments have attempted to bring public spending under control. Thatcher in the UK, Reagan in the US, Chirac and Juppe in France, Clinton in the US, Chretien in Canada, and later Schroeder in Germany, all attempted to 'streamline' government services, and cut taxes on business. This was justified by the ideology of 'globalisation'—to be competitive in a more integrated world economy, national states had to spend less on 'unproductive' welfare recipients and promote 'enterprise'. The reality was more complex. Leading capitalist economies were declining in productivity and growth, while investment was shifting to less-profitable service industries. The population was becoming older and thus had more dependent citizens. States can race to counteract these trends with cost-cutting, but they're up against a stubborn fact: fiscal crisis is built-in to modern states.

In 1973, just as the post-war social compromise was falling to pieces, the sociologist James O'Connor identified a long-term 'tendency for government expenditure to outrace revenues.' He said this was rooted in two basic functions facilitated by the state: accumulation and legitimation. The first included measures that benefited the economy, such as stimulus spending, tax breaks, bailouts, nationalisations, shutting down failing businesses, building new infrastructure and so on. The second involved the organisation of consent through the mediation of class struggles, the creation and maintenance of the shared cultural and social space within which production takes place, and the deployment of material incentives to encourage integration. For O'Connor, the costs of these functions tended to rise beyond the ability of the state to recover revenues.

This was ultimately rooted in a conflict between democracy and capitalism. No matter how many economic functions the state takes on, the control of profits remains in private hands, and the state cannot take control of these profits in the interests of carrying out its legitimation functions without seriously curtailing capitalist power.

This makes perfect sense. Yet one cannot infer state behaviour from various 'functions' that it supposedly has to perform. A lot of what states do is dysfunctional. And in fact, all accumulation functions can in principle be carried out in the private sector. Why do states even bother to take on economic functions? Why don't they just cut the bureaucracy out entirely? Part of the answer, as Mariana Mazzucato has shown, is that private capital is dependent upon the innovation and dynamism of the public sector. Some types of accumulation function aren't profitable enough, or are too risky, for private firms to take them on. Yet, neoliberal states often fail to take on essential accumulation functions, even where the private sector neglects them. Another reason might be that some functions are too important to be trusted to a narrow sector of capital devoted to short-term profits. But the case of US healthcare reminds us that all kinds of irrational and excessively costly privatised arrangements can be tolerated for a long time. Dysfunction is normal in capitalist states.

Ceci n'est pas un état

There is no such 'thing' as 'the state'. In a way, we all know this. The police truncheon is a tangible object, and the cop wielding it is a person: the state is neither. But it's a lot harder to figure out exactly what the state is.

What we experience as 'the state'—traffic wardens, hospitals, death certificates, statutes, local elections, binmen, job centres, arms fairs, and so on—is itself just a series of outcomes. Rather than starting with these things and trying to work out what their internal coherence is on the basis of their functionality to the system, we should inquire as to the processes of which they are outcomes. Think of elections. These are themselves the outcome of a prolonged class struggle in the UK, beginning with the English Civil War and culminating in successive Reform Acts that eventually enfranchised the entire adult population. Hospitals fall into a similar category, inasmuch as the NHS is the outcome of a particular type of social democratic class politics. Much of the welfare state is the product of other types of political conflict, such as feminist or anti-racist struggle. These are gross simplifications, but they illustrate the point. The processes which go into the making of the state are political struggles structured by antagonistic social relations.

The state can thus be understood as the outcome, or the 'material condensation' as Nicos Poulantzas put it, of the balance of class and political forces in a society. And if the state's format—personnel and institutional linkages—all tend to support the existing patterns of domination in a society, it is because that is the accumulated outcome of centuries of political struggle. But the institutions that result from these processes are subject to ongoing struggles both internally and externally. Given this, whatever 'functions' the state carries out, it does so in a permanently fluctuating and unstable field of forces. Any 'line' that emerges within the state arises from the interaction of opposing forces.

Thus, when the state carries out legitimation and accumulation functions, it doesn't simply read off its objectives from whatever is 'functional' to the system. What is good for the system is rarely transparent and always contested. Rather, it organises a series of compromises between the dominant and dominated, and between different elite sectors. These compromises are expressed not just in institutional outcomes, but also in the ideological and technical discourses of the state. Such compromises overwhelmingly favour the dominant classes, but are represented as reflecting the 'national interest'. And they are subject to constant revision as the balance of forces shifts due to recession, a rightward lurch, or a collapse in trade unionism.

Understanding it like this helps us to better understand the permanent fiscal crisis of modern states, and the austerian answer to it.

Capitalism vs democracy

The dilemma of modern states is this. As the core economies become less productive and profitable over the long term, businesses become less willing and able to fund interventionist states. At the same time, however, as economies become more crisis-prone, and as these crises get deeper, the need for state intervention increases. Bailouts, unemployment benefits, public-private scams, all cost money. States can try to cut costs, but political opposition may prevent this. They can borrow against future growth, but only if such borrowing is part of a viable growth strategy. That again is subject to the contest of opposing political forces.

And this is where the austerians come in. They represent the neoliberal faction of the capitalist class, and they know that their problem is democracy. They may not use exactly this language, but they know that the egalitarian and collective ends of democracy are at odds with the competitive and hierarchical ends of capitalism. Their objective is to limit the claims of democracy on capitalism, and the opportunity to do so is rare. And they know that a crisis presents opportunities for the left to expand the democratic constraints on capitalism. This is why they 'never let a serious crisis go to waste', never miss an opportunity to disrupt the continuum of democratic negotiation on their own terms, and revoke and reorganise the compromises through which legitimacy was previously secured.

The fiscal crisis is their cue, but their objective is bigger. They haven't forgotten that the crisis is one of capitalism and they wage war in and through the state to address that crisis on terms favourable to capital. That means changing the relations of forces that are condensed in the state, retooling the state to meet business needs. It means less democracy, more capitalism.

IMG: HANNAH BLOWS
& ROBBIE BLUNDELL

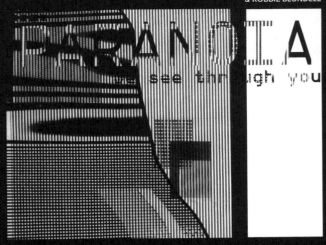

PARANOIA
see through you

Paranoia
We See Through You

As Lacan noted, there is something fundamentally paranoid about knowledge. In order to understand the least thing about the world, we operate with necessary misapprehensions about what we can and do not know, our place in the world, and the relationship between what we know and what we can do with it. While we do not usually believe we can understand or control everything or even very much at all, behind the scenes there always lurks an implicit theory of knowledge: we might regard knowledge as cumulative, as additive, or we might see it as functioning on different levels: this kind of knowledge works here, this other kind works there. Only in moments of rare lucidity or delusion do we believe that we have understood everything, as much as we think we might want to. We are neither God nor are we usually to blame for most of the quotidian crap we usually feel guilty for.

Knowledge can be seen as power, or as a tool, or as useless but interesting, or as incomplete but progressive. Even though 'grand narratives' are supposed to be over, we might nevertheless be Marxists, feminists, historical pessimists, catastrophists, ecological thinkers, anarchists, etc.—or even many of these things at once. In other words, there might be some kind of overarching framework that we use as individuals and collectives that attempts to uncover structures and patterns that enable us to predict and even resist the future. We can argue about and refine these frameworks, or even radically break with them as time passes. But they are generally open-ended, nuanced, flexible, if firm in various places. Those who claim to understand exactly how everything works, or have an explanation or a reason for every event that happens, we might think are assuming too much, or are desperately seeking some sort of principle that describes the lot: the New World Order, perhaps, and the cry of 'false flag!' that greets every major bombing, attack or accident; this is not of course to say that there haven't been such operations and cover-ups, merely that to assume that they always are indicates a mindset that sees conspiracies everywhere. In a world where there are no accidents, errors, coincidences, everything starts to take on a horrible, terrifying meaning: if there are no gaps, then everything is full to the brim with a grotesque weight, and someone or something ends up being responsible and consequently blamed, feared and/or worshipped.

But as the old phrase 'just because you're paranoid, doesn't mean they're not out to get you' implies there is an important separation between the form of paranoia and its content—a paranoid feeling that turns out to be true is no less paranoid for all that. But what we are witnessing lately with the grim breaking waves of stories about institutionalised child abuse and other ruling-class corruption is less confirmation of pre-existing paranoias than the revelation that paranoid content is outstripping paranoid form: even the very worst mind could hardly have grasped the extent and reach of such violent abuse and exploitation of the most vulnerable, whether it be Savile's hospital patients or care-home children drugged and raped by MPs and peers. The paranoid understanding of class—these people are not like us—is revealed to be true in the case of establishment abuse and those who colluded in covering it up even if they did not directly participate. How can we describe this kind of knowledge that those at the top surely had and continue to have? As hundreds come forward to report abuse at the hands of celebrities and politicians, we have a very clear indication of how much fear and power is involved in discrediting and undermining the experiences of the abused, where their knowledge and lives are trashed because someone much more powerful can just bury them, figuratively and literally.

Classic paranoid thoughts—anxiety about being watched, being spied on, agencies reading thoughts or implanting them—are, it turns out, in fact, all correct. In the wake of the NSA revelations, how to distinguish between formal and content paranoia becomes increasingly difficult. In an interview with Melissa Dahl for the *Science of Us* website, psychiatrist Joel Gold puts the problem like this:

So how do you talk to someone who is delusional but, at the same time, isn't wholly wrong? If this happened ten years ago, and my patients were saying, 'There are cameras everywhere, the government is watching me, they're listening to my phone calls,' we'd believe they were paranoid. Today, we can't really automatically say that, because it's true—the government might be listening to this conversation right now.

The political question concerns the definition of mental illness—is someone really paranoid when the form of their supposed illness in fact matches the content? How usefully paranoid should one be when UK reality itself looks like a Philip K Dick multiverse crossed with the class politics of Lindsey Anderson films, scripted by David Peace with all the morality of *Kind Hearts & Coronets*? Is it better to take a cool, well-rested distance or to triumphantly declare from the pinnacle of red-eyed anxiety that this is what we suspected all along? Does it make a difference what our formal framework for understanding knowledge is when the content is just simply rotten? What is the best way of getting back control of knowledge as such, to ensure that those with secrets to hide are never again in a position to be able to hide from what they've done because—simply—they won't be able to do it again?

If we are all expected to lead transparent lives—that is to say, lives that are open at every point to surveillance, monitoring, suspicion, harassment, prosecution—how do we demand transparency of those who do the watching and who cover-up their secrets from the majority? Detective shows, as ubiquitous as they are popular, appeal in part because of the sheer will of the flawed cop tracking his or her quarry towards some sort of uneasy conclusion. We are supposed to believe that the state is the detective, damaged maybe, but ultimately on the side of the good, pretending to self-investigate when necessary, self-correcting when random innocents get killed along the way. But, above all, we are supposed to believe in the detective as the entity that combines knowledge and good intentions. We need not only to kill the cop in our head, but the entire police station, the IPCC, the courts, prisons and the state that oversees, and in fact is them.

Some have suggested that Snowden's revelations are perversely ultimately useful for governments—after all, if people know their backs are being watched wouldn't they spontaneously police themselves?—but at the same time, the stakes—global transparency and knowledge-control— couldn't be, well, clearer: if understanding about what is going on means being paranoid from time to time, then, in the name of all that is real, bring on the fear.

How We Might Better School Ourselves

A View From 100 Years Hence

We cannot know what the future will bring, but we can use the idea of the future to look at the present in new light.

I hope that one day I might have grandchildren. If I am really lucky I might even live long enough to get to talk to my grandchildren when they are adults, but I know that is unlikely. Even if my future health is fair and my children become parents, it may be too late for me. Like most of today's English middle class I became a parent too late. So this is a letter for an imagined adult grandchild. I'm trying to explain to her something about how we live today. I am far from the first person to carry out a thought experiment in this way.

The year is 2064. I want to tell you about how schools in England worked in 2014. As always there were good and bad. We concentrated most on what we thought was bad. Often it wasn't bad at all, we just had very strange ideas of what good was. In hindsight we were in a mess, but if you are in a mess you may not know it. And we were largely in a mess because we had forgotten what education, life and caring, should be about. Schools had become competitive, education a competition, children had to compete to be 'the best'. There were many unforeseen consequences.

Not all children were in school in 2014. Huge numbers were excluded from education every year. In any one year a fifth of children with autism were formally, although illegally, excluded from schools. Of all children, boys were three-times more likely to be excluded than girls. Children receiving free school meals were four times more likely to be excluded than those from better-off families. Children from particular ethnic minority groups more likely still, and those with a statement of special education need even more likely. The numbers being permanently excluded a year, normally for violent or disruptive behaviour had been falling. However, by 2012 the number permanently excluded that year rose to 5170, more than one in ten of whom were in a primary school. Many tens of thousands more school children were expelled for a short period. Others were not missed much when they were not at school. Their presence did not help the school 'excel'.

Every so often if a story was extreme enough a small part of the world of missing children was revealed. In 2013 in Oxford the story of six local girls who were abused between ages 12 to 15 was revealed in the press. The men who abused them were sentenced to 95 years in prison. But just as they had been almost totally ignored when they first complained, the girls' story was quickly forgotten. No one by 2018 was asking whether it could be happening again. It was old news. There were many adults responsible for caring for children on the margins of education, but the overall system didn't care that much. The overriding ethos of the time was all about aspiration and getting better and better 'results'. The products were children.

Children in England had never been scored against each other as much as they were in the early decades of the twenty-first century. Each child was repeatedly tested, given individual learning targets. Each teacher was individually assessed and monitored. Each school was repeatedly evaluated and schools that tested and trained their charges in the prescribed manner were labelled 'outstanding'. Segregating primary school children on different tables within a classroom by ability was apparently an outstanding thing to do; despite evidence that such setting or streaming of kids reduced their overall achievements by the equivalent of losing a whole month of schooling for every child in the class. Squeezing the most out of every child to realize what was then called their 'potential' was what mattered most. England had to do this, it was said, if the country was to compete in what its politicians called 'the global race'.

England's leading politicians had been taught to compete. They had done well at school, got to the right university, done the right course (often the same course), crushed the ambitions of others who might have wanted to have led their political parties, former school-friends, colleagues, partners and siblings. They had become adults and later parents surrounded by the ethos of educational competition, of winners and losers. In hindsight we were silly to expect more of them, but all the time they thought they were racing to the top, they were actually striving for changes that damaged the education of the nation's children. Children were taught more and more about how to pass the next test, and less and less about what it was they were supposed to be studying. They appeared to be learning—but weren't.

It took us a long time to work out what was going wrong with education in England. Some of the early evidence became clear when it was revealed that children who had gone to private schools were 10% less likely than children from state school to gain a good (2.1) degree at university even if they had identical entry grades at A level. The private school children had been taught-to-the-test even more rigorously than state school children were and so, although they inevitably gained higher scores in the tests, they had actually learnt less. This only became evident when they were tested at the next level, at university. Their private school 'education' had not equipped them with the skills they needed to continue learning. Instead it had maximised what could be squeezed out of each child in the short term. Their parents had paid for those short-term results.

It was international comparisons that most clearly revealed that the English schooling system was turning into a race to the bottom. Of all the statistics revealed, the most dramatic showed that out of 22 countries that were compared, England ranked among the three lowest in terms of the mean proficiency in numeracy achieved by its young people. Only the United States scored significantly worse. The countries that scored highest were Finland and the Netherlands. However, when ministers were confronted with these figures, rather than travel to those two countries they jetted off to the highest scoring small area, the Chinese city of Shanghai. Within two months of the minister's visit it was revealed that that city was considering withdrawing from the international comparisons because they were causing teachers to teach too much to the test, exposing students to dangerous levels of study and causing teachers to devote 'between two and five hours every day to designing, reviewing, analysing and discussing homework assignments.'

Any group of children can be forced to score highly on a test if trained long and hard enough. That is not the same as a good education or a good life. In England boarding schools showed the extreme of what was possible. In 2014 campaigners lead by psychiatrists wrote of the damage that could result from a boarding school education, especially one where the emphasis was on wringing the highest possible marks out of every single child, a child who spends all day and all night at school. And a child who was told that their parents' lives were so busy and important that they could not be there for them.

You're probably wondering how it all got this bad. The problem was that the competitive ethos was self-reinforcing. The more that children were tested the more testing was accepted as normal and doing well at tests became seen as more and more important and valid as a measure of success. Children brought up in this way became teachers who had never known anything else. The most aspirational teachers joined school senior management teams and further reinforced the sentiment. Dissenters were chastised. Entire management teams were replaced if a school was seen as not trying hard enough to compete.

Eventually schools became one of the main determinants of how much housing costs in each local area. The average increase in housing prices around a so-called good school anywhere in England was much higher than any within Paris, the most economically competitive area of France. Private-school fees soared, even during the great recession. Universities entered this game and from summer 2014 almost all undergraduate students in English universities were paying around £9,000 a year in fees, most through loans. They were told they would easily recoup this money in future earnings. Over half of all young women in England were going to university at this time. It was no surprise when they did not all become rich enough to pay off their enhanced debts with little effect, especially the women who continued to be paid less than men for many years to come.

I know you know how it all ended, and of course it had to end. It was unsustainable. But I thought I should write this down because I know it's so hard to imagine that all those parents and teachers and politicians put up with such a situation for so long—let alone the children. But in 2014 it just appeared inevitable to most people that this was what good education was about. Some of those who had been most taught-to-the-test even described their school experience as 'privileged'. A whole nation had become obsessed with marks, subservient to letters and numbers, and when they ran out of enough letters they even created * marks (yes there really was an A*). At the height of the idiocy a new geneticism became popular and the mayor of London, a man now long forgotten called Boris, talked of supposedly clever children as 'top cornflakes'.

The English became so educationally myopic that they no-longer looked back about what had been better in their recent past, or what was happening in neighbouring countries or just over the channel in most of Europe, or even imagined what a better way might be that was not just an even more concentrated version of more of the same. They had taught themselves how to be stupid. It's easily done and well worth remembering how it happened back in 2014.

Politics
It Still Matters

Societies that fail to adapt to the challenges they face eventually fall apart. The planet is littered with monuments to political systems that finally ran out of road, leaving only their relics behind. The Parthenon in Athens stands as a testament to the passing glory of ancient Athenian democracy, which flourished for two hundred years and then died at the hands of Philip of Macedon and his son Alexander the Great. The huge monolithic stone heads on Easter Island were produced by a flourishing island community as symbols of the power and purpose of its leading inhabitants; the competition to build bigger and better statues eventually used up the island's natural resources, resulting in starvation and ruin. Lenin's tomb in Moscow once stood as the focal point for global communism, honouring the man who had devised a politics that was going to conquer the future; now that the future is here, his mausoleum has become just another tourist trap. Are the liberal democracies that Fukuyama said were the end of history destined to go the same way? Will the Capitol in Washington sooner or later join the list of magnificent ruins?

There are two reasons to think that the fate of democracy may be different. The first is that the most successful states of the present have access to resources that no previous society could match. We are enormously richer, better educated, better informed, healthier and longer-lived than any human beings have ever been. We can draw on vast and sophisticated networks of communication. We keep inventing new stuff at a prodigious rate. The pace of change is only going to accelerate. It is hard to see how societies like these could get stuck for long.

The second reason is that modern democracy is inherently adaptable. Democracies are good at avoiding the worst political outcomes because democratic citizens are so irritable and impatient, constantly pushing for something a little better than what they have. When democracies make mistakes—which they frequently do—they don't plough on with them to the bitter end. They change course. The politics of restraint has proved good at correcting for the most serious errors of judgement that politicians can make. Bad leaders get kicked out of office; slightly less bad leaders replace them. Slowly, painfully, the system rights itself. Autocratic regimes, which are often better at taking snap decisions, are worse at spotting when those decisions are the wrong ones. Dictators and tyrants are the ones who lead their people over a cliff.

However, there are other reasons for thinking that these might be false consolations. The first is that the democracies are not masters of their own fate. Our world is now so interconnected that failure in one place can lead to a cascade of disastrous consequences for everyone. Contemporary Denmark is as comfortable a place to live as human beings have ever found. But Denmark would be powerless to protect itself from disastrous mismanagement somewhere else on the planet. Even the most powerful states are too dependent on each other to be confident that they can be immunised from each other's mistakes. The United States and China are competing experiments in forms of technocratic government. The democratic version, which combines elections with financial expertise—professional politicians with central bankers—is the more adaptable. The autocratic version, which combines one-party rule with managerial expertise—party cadres with engineers—is the more decisive. The problem with the adaptable system is that it can be indecisive. The problem with the decisive system is that it can struggle to adapt. When either of these experiments goes wrong, the knock-on effects will be felt everywhere. Another financial crash in the US or a political revolution in China would have consequences that are very hard to predict. In the worst-case scenario, the two systems could still find themselves at war. If that happens, all bets are off. Even in Denmark.

The second reason to be worried is that history may not be a reliable guide. The challenges that states face in the twenty-first century are different from those they have faced in the past. The difference is in the time-scale. The advantage of democratic adaptability depends on there being time to adapt. That may not be the case for the most serious threats democracies are likely to face. In some respects time is too short. One of the striking features of the financial crash of 2008 was just how quickly politicians had to act to stave off disaster. They got through that one by the skin of their teeth, but there is no guarantee that next time they will be so lucky. Meanwhile, the consequences of the crash will be playing out for a generation or more. Recovery has been slower than for any previous recession, slower even than the Great Depression in the early 1930s. A large cohort of young people across the Western world is out of employment, with no prospect of finding a job any time soon. Austerity and the paying down of public and private debt are liable to continue for the foreseeable future. Voters are told that in the long run they will benefit. Yet democracy still works to the timetable of the electoral cycle, with its premium on regular, incremental improvements in people's standard of living. The time-scales are out of joint. Politicians have a few hours to save the world; voters have to wait decades to see the benefits. It is not clear how democracy will adapt to this challenge.

The most acute version of the conundrum relates to climate change and the threat of environmental catastrophe. The long lag before the effects of climate change will be felt make it very difficult for elected politicians to take pre-emptive action, conscious as they are that the people who pay the price won't be the people who see the benefits. Yet if we never take pre-emptive action, and if the gloomier scenarios predicted by the current science turn out to be correct, then the consequences are likely to catch us unawares. At some point, the long-term threat of environmental degradation will reveal itself as an immediate disaster: a massive flood, a calamitous harvest failure, the mass movement of peoples, another war. At that point democratic adaptability will kick in. But by then it may be too late. Autocratic regimes like China might be able to take more decisive action in the present to deal with the long-term effects of climate change. China's rulers do not have to worry about getting re-elected. So if China's technocrats decide to green a Chinese city, they can, within practical limits, make it happen. However, Chinese technocracy won't resolve climate change on its own. And when the consequences of democratic inaction reveal themselves in the future, the Chinese political system may be insufficiently adaptable to cope.

The final problem is that democratic adaptability can morph into democratic complacency. We have reached the point where there is good historical evidence that democracies eventually rise to meet the challenges they face. The transition from Hobbes' world to our world is a story of the successful adaptation by inclusive states to whatever history could throw at them. Democracy survived the Great Depression. It eventually enfranchised almost all its citizens. Violence fell away. Prosperity spread. Democracies have not always responded to threats and injustices in a timely fashion, but they have usually got there in the end. It is tempting to assume that this process can continue indefinitely. We will get our act together when we need to.

In late October 2013, the US Congress shut down the Federal government as part of an intractable and poisonously partisan dispute over the funding of President Obama's healthcare reforms. It looked like a recklessly cavalier act: politicians choosing to pull the plug on government because they can't agree on an important piece of legislation. The causes of the growing partisanship and rancour in American politics are many. But one of them must be this: politicians behave so cavalierly because they think the system can survive it. They don't believe that they have really pulled the plug on government. American democracy has got through much worse in the past and survived. So it's assumed it can survive this. When the dust settles, the system will adapt. And perhaps it will. But this is brink-manship that imagines the real brink is always some way off. You can flirt with disaster because it is only flirting. No American politician wants to renege on America's debt or stop paying the bills. They threaten to do it only because they believe it will never happen.

This is politics as a game of chicken. Games of chicken are harmless, until they go wrong, at which point they become fatal. Flirting with disaster at a time of rapid change and increasing global interconnectivity risks meeting with disaster just when you least expect it. The US government may believe it will always honour its debts in the end. But its creditors, which include the Chinese government, may get tired of all the games. China's technocrats could choose to pull the plug themselves by looking for somewhere else to park their cash. Then the US is in real trouble. Cavalier democratic politicians can easily lose control of events. Relying on adaptability to save them only makes it more likely that they will eventually hit the rocks.

None of this means democracy is doomed. Nothing in politics is pre-ordained. There are still plenty of grounds for optimism in a world that is better-off than it has ever been, in which poverty as well as violence is on the retreat and where technology promises limitless new opportunities. The threat of catastrophe remains real, however. Things could still go terribly wrong. Relying on technology to save us will not be enough. We need to recognise the risks posed by global interconnectivity, by the time-lags between our present actions and their long-term consequences, and by our growing complacency about what politics can achieve. Given the size of those challenges, the institutions of the state will almost certainly have to be scaled up to match them as well as being scaled down to prevent them from becoming too remote. This will involve difficult choices and dangerous moments. Nothing about it will be easy. But it can't be done by stealth or by crossing our fingers. It can only be done through politics.

Politics still matters.

ROLE MODEL

START:

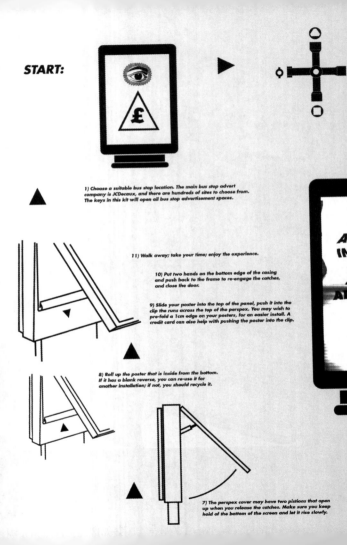

1) Choose a suitable bus stop location. The main bus stop advert company is JCDecaux, and there are hundreds of sites to choose from. The keys in this kit will open all bus stop advertisement spaces.

11) Walk away; take your time; enjoy the experience.

10) Put two hands on the bottom edge of the casing and push back to the frame to re-engage the catches, and close the door.

9) Slide your poster into the top of the panel, push it into the clip the runs across the top of the perspex. You may wish to pre-fold a 1cm edge on your posters, for an easier install. A credit card can also help with pushing the poster into the clip.

8) Roll up the poster that is inside from the bottom. If it has a blank reverse, you can re-use it for another installation; if not, you should recycle it.

7) The perspex cover may have two pistions that open up when you release the catches. Make sure you keep hold of the bottom of the screen and let it rise slowly.

2) S
att
op

No
ins
ex

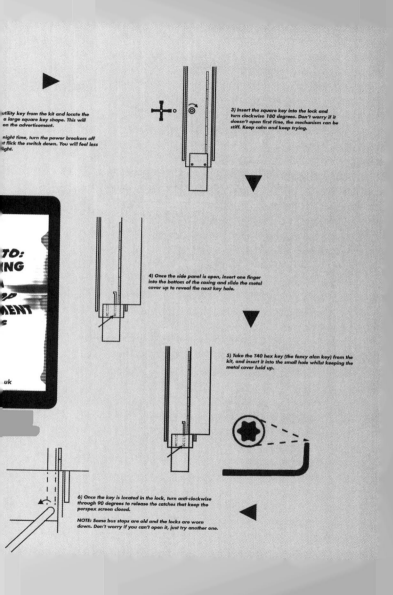

utility key from the kit and locate the
a large square key shape. This will
on the advertisement.

night time, turn the power breakers off
t flick the switch down. You will feel less
ight.

TO:
ING

MENT

.uk

3) Insert the square key into the lock and
turn clockwise 180 degrees. Don't worry if it
doesn't open first time, the mechanism can be
stiff. Keep calm and keep trying.

4) Once the side panel is open, insert one finger
into the bottom of the casing and slide the metal
cover up to reveal the next key hole.

5) Take the T40 hex key (the fancy alan key) from the
kit, and insert it into the small hole whilst keeping the
metal cover held up.

6) Once the key is located in the lock, turn anti-clockwise
through 90 degrees to release the catches that keep the
perspex screen closed.

NOTE: Some bus stops are old and the locks are worn
down. Don't worry if you can't open it, just try another one.

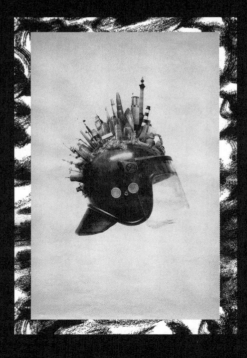

Advertising Shits in Your Head

On Brandalism

Advertising shits in your head—but, first, its torrential, golden flow stains your magazines, your phone, your computer, your newspapers and your streets. Advertising dominates and shits all over our culture. It is a visceral, powerful form of pollution that not only affects our common public and cultural spaces, but also our deeply private intimate spaces. Advertisers want your 'brain time'—to shit in your head without your knowledge. We want to stop them.

First Thing's First

As you read these words, the UN's Special Rapporteur in the field of cultural rights is preparing a landmark report into the effects of advertising and marketing on our cultural rights—specifically the right for us to choose our own identities without coercion or persuasion. The report focuses on the development of conventional advertising and marketing practices and also emerging ones linked to behavioural targeting and neuromarketing. It is becoming increasingly apparent that from the sides of entire buildings to the individual neurons in our brains (the microscopic cells in our brains that inform us of our reality), advertising, media and marketing corporations are waging a war of perception on our individual and collective consciousnesses. So citizens and artists across the UK, with help from others across the world, have begun fighting back.

The Brandalism project started in 2012, as an extension of the guerilla art traditions of the 20th century, and a manifestation of various elements influenced by agit-prop, the Situationists and graffiti movements. We began by merging the arts, the social and the political in the UK's largest unauthorised exhibition, taking-over 36 billboards in 5 UK cities. Internationally recognised artists were involved, but on the street you wouldn't know it: all the works were unsigned and anonymously installed within public space, as gifts to society.

We attempted to connect individual forms of expression with collective bigger-than-self issues. It was part propaganda, part art—or 'popaganda' as radical artist Ron English calls it. They were installed in spaces traditionally associated with commodity exchange but the artworks spoke of something else. It was a threat and the result was the national mobilisation of the big 3 outdoor advertisers (JCDecaux, ClearChannel and Primesight) to hunt down our art works and remove them.

It is important to consider here that the sites reclaimed by artists are in public space, despite being privately owned and operated by multinational advertising corporations. There are hundreds of thousands of these sites across the UK, but we have never consented to being pissed on from above by their messages and their branded advertisements. This is fundamentally different to the other forms of advertising that we come into contact with and have, to a greater extent, some agency over. We can choose to turn a page, a channel or install software on our computers to remove these trespassers on our visual realm. We have no such luxury concerning the public realm.

How they got in your head

The drive to consumerism that infiltrated society told citizens to become more concerned about consumption than political action. The expansion of capitalist economies inevitably led to an uneven distribution of wealth, thus widening economic disparity. Suddenly the media (and the art created by designers) became a tool of political forces and a medium for advertising, rather than the medium from which the public got their information on political matters. This limiting of access to the public sphere, by the political control of the public sphere, was necessary for the modern capitalistic forces to operate and thrive in the competitive economy.

We have always seen culture as the spaces and places where society tells stories about itself. Every society has a space where these stories are told and in our culture it's advertising that dominates these spaces (both physical and digital). If we want to understand the messages that define (popular) culture then we have to look at the main storytellers. In our culture that is the storytellers that have the most money—the advertisers. Advertisers underwrite and subsidise most forms of communication (print, radio, TV, outdoor, digital, online) in the UK and their spending topped £14 billion in 2013; with the digital outdoor sector showing growth rates of 17% in 2013, it isn't about to slow down any time soon.

Cognitive and social science (neuroscience, psychology and sociology in particular) studies have shown that advertising distorts our most automatic behaviours, including unconscious behaviours (low attention processing model). Using brain imaging, neuroscientists have recently begun to look at the effects of branding on our brains. Focussing on our reward systems, the region of the brain that interacts with emotions and decision-making, they found it is highly sensitive to signals from our environment, which can influence our behavior even when they are not consciously perceived.

These studies are finally proving what many have suspected for decades: advertising affects and normalises attitudes, behaviours and values. Advertising doesn't just reflect culture, as the industry purports, it actively shapes our values. Could we now say that the control of our collective values lies with those who can afford it?

If we want to understand our culture and society we had better come to terms with the role and power of commercial images. Consumerism does not stress the value of a collective, sustainable future, and the prevailing values of the commercial system provide no incentives to develop bonds with future generations. Faced with growing ecological and social crises, and with advertising being the engine of an unsustainable and detrimental economic system, we have to manifest alternative values that will provide a humane, collective solution to these global crises. With so much of our culture focussed on consuming, to accept that you can't make a mark on the world—that your only pleasure is to say, 'I bought,' never to say, 'I made'—is a form of disempowerment that we need to reverse, quickly. We have to give them their shit back. And we are stronger together.

If we are to fundamentally alter this reality, we must begin from the understanding that we need to create—with rediscovered knowledge of our inherent abilities as creative humans, as cultural producers, and not as the consumers we have been told we are from day one.

Re-democratising Public Space

Every citizen should be guaranteed the right to choose where and when they want to access advertising information. This would protect citizens from unwanted influence, or simply allow them to rest from information overload. In the UK we see on average 4,000 brand impressions in the city, every day. In the face of this daily grind, the mental freedom of citizens must be ensured, especially in public space. We as citizens must be the guarantors of our own intellectual freedom, as well as helping to provide psychological security for everyone. We don't need anyone else to do it for us. We are the city. We are the streets.

This understanding of the public sphere forged the starting point of the Brandalism project. How could we, as creative people, help re-democratise public space and share alternative messages about the social and environmental injustices caused by consumerism? How can we break their monopoly over message and meaning in public space?

So the idea behind Brandalism was to create new ideas and perceptions of public space at a time when its democracy is highly contested. On reflection, the first foray fell short: even though the project received international acclaim, striking cords of discontent across the world, in the end it was two pissed-off people in a van intervening directly. What emerged in 2012 was clearly a temporary intervention, a starting point for further dialogue and development. It didn't offer a solution to the problem of who gets the chance, opportunity and right to share messages and create meaning within public space and culture.

When the Brandalism project returned in 2014, we were fundamentally concerned with movement. We asked ourselves the question: what can we as a global network of citizens do to challenge the cultural pessimism arising from the power of consumerism? How can we facilitate the reclamation of our right to the city and the revolution of everyday life?

Across the globe the chasm between citizens and political institutions is growing and privatization of our public spaces is increasing. Neoliberal values ensure that the logic of the market dictates social relations via commodification. In response to this, a networked culture, a 'movement of movements', centered around global solidarity—a worldwide activism spawned by globalisation and driven by citizens, new media technologies and the expansion of art's urban context—has emerged in the last decade.

Brandalism's most recent attacks on the spaces of corporate advertising form part of this emerging movement in an attempt to shift artists' and public attention to grassroots activism, as a means to combat the privatisation and corporate takeover of our cities, public spaces and culture. Public space is an arena in which no single authority should reign and multiple voices should be heard, so we started from a profoundly democratic conviction that the public sphere is a place for communication, a place where people can speak, establish their presence, and assert their rights. By raising issues via art works, viewers could interpret and debate: Brandalism therefore attempts to wrest authority away from the wealthy and return it to the public. The public sphere should not be an arena of market relations but rather one of discursive relations, a theater for debating and deliberating rather than for buying and selling.

Our project saw a global network of artists transferring art works to us to print. We voted with consensus as to whether each artwork should be included in what became the world's largest unauthorised outdoor exhibition. On home-made printing equipment, 400 art works were collectively screen-printed, each one an original. They were then installed by teams in 10 major UK cities (teams who are now a network of citizens as artists/activists). The art was revealed and existing when the works were installed and observed in situ: at once, privatized parts of public space became user-generated. Occupied spaces that are usually the preserve of powerful advertisers and political parties shared alternative messages, ideas and perceptions of what the public realm could be.

To build the movement, we now run workshops showing other people how to intervene and take back these spaces. And we are already planning the next project with others from around the world. We are working together to position the citizen as narrator, and in the telling reveal to others how the city can become a playground, stage and instrument for unsanctioned artworks and activist interventions. This is the terrain of arts activism that re-democratises message, meaning and cultural forms of communication dominated by global mass-media corporations. We want to force them out of public space permanently. They do not have the right to our cities, our head-space, our culture. We do. Reclaim your right to both the city and to your self.

'COMPANIES FILL THE SPACE NOW WITH THEIR HIDEOUS BRANDS, WAGING THE SAME FRENZIED BATTLE AS THE JUNGLE SPECIES IN ORDER TO APPROPRIATE THE PUBLIC SPACE AND ATTENTION WITH IMAGES AND WORDS, LIKE ANIMALS WITH THEIR SCREAMS AND PISS'

-MICHEL SERRES

#WeDoNotConsent
A Discussion on the Post-Police World

On July 8th 2014, we took over Committee Room 9—The Sir Robert Peel Room—of the Houses of Parliament, as part of John McDonnell MP's People's Parliament initiative. David Graeber was our chair, and was joined by a panel comprising Hannah Dee, co-founder of Defend the Right to Protest, Richard Garside, co-director of the Centre for Crime and Justice Studies and Fahim Alam, director of the film Riots Reframed.

It was a discussion and critique of police forces, and an attempt to answer the question: What would it take to move towards a world without them?

David Graeber

There is a deep assumption that if there were no police everyone would start killing each other, society would break down, this is the only thing that's holding us together. Well just 200 years ago there weren't police. If you had noisy neighbours you had to work it out directly, people did this sort of thing all the time without normally killing each other.

Hannah Dee

There's a fear, a concern in the establishment, that the way in which the various scandals have erupted over recent times (Hillsborough, Plebgate, the treatment of the Lawrence family and undercover cops and now we're looking at the police in the midst of the child-abuse scandal) is beginning to unravel the myth of the police as a kind of neutral force and that notion of Robert Peel, the founder of the modern police force in 1829, that the police are the public and the public are the police. I think very clearly it was a myth when the police were founded.

The politicians and the media collude with each other to defend each other's interests and I think that's one of the reasons why getting accountability is so hard.

In rural Madagascar at some point in the late 80s–early 90s, the police just left. I was there and people didn't just start killing each other, they mainly just carried on with their lives, much as they had before.

I think the most insightful thing I've heard about police is that the police are basically bureaucrats with guns or sticks, they're the point where the state's monopoly of force actually hits the dirt.

Richard Garside

It does strike me as a peculiarly lacking in any kind of historic imagination to think that the prisons will always be with us and the police will always be with us. Societies change and evolve and we can play our part in making that happen.

When someone pulls out their phone and calls their lawyer it's equivalent to pulling out a gun, they are evoking the armed power of the state and as soon as you have that armed power of the state you don't have to think what another person is thinking, you don't have to be reasonable.

That idea of the role of the police being to preserve disorder gets absolutely to the heart of what their function is in capitalist society, because it's a society based on perverse priorities. It's a society where a bottle of water is considered more valuable than the life of a black man from Tottenham. That was the lesson we drew from the shooting of Mark Duggan, the riots and how people that fought back against police brutality were treated, rounded up and sent to prison for up to years for stealing a bottle of water or taking a lick of ice cream. And I think the point about that is that the corruption, the violence, the racism that we see exposed in the scandals time and again in the police is that they're not isolated accidents, they flow precisely from the role that the police play as guards and defenders of this system.

If we're revolutionary then ultimately we can't beat them in a battle, especially right now, they're armed to the teeth, the only way to win is if those guys flying the helicopters or the ones with the water canons or the guns eventually throw them down and give up and decide they don't want to kill us. You know the big strategic question for us is how we get to the point where those guys have to make that decision. That gigantic instrument of repression is a huge machine, it's incredibly effective. But the lethal element is that it's made up of human beings and when you look at what actually happens when revolutionaries win is that systems like that crash because the people operating the system just can't take anymore and refuse to do it. Armies go home and refuse to fire.

You think about Ian Tomlinson, it should have been so easy. PC Harwood caught on camera pushing him over moments before he died and yet PC Harwood walks away a free man. I think one of the reasons for that—and when you read about the individual stories the same patterns emerge, that closing of ranks, the way the autopsies are ordered, the role of the coroner, the role of the media in getting the narrative of the police out and so on—is because to hold the police to account for violence would be to question their right to use force, their monopoly on force if you like. So there's a sense in which the police are in one sense too big to fail. But I think it's also the case that, in a society that is run in the interests of a very small minority, that actually you can't run things by force alone and this is why this idea of policing by consent is so very important to the establishment.

Fahim Alam

We cannot consider the police, without considering prison, without considering war, without considering colonialism, without considering terror, without considering poverty, without considering weapons, violence, and the rest of it.

Most of the time British society is generally fairly orderly, compared with many parts of the world, and the role of the police in maintaining that order is frankly minimal.

What is consent? Consent has to be free, and informed, in order for it to be meaningful. The consent that most of the public give to the police to police them, comes not from knowledge, but comes from the propagation of ideas which are counter to that knowledge.

Yes, I am a dreamer, I'm living in dreamland, I like to dream, I like to dream of a different society, I like to dream of a different possibility, I like to imagine that.

But that does not limit my ability to conceive of how we might deal with solutions, in the short term, within the current system.

The crucial question as always, and this is the case with the police and any other agency, is who sets the laws and in whose interests are they set?

If you look at how the modern police force was established it was in the wake of what was known as the Peterloo Massacre, huge mass demonstration against hunger and for the vote and the army wade in and dozens of people got killed and it caused an outcry, not just against the people that had been protesting, but it went right into the liberal elite and the establishment were worried about that so began to establish an idea about how you could build a police force that would maintain order but in a less obviously violent way, in a more sophisticated way. So they got rid of the cutlass and the gun and they were given the truncheon and the idea of the truncheon was using less than lethal force, that you could hit someone without killing them and use the other hand to catch them and put them through the courts so justice could be seen to be done. And alongside that this notion of the police as citizens in uniform, as they were called, there to protect us all, public safety, protect us from murder and theft and this kind of dark anarchy and chaos that society would descend into without them.

A lot of those units that were developed and funded in the wake of the miners' strike to spy on activists, trade unionists, environmentalists, families complaining over deaths in custody and so on, in order that the state could be aware of what was happening and it wouldn't be caught out again. A similar thing is the Public Order Act making it easier to criminalise protestors. If you think about how violent disorder and so on have been used to criminalise students and other protestors. That was something that was made easier in terms of how the public order act was developed, but also these powers given to the police that impose various conditions so our protests are no longer protests but managed events where we have to conform to these conditions in order for it to be a 'legitimate protest'.

But those in power have an army of people, an army of people to reinforce that power, they have guns, they have fortresses around their buildings, they have cameras, they have machines, they have fleets of cars and vans and helicopters, how can we defeat that?

So I think reframing the whole idea of what the police are and what they're about is really important if we are to understand the invasion of police in places they never existed before comes along with other things, like the marketisation and privatisation of education means we suddenly have cops on campus. All of these things, the market, bureaucracy, cops, violence, you know they all form a package, they come together and we need to take them all out at once.

An Anarchist Guide To...
Bookfairs

How did a few stalls of photocopied fanzines and a pool table in a broken down warehouse in Wapping go to being the all-singing, all-dancing London Anarchist Bookfair corporation in the space of a mere thirty years? Moreover, what is the point of travelling halfway across the country to fight your way through a hall full of crusties to buy some books you could have ordered over the internet? Why bother going to a meeting on the relevance of class struggle when you could have it out on some message board or on twitter?

Bookfairs are the mainstay of anarchist movements in dozens of countries all over the world. Even in countries where there is a substantial anarchist movement with a big presence in workplaces or on the streets, you'll still find people hanging up the red-and-black flags and setting out stalls.

The fact that anarchist bookfairs here have gone from strength to strength, getting bigger and more widespread regardless of the relative strength or level of activity of the anarchist movement in the UK, is undeniable—but does it tell us anything useful?

Anarchist bookfairs are the liveliest political events across the country, and this year there'll be four of them—Bristol, Manchester, Sheffield and Leeds & Bradford—in addition to the London anarchist bookfair. On top of this the London Radical Bookfair has now re-established itself. And straightaway it's growing too, this time with the anarchist publishers and distros as the most popular stalls.

We think bookfair success comes from two things: firstly the buzz of coming together with a huge number of people who are interested in the same thing; secondly, a desire to provide an open, welcoming introduction to the millions of people we know are sick of the political parties but still desperate to do something to take more control of their lives.

So anarchists and people interested in anarchist and anti-authoritarian ideas want to get off the internet, meet people face to face and do something to break down the barriers that keep us apart. This can be asking the publisher of a communist tract what it meant, or scrabbling through punk CDs at Active's stall instead of scrolling through some website. It's good to know that the fanzines, papers and posters are put out by real people, and you get to meet them in person at the Bookfair.

Putting on a Bookfair itself is obviously a lot of work, made possible by the fact that ultimately there are a lot of people in the anarchist movement who take responsibility, understand mutual aid and get stuck-in to get things done— publicising, getting stalls there, setting up meetings, helping out setting up or on the day. In the London collective we moan sometimes but in the end it works and serves as a real example of the possibilities of self organisation.

That said we do have to take decisions and plan things and, unsurprisingly, not everyone is happy all the time.

Take the question of getting in the big names. Instinctively, anarchists are against leader figures but we have invited people like John Pilger and Paul Mason. They might not be as anarchist as we'd like, and inevitably take up positions that most anarchists would get pissed-off about, but we aren't presenting them as anarchists. A lot more people come to these meetings, a broader group, who are sympathetic to left-wing ideas but may know little about anarchism or the anarchist movement. But once they pick up a copy of Freedom, Fighting to Win or Organise, their politics and their lives are going to be changed forever. Or that's the theory. The media portrayal of anarchism, backed up by political rivals and opponents, is either that of masked-up thugs espousing nihilism or of head-in-the-clouds hippy idealists.

And it has to be said: we sometimes play up to either or both. So getting a broad message about the possibilities of anti-authoritarian revolutionary class struggle, and getting that message out as widely as possible is key for bookfair organisers, along with everyone else who wants to make the event a success.

But if we can persuade people they want to come, we have to make sure they are able to—so access is important. Mobility, hearing and sight are things a lot of us take for granted, but bookfair organisers need to try and remove or reduce barriers to participation in the event (in the same way we should be doing with meetings and events and our movement generally). This is not just tokenism: some of the most militant and effective protest actions and organising in recent years has come from groups like DPAC (Disabled People Against Cuts). Proper childcare is another aspect of making the event and the movement accessible. If having kids means you drop out of anarchist politics or you have to leave the discussions and decisions to people with no kids, then we know where that's going to end up. So over the years the London Bookfair has moved on from the random crèches of the 80s to giving parents and carers more of a chance to get something out of the day.

Some critics might say that bookfairs should all be in squatted venues or social centres. Since the demise of the Autonomy Centre the London Bookfair has gone steadily upmarket, from the Tonbridge Club on Cromer Street to Conway Hall, until it became too big even for that. That was the last venue with any real connection to the movement. But without the security of a fixed venue we can't have the childcare, physical access or the ability to publicise the event widely to different groups of people.

Using a venue like Queen Mary's College in London, as we do now, needs money, and that has to come from the stall-holders and the groups putting on meetings, collections and donations (we also get sponsored a pound for every time someone says, 'I thought anarchists were against organisation').

But however grown up/well organised/sterile the organisation of the event has become, the ideas behind it—that you find in the fliers, the books and magazines, on stickers or in the meetings—still have the fight and passion.

Go to any of the meetings at the London Bookfair and they are packed with dissent and questioning: dissent from the current state of the world, dissent and frustration at our own failures, but also a confidence in our history and our future. Revolutionary ideas, ideas against the current, have to court controversy and provoke argument. And you will get that whether it's the Anarchist Federation or Sol Fed, institutions like Ian Bone and Martin Wright's address to the movement, or meetings on organising by sex workers. And this year a group of anarcha-feminists have taken on organising AFem2014, an anarcha-feminist conference the next day, so it'll be a full weekend of radical action.

Whatever happens at an anarchist bookfair, whatever big plans are set or packed meetings are held, whether it's a massive french brass band falling into a pile playing punk songs, a Chinese union activist setting out the real story behind your Iphone, or a heated debate on austerity and the crisis, people have come together. And those people know that there is a whole bunch of other people that want a better world and are prepared to do something to make it happen.

TXT: NIALL MCDEVITT

LABOURGEOIS (arbeit macht fries)

1.

Labour to be free. Labour, children! Labour, adults!
And the freedoms will descend like a white christmas
But there is too much work to do for the generations
Of workers to be able to do it, and the pay is next to
Useless. There is less and less money to pay workers,
Rightly or wrongly. So we'll pay some of us. We'll pay
Godot but not the tramps. It's tricky. No one wants to pay
Existing wages to existing employees. Non-existence
Opens its factory gates and the workers flood in, angrily
Insisting on better conditions. These too are non-existent
So the unemployed dead are balloting for strike action.

2.

Labour is no longer a party in the political sense but an
After-party in the showbusiness sense. Showbusiness and
Business are now the exact same thing. Businessmen are
Orangemen are matchstalkmen are supermen are madmen are
Unionmen are funnymen are men's men. Business is the new
Rock n'roll. The Sex Pistols have signed Richard Branson. They've
Granted him custody of the CDs. The company's called Whore.
Everything is matesy-matesy 'twixt Branson and Whore
Or maybe not. Maybe it's a biblical illusion, and Branson
Is really the devil? He looks like Mr. 666. He smiles. He
Simpers like Satan. But maybe he's God or England or Elvis?

3.

Lavatories have to be cleaned. We need our untouchables
And thankfully the majority of us are touched enough to
Be willing and able to clean lavatories. Okay, the work is an
Ordeal but we know our children will one day inherit it
Unless they're lucky enough to become pro-footballers
Running around chasing balls. But they won't be.
Good luck is also a commodity and the 'opera prices' are a tad
Exclusive. I can't live on what I find on the ground anymore.
Our deal has changed, or we've seen through it. A human being
Is no longer a human being. We are not hands, but digits
Signing on as Poundland neophytes. We're toys (are us)...

4.

Love work. Live for your work. It is the ultimate reality
And can lead in the long run to even more ultimate realities,
Boring us to death – that cigarette break before the afterlife –
Or bringing us back to life... from zero-hours to eternity.
Unions are bad for morale. Hate unions. Do not pay union
Rates. You cannot afford them in these times of dearth...
God knows, you can't afford the busfare to the foodbank!
Everything is a test. This is a film or a Playstation game
Or a reality show. But it is not you or me or us or them
Insistently knocking on the door. 'Hi! We're from Resolve Call.'
Shit. I see the riches. I'm invisible. Hand me that tin-opener

TXT: DECCA MULDOWNEY

Witness this Day My Hand

and I remember
ice between my teeth
ice under our feet

we were strung out
over street corners
padded sleeves with
abandoned cardboard
bicycle helmet bandana
and yes after a while
it did feel like
going into battle

sleeping on rough carpet floor
of occupied classrooms
long meetings in a drafty
hallway raised hands soy milk
dream lightly under watch of
security guards and neon bars

secret caucus in a travelodge
hotel in central london
take out your sim card and
leave it in the bathroom sink
how many people can you bring
to the brink to the edge of the
march and push beyond?

it's hard to beat that feeling beating
back the cops and breaking kettle
walls with nothing but our hands
it's hard to beat the black bloc
but I've seen them beaten down
huddled in foetal knees drawn up
on grey cracked pavement stone
cops raining down blows

banners draped down multi story
arts school build costumes book blocs
face off with theatre of the oppressed
against pepper spray mad plainclothes
charging wild horses in uniform into
crowds of students with essay deadlines
that's what they call priorities

spent five hours hemmed in on westminster
bridge burnt placards and a level homework
kids get wild eyes looking down into thames
flow far from soft into these restless hearts
hard to find a song we all know
goddamn those words are illusive

downtime in squatted social centres
collecting witness statement marks
of trained dog teeth on loose elbow
first aid kit hopeless for what could
bleed internally what could follow us
through rooms for our whole lives

some battles you don't win or lose
they just fight you

WE'VE HAD MANY UPS AND DOWNS AND U-TURNS IN THE TEN YEARS WE'VE BEEN TOGETHER

JUST LIKE ANY-BODY ELSE

AUNTY

I FIRST MET MY OWNER IN 'CLINTON CARDS' IN ASHFORD.

MY OWNER WAS LIVING IN A RESIDENTIAL CARE HOME-'SPRINGS COMMUNI

I AM OFTEN REFERRED TO AS MALE-WHICH IS ABSURD...

I ALSO GET MISTAKEN FOR A BLOW FISH AMONGST OTHER THINGS

WHEN I TALK THEY GET CONFUSED AND THINK IT'S MY OWNER...

IT'S NOT DIFFICULT TO UNDERSTAND -

I AM **DEL**, HER PIGGIE FRIEND!!!

SHE IS MY OWNER - TILLEY

SHE OWNS ME BUT DOES NOT SPEAK FOR ME

WE LEFT 'SPRINGS COMMUNITY' SIX YEARS AGO. IT WASN'T EASY.

LIFE CAN BE STRESSFUL FOR A PIGGIE LIKE ME...

SOMETIMES· OUR INDEPENDENCE COMES WITH A HIGH PRICE,

GASP

WE LIVE TOGETHER IN A FLAT THAT'S INDEPENDENT

THE TROUBLE IS, MY OWNER NEEDS SOME SUPPORT STILL

?   ?

THIS IS HARD TO COME BY THESE DA—

RING RING

NOV—DEC

2014

ISSUE____ 8

DEBT WORRIES?

Get ▆ bank or payday moneylender▎ problems off your mind in one easy step:

DON'T PAY

the bast&rds. *Don't they have enough already?*

Citizen's Income
Freedom From Fear

Once, many years ago, I found myself absolutely penniless, flat broke, in Cairo.

It was in the days after cash machines appeared, so I'd expected to just be able to draw out the money I needed to travel as I went along. It was even after the days that email existed, so I could make frantic pleas—if not necessarily expecting a response—to the origins of the difficulties.

But it was before Skype and cheap international calls, so attempts to sort it out required long, expensive calls from phone boxes on the cacophonous streets—chewing into my fast-diminishing supply of cash. I remember the panic.

Yet I also understand that it was nothing like the panic experienced by a man who the volunteers at a foodbank I've visited told me about. I won't say where, to avoid any risk of identifying—in the past two years as Green Party leader I've visited lots of food banks, representing, as they do, one of Britain's fastest-growing 'industries'.

He was the single father of two children and, through absolutely no fault of his own, he hadn't attended an interview at the Job Centre because the text about the interview had been sent to the wrong number—he'd gone to get the money to buy food and found there was nothing in his account.

He'd been to the Job Centre, they'd recognised he wasn't at fault, and promised him his money in full 'in a couple of weeks'. And he'd been left with two children, and empty cupboards. The staff particularly remembered him because they were really worried about the state he was in.

The story is very different to mine because no one depended on me; only I was going to suffer as I sorted the problem out. And it was very different because in my relatively privileged life such circumstances have been rare, and I've always been confident that they wouldn't last long—they were temporary hiccups, not a permanent state of being, a permanent state of fear.

In today's Britain, living in that permanent state of fear, never knowing from week to week if you'll be able to buy food or have to rely on charity, not knowing if a stuff-up in your housing benefit will leave you homeless, or a sanction for something that you couldn't possibly have known about leave you in a state of total penury, is a reality for more and more people.

Benefit sanctions are being applied harshly, unreasonably, savagely. It's hard to blame the staff: they're under immense pressure—not 'targets', we're told, but 'benchmarks' to deal with a certain number of their 'clients' each week.

Add to that the untender mercies of Atos and the Work Capability Assessment that sees huge numbers of ill and disabled people told they're 'fit to work' when they're clearly nothing like that.

Then there's the asylum seekers who clearly are refugees, straightforward cases under the Geneva Convention, that are turned away, left with no recourse to public funds, and threatened with deportation to torture or worse. 'No recourse to public funds' means, if you're lucky, finding a refuge with an organisation like the wonderful Southampton and Winchester Visitors Group, or if you're not, sleeping on the streets, or in conditions of extreme exploitation.

This is neo-liberalism 21st-century style, the final outcome of 35 years of Thatcherite ideology dominating our political debate. The welfare safety-net has been rent asunder, and increasing numbers fear they could be next to fall through. For the rightwing media and far too many politicians, the 'undeserving poor' are back, and if they don't quite say 'workhouse', they're thinking it, and delivering it with mindless, pointless workfare jobs like stacking shelves in Poundland—while the workers who might have had that paid work languish.

That's no doubt one reason why the idea of a basic or citizen's income is gaining increasing traction. The idea that once you've been accepted as a member of a society—i.e. been born, or moved in—you'll get a basic payment every week, enough to meet your essential needs, would, a couple of decades ago, have appeared largely unnecessary. Now it looks potentially revolutionary.

It offers a new prospect: freedom from fear, from the worry of not being able to put food on the table, or catch a bus to where you need to go.

And it's an idea that's found purchase in some seemingly unlikely places. Not-exactly-radical Switzerland is having a citizen-initiated referendum on it next year. There's plans for a second European Citizen's Initiative on it, proposing an EU-wide basic income. And I find that when I go around the country more and more groups are debating it.

It's enough to send a conventional economist into a spin. One problem for them is that it's hard to model how individuals would behave when the necessity of taking a truly horrible, soul-destroying job (like those call centres where your loo break is timed) was taken away (although the rest of us could imagine the pleasure of not having to deal with such call centres). And it's hard to model what would happen to wages (I often suggest that a sewer-worker might have to be paid more than a banker, and get lots of 'too rights'). Maybe lots of people would decide to really explore their vocation as a poet. A bit tough on their loyal friends who have to listen to the work in progress perhaps, but people spending time writing bad (and possibly also some good) poetry has many positives—you don't get output much lower in carbon emissions for one thing.

And there's the huge practical outcome of ending benefit traps. No sudden disappearance of housing ben-efits and JSA, or resulting to hideous payday-lenders to bridge income gaps. If you earn a reasonable amount you'll simply be paying the basic income back in tax, and there's no immense, hopelessly complicated computer system as with Iain Duncan Smith's Universal Credit.

And with a foundation of security, a comfortable cushion at the bottom of the financial ladder, there'll be less need to fear the bottom rungs of the income ladder, less need for the kind of stressful scrambling whose damage The Spirit Level charted so well. For women, in particular, the advantages are obvious. No soul-destroying hoops to jump through for carers' benefit, no questions of frozen or removed child benefit—simple security that's there if you decide to spend time on unpaid but hugely important employment of child or elder care.

Basic income has been Green Party policy for many years—the foundation of security seen as essential to the transition to a society in which we live within the physical limits of our one planet. Now we, and many others, are talking about it more and more—and I know members who've joined the party on the basis of this one policy.

We need to transform our economy—rein back our financial sector to a much smaller, less risky shape, bring manufacturing and food production back to Britain, work out how to have a decent standard of living for all within the environmental limits of one planet. Basic income won't achieve all, or even a lot of that, but it's a foundation that could make much of it possible.

Voices From the Edge
Change vs. Charity

It's increasingly difficult to find people who disagree with the Edge Fund's view that the dominant financial and political systems reinforce existing power and privilege, and prioritise economic growth whatever the human and environmental cost. Mainstream philanthropists and large charities, despite their merits, maintain their existence within this framework and, thus, are unlikely to create meaningful systemic change. So when I first heard of the Edge Fund in early 2013 from a fellow grassroots activist, my interest was immediately piqued. I knew I wanted to join as a member. I felt, and my experience with Edge has confirmed this, that the fund, because of its radical, democratic and participatory nature, is a groundbreaking, paradigm-shifting political project.

Edge is radical because Edge exists to support those very individuals and groups that swim against the tide and fundamentally challenge the status quo. Most of these groups are unconstituted and silently deemed 'unfundable' by grant-giving bodies. While providing support services (for example, medical, counselling, job advice and so on) to marginalised communities can be crucial in the short-term, Edge recognises that simply giving while not empowering perversely reinforces oppressive structures. Edge exists to create change not to give charity.

Edge is democratic because Edge will not fund groups that are not representative of the community the applicants are claiming to speak on behalf of. The rationale behind this thinking is twofold. How can those not affected possibly know what it takes to create systemic change? And it is hugely disempowering for those who are directly oppressed by existing structures to not be in control of their own destiny.

The one exception to this rule is that if the project is fundamentally challenging systemic oppression, the application is accepted. For example, environmental groups in the UK usually, but not always, fall into this category as most of environmental and human destruction happens in localities outside the UK. However, the solidarity efforts of these groups are key to the struggles of communities elsewhere.

Edge is also democratic in the makeup of its membership. The fund actively seeks to recruit individuals who are not from privileged backgrounds. Since every member gets an equal say, Edge hopes that the more diverse the membership the less bias there will be towards funding any single issue. Criteria for joining is simple: you believe in Edge's values.

Edge is participatory because each and every member is given the opportunity to have a voice in deciding which groups are funded. Extent of participation is entirely up to the individual—members can score as many or as few applications as they want. Edge is run by working groups— Facilitating Group, Communications Group and so on—to which all members are invited to join. Edge is not a rich individual, a board of trustees or a senior management team. Edge is its membership.

Although Edge provides only small amounts—ranging from £500 to £5,000—the funding can be crucial. Usually applicants ask for funding to cover meeting and project expenses such as room hire, equipment hire, travel, printing and other admin costs. Before I became an Edge member, I did not realise how much of a life support such small amounts of money can be to radical groups.

Edge has existed since 2012 and is currently in its fourth funding round. Amongst others, Edge has funded a mobile phone app that informs people of their legal rights and records experiences and officer IDs when their rights have been violated (Stop and Search Mobile App), legal observers (Green and Black Cross), physical spaces that enable groups to organise and build infrastructure (The Common House, Next to Nowhere), communities empowering themselves by ensuring their sisters and brothers are treated with dignity (Why Refugee Women, London Coalition Against Poverty, Lesbian Immigration Support Group, Disabled People Against Cuts), groups using creative expression as a tool to inform, inspire and disrupt (Space Hijackers, CoResist), groups monitoring and recording environmental injustice so that silenced voices do not disappear unheard (Coal Action Network, Foil Vedanta) and many many more. The list is long and humbling.

Edge, of course, is not perfect. Our membership remains predominantly white, and underrepresented by young people, those who live outside London, and those who are from migrant backgrounds, Black, Gypsy, Traveller and Roma communities. Much work needs to be done to break down power and privilege structures. While every member is Edge, many members feel ill-equipped to represent Edge publicly. We also have to turn down a majority of applicants, reiterating that raising funds is a constant struggle. Much more work needs to be done to facilitate the sharing of knowledge within the membership and between applicants. Edge would like to support applicants in non-monetary ways, and this is not easy. While Edge has attracted the curiosity of the more progressive mainstream grant-giving bodies (for example, the Tudor Trust and Joseph Rowntree Charitable Trust), Edge has not yet changed the behaviour of the larger bodies. Edge recognises its shortcomings and work is underway by various working-groups to address many of these issues.

Despite the long road Edge has yet to travel, I remain cheerful. Perhaps I am naive or perhaps the enormous energy, commitment, creativity and resilience of the groups that I have come in contact with because of Edge is contagious. My experience tells me that Edge is more than a funding body. It is a political project that brings together a network of diverse groups and individuals all working to create another world where voices from the edge don't go unheard.

TXT: ROBBY WRONGFOOT

Frack Off
Reclaim the Power

It's 5am on a cold December morning and a 56-foot wind turbine blade has just been assembled across the entrance to a fracking site at Barton Moss, Salford, blocking access for the rest of the morning. As dawn breaks and the assembly team scarpers back across the fields from whence they came, the nearby Protectors' Camp awakes to find this sleek large lump, tied with a red ribbon to mark the Christmas season. The group, acting under the name of No Dash for Gas, had met at the Reclaim the Power camp in Balcombe, Sussex in August 2013. Later in the morning, Salford residents and a woman in a Santa's outfit gather for selfies in front of the turbine—and the ongoing battle for the UK's energy future rages in the media.

Over the last three years, resistance to unconventional gas extractions has steadily been growing, with increasing effectiveness. Research by the University of Nottingham shows a continuing decline in public support for fracking, falling from 54% in September 2013 to 49.7% in May 2014. There are now 160 anti-fracking community groups in the UK and Ireland listed on the national Frack Off website. Where drilling rigs have been set up, these residents' groups have combined effectively with frontline direct action 'Protector Camps' (squatted roadside protest camps), whose lineage partly goes back to the Occupy movement.

The frontline is very literal at these sites, with rows of protesters linked arm-in-arm walking in front of trucks carrying fracking equipment. Violent police repression has been extensive—as have the acquittals for many of the trumped-up charges. Together with strategic legal pressure from major NGOs, this resistance needs to be celebrated for having already dealt a hefty blow to the industry before it has been allowed to gain a foothold. As one observer at a shale-industry conference noted: 'Every truck that is blockaded, every planning application that is mired in bureaucracy: it's killing the industry.'

Reclaim the Power, with its roots (and tent pegs) in the Climate Camp movement, has played a part in this resistance. It currently exists as a loose network, drawn from different corners of the UK (mostly cities), which has organized two mass-action camps to skill-up new people in direct action. It's a different demographic from those who regularly attend or live on Protector Camps—but there is significant overlap. Drawing the links between environmental destruction, corporate control and economic austerity, Reclaim the Power also aims to reassert a climate justice narrative into the anti-fracking debate, especially given the climate denialism that is quietly nestled amongst other conspiracy theories at some Protector Camps.

In August 2013, Reclaim the Power held the first camp in Balcombe. In response, Cuadrilla were forced to stop drilling for six days. Successfully disrupting the industry provided a motivation, despite the huge workload involved, to hold another camp in August the following year. Since a key aim of the network is to create uncertainty for the industry, Reclaim the Power announced that a camp would be held in August 2014 but chose not to disclose the location until much later. Who would be targeted? IGas in the Midlands? Cuadrilla in Lancashire? Rathlin in Hull? Invitations were received from lots of different communities fighting fracking.

Eventually, a decision was taken at openly advertised gatherings to hold the camp in Fylde near Blackpool, where Cuadrilla (again) had submitted two applications to drill, this time for the production of shale gas rather than just exploration. As the only area to be fracked in the country in 2010, community opposition in Lancashire has grown from strength to strength. Seventeen local groups signed an open letter welcoming the decision to locate the camp in

Blackpool. Better still, a women-led group of Lancashire residents, 'Operation Mothers and Grandmas' (#OMG) dressed
in yellow headscarves and tabards, took and held the field
where Reclaim the Power would take place one week before
the start of the camp. The invitation from this community to
host Reclaim the Power could not have been more explicit.

Planning effective mass actions using open decision-making processes (meaning anyone can attend) has always been
difficult to pull off. When the collective decision is made, the
target is also announced, usually giving police and security
ample time to prepare in advance.

Many mass actions over the last decade in the environmental movement have followed this process including the
Gleneagles G8 Counter-Summit action, and Drax, Heathrow
and Kingsnorth Climate Camps. Despite open decision-making processes being easy to infiltrate, the actions have still
been successful. The British Airport Authority, for example,
were forced to abandon their offices at Heathrow for a day
in 2007 when a meeting of over 300 people collectively
decided to target the company's HQ in a pre-announced day
of action. Laying siege to a particular piece of infrastructure
or a summit shows the movement's strength and unwilling-
ness to comply with prescribed protest methods, as well as
stirring up wider public support. Alternatively, unannounced
actions retain the element of surprise, catching police and
security services off-guard.

Reclaim the Power used an intensive 'monster-match-
speed-dating' process to facilitate large numbers of new people planning and taking action together in a short period of
time. The recipe ran as follows: people attending were asked
to fill out paper forms indicating the extent to which they
were willing to be arrested, their experience, mobility levels
and what type of action they're up for. 'Getting over fences',
'dressing for the office' and 'staying invisible' were amongst
the options. These paper forms were then processed by a
trusted crew, who teamed people up to ensure each group
had a good mix of experience and arrestability. Once teams

had formed, they each received a unique mission. Some of these missions had been researched in advance, other targets had been chosen on short notice.

The results in Blackpool were impressive. The camp successfully facilitated hundreds of people arriving on Thursday, attending workshops on Friday and Saturday, and marching along Blackpool promenade en masse on Sunday—and still found time to plan thirteen direct actions that took place on Monday. The actions included blockades of a drilling site at Crawberry Hill near Hull, iGas headquarters, DEFRA offices as well as a new extreme-energy research lab at Swansea University. The regional headquarters of Cuadrilla were also occupied, corrupt councilors and PR companies visited, a banner dropped above the Manchester Ship Canal, plus street theatre actions and a die-in at the local HSBC branch (the frackers' bank) for good measure. Surprisingly, not one arrest was made for any of the actions, which took place in several different police constabularies. We can only speculate on the reasons for this no-arrests-decision by Her Majesty's Plod.

The success or not of a political project can often be measured by the energy it generates amongst those who take part. Direct action, done well, can be creative, fun and empowering for its participants and can generate momentum and enthusiasm for others. In this regard, the immediate outlook looks good for the Reclaim the Power network, with regional follow-up meetings taking place in Leeds, Bristol, Edinburgh, Lancaster, Oxford and London, deepening links with trade unions as well as follow-up actions at the People's Climate March. Direct-action campaigns can generate an unpredictability for corporate operations and their PR strategies, and over time can halt entire industries.

In fighting what we're against, we also have the opportunity to communicate what we're for. On the final days of the Reclaim the Power camp, the plenary sessions endorsed Fuel Poverty Action's 'Energy Bill of Rights', calling for a clean, fair and affordable energy system. A wind-turbine blade across a fracking site can articulate this symbolically—but emerging community renewable initiatives such as 'Re:Power Balcombe' show how extreme-energy industries could be ditched in favour of a cleaner, safer, equitable future. The anti-fracking movement is forcing these discussions onto the table, and in doing so, radicalising a new generation of activists.

FRACK OFF

Work

A View From 100 Years Hence

Imagining the future and then looking back at the recent past from that place can create a clearer image of where we are today. Today, more of us are working at older and older ages. Usually elderly people would rather not undertake the mundane jobs that increasingly they have to apply for. Suicide rates among the elderly are highest in those towns and cities of Britain where more of the elderly are in paid work after age 65. If current trends continue then more of us will live to work as employees into our old age in the future and fewer and fewer of us will be happy with the work we are offered.

Only a few very affluent people are likely to have pensions large enough to enable them to avoid paid employment in part of their old age. More and more of today's young adults have no pension provision other than the state pension. Of any age group the greatest wealth inequalities of all are found between groups of pensioners. By pensionable age people have either amassed very little wealth or have great savings including a pension, and own valuable property. Among the affluent only the very rich have no pension. It is a form of insurance they do not need.

As the riches of the best-off 1% of people grow and grow, more jobs in future will be focussed on serving their needs. Today that small group secure about 15% of all income in Britain, about 10% after income tax is taken. If top income tax rates in the future are to fall, as they have mostly fallen over current lifetimes, then there will be fewer jobs provided by the state and more people directly employed by the very richest minority. More cleaners, cooks, nannies, gardeners, personal accountants, housekeepers, drivers, personal shoppers, trainers and more employed in jobs that currently don't exist but which will be created to pander for new tastes and fashions among those who believe they are most worth it.

In the future people near the very top may well work longer hours than they do today. Those at the very top can choose their hours, but those just beneath them cannot. The need to beat the morning commute may lead to greater numbers starting paid work earlier and earlier in the morning. Even if this is not through physically being at the office, scanning emails and reminders every waking hour can easily turn what used to be an eight-hour working day into something much longer. In Britain in 2014, millions in part-time employment said they would prefer to have a full-time job, yet we had never collectively worked as many paid hours. Part-time work simply did not pay enough.

People don't really want to work longer and longer hours. They are given little choice as hourly wage rates fall and the cost of living rises. In areas where the jobs are better paid the cost of living rises faster than salaries. You can, if paid enough, live a long way out, work long hours and get a nanny or two in to cover for never being home before the children go to bed. But to make all the finances work you have to ensure you do not pay the nannies too much. High paid and low paid jobs in the future will increase in number. There will be fewer 'average' occupations.

In 2014 more people than ever before believed they were average while fewer than ever were. At first the government subsidized mass childcare to ensure that having small children to look after was not an excuse against taking paid employment. They reduced benefit levels year on year to make the punishment for not working for someone else a more grinding poverty than each year before. Numerous sanctions were imposed, cutting all welfare benefits for a time if a 'claimant'—as people came to be called—transgressed and missed a meeting.

Out of desperation more people took jobs with zero-hours

contracts, or started their own business. The Royal Society of Arts (and Commerce) reported that people who started their own business were less well paid but happier than those with direct employers. They could have put it the other way round and said that for most employees the experience of having a boss was so bad that despite the slightly greater job security they were more miserable than self-employed taxi drivers.

Taxi drivers were a case in point. More and more people took to driving around in their cars, having paid for taxi plates and a radio, looking for someone who wanted a lift. As more people became drivers all the drivers had to drive for longer and longer each day to pick up the same number of fares. They became more tired, more irritable, less safe drivers, but the overall numbers in employment rose. When bus subsidies were removed more people without cars had to use taxis. Fewer buses meant more private sector employment, more cars, more congestion and more pollution. However, more employment is not necessarily better employment. Few taxi drivers talk of the great enjoyment they got from ferrying passengers along the clogged roads.

As the state was pulled out of areas of subsidizing areas like transport, education and health care, wages in each area fell. People moved from job to job more often than they had in the past. Those taxi drivers who could no longer endure 14 or 15 hour days gave up when they could find another job, often caring for the elderly, the mentally ill or young children. Driving a taxi had only required a driving license. Many of these jobs did not require any qualifications or much experience. You needed qualifications to be promoted but not to do the basic job.

There were also more and more guest workers to carry out the menial work. A very economically unequal country tends to generate a lot of opportunities for poorer migrants. Even by 2014 most young women in England by age 19 were going to university to try to avoid having to take menial work later in life. Childcare had become menial work. A qualifications bonanza bloomed. But that first degree would not guarantee you good employment, you needed a post-graduate qualification, and an internship you paid for the privilege of undertaking, or an apprenticeship where you were paid far less than the minimum wage.

Of course many people in 2014 enjoyed their work. Many had worked in the same institution for some time and had got good at what they did. Their customers, colleagues, patients, claimants, fares and students got to know them. It wasn't all about making money and the bottom-line. But such relationships became seen as quaint in time. And younger employees were not taken on with the idea of keeping them on for that long. The young knew that and so jumped from firm to firm almost as fast as they were pushed. The idea of having any loyalty to an enterprise, a school, a hairdressing business, a garage, a construction plant or a building firm went out of fashion.

As wealth polarised further, those who wanted to start their own business increasingly had to borrow to do so. Algorithms, not people, ran banks. At any sign of default they quickly moved to seize the assets of the business, the home that had been mortgaged to finance it. Even before the financial crash of 2008 some 99% of business newly registered to pay VAT folded within ten years. Otherwise the UK would have been awash with antique shops and other ventures that so many people had dreamt so long about starting up. As many firms have to die as are born. The more that are born the more that must die.

Big corporations grew larger but almost all also eventually folded. The majority of the largest firms in the UK in 2014 had not existed a hundred years earlier, almost all were gone a hundred years later, and yet they exuded an air of permanence. Young graduates fought to get places in their 'starter streams'—greedy for the high salaries promised later, desperate for some security and unaware that every year their intake would be decimated. Within eight years less than half those who started with such fanfare were still employed, just a seventh of all those selected as being so promising managed twenty years in the firm. But it had to be that way, almost every firm in London employed hundreds of people aged below 35, and just a few dozen aged over 40. Those who didn't make the grade could drive taxis, manage guest-worker cleaners or stack shelves in their non-retirement.

No one should have been surprised. All that had happened was a continuation of what had already been in play by 2014. Every year (for a hundred years) the trends continued onwards with only the occasional blip. By 2114 most people knew they were poor and insecure, more were working longer for less than their parents or grandparents had, but a tiny few—now much less than 1%—were taking more than the best-off ever had. They told those below them that if only they, or their parents, or grandparents or great-grandparents had tried hard enough—had been good enough—they too would have got what they deserved. And in a way they were right. If we'd all just tried harder in 2014 all of this could have been different. But we'd already been taught to worry about just ourselves.

Materialism, Old and New

No Gods? No Matter

Materialism appears today in four main versions: Reductionist 'vulgar' materialism (cognitivism, neo-Darwinism); The new wave of atheism that aggressively denounces religion (Hitchens, Dawkins, et al.); Whatever remains of 'discursive materialism' (Foucauldian analyses of discursive material practices); Deleuzian 'new materialism'. Consequently, we should not be afraid to look for true materialism in what cannot but appear as (a return to German) idealism—or, as Frank Ruda put it, apropos Alain Badiou, true materialism is a 'materialism without materialism' in which substantial 'matter' disappears in a network of purely formal/ideal relations.

This paradox is grounded in the fact that, today, it is idealism that emphasizes our bodily finitude and endeavors to demonstrate how this very finitude opens up the abyss of a transcendent divine Otherness beyond our reach (no wonder that the most spiritual of twentieth-century film-makers, Tarkovsky, is simultaneously the one who was most obsessed with the impenetrable humid inertia of earth), while scientific materialists keep alive the techno-utopian dream of immortality, of getting rid of our bodily constraints. Along these lines, Jean-Michel Besnier has drawn attention to the fact that contemporary scientific naturalism seems to revive the most radical idealist program of Fichte and Hegel: the idea that reason can make nature totally transparent. Does not the biogenetic goal of reproducing humans scientifically through biogenetic procedures turn humanity into a self-made entity, thereby realizing Fichte's speculative notion of a self-positing I? Today's ultimate 'infinite judgment' (coincidence of opposites) thus seems to be: absolute idealism is radical naturalist reductionism.

This orientation marks a fourth stage in the development of anti-humanism: neither theocentric anti-humanism (on account of which US religious fundamentalists treat the term 'humanism' as synonymous with secular culture), nor the French 'theoretical anti-humanism' that accompanied the structuralist revolution in the 1960s (Althusser, Foucault, Lacan), nor the 'deep-ecological' reduction of humanity to just one of the many animal species on Earth, but the one which has upset the balance of life on the planet through its hubris, and is now justifiably facing the revenge of Mother Earth.

However, even this fourth stage is not without a history. In the first decade of the Soviet Union, so-called 'bio-cosmism' enjoyed an extraordinary popularity—as a strange combination of vulgar materialism and Gnostic spirituality that formed the occult shadow-ideology, or obscene secret teaching, of Soviet Marxism. It is as if, today, 'bio-cosmism' is reemerging in a new wave of 'post-human' thought. The spectacular development of biogenetics (cloning, direct DNA interventions, etc.) is gradually dissolving the frontiers between humans and animals on the one side and between humans and machines on the other, giving rise to the idea that we are on the threshold of a new form of Intelligence, a 'more-than-human' singularity in which mind will no longer be subject to bodily constraints, including those of sexual reproduction.

Out of this prospect a weird shame has emerged: a shame about our biological limitations, our mortality, the ridiculous way in which we reproduce ourselves—what Günther Anders has called 'Promethean shame'—ultimately simply the shame that 'we were born and not manufactured.' Nietzsche's idea that we are the 'last men' laying the ground for our own extinction and the arrival of a new Over-Man is thereby given a scientific-technological twist. However, we should not reduce this 'post-human' stance to the paradigmatically modern belief in the possibility of total technological domination over nature—what we are witnessing today is an exemplary dialectical reversal: the slogan of today's 'post-human' sciences is no longer domination but surprise (contingent, non-planned emergence).

Should we see an unexpected sign of hope in this reemergence of surprise at the very heart of the most radical naturalism? Or should we look for a way to overcome the impasses of cognitivist radical naturalism in Deleuzian 'New Materialism,' whose main representative is Jane Bennett with her notion of 'vibrant matter'?

Fredric Jameson was correct to claim that Deleuzianism is today the predominant form of idealism: as did Deleuze, New Materialism relies on the implicit equation: matter = life = stream of agential self-awareness—no wonder New Materialism is often characterized as 'weak panpsychism' or 'terrestrial animism'. When New Materialists oppose the reduction of matter to a passive mixture of mechanical parts, they are, of course, asserting not an old-fashioned teleology but an aleatory dynamic immanent to matter: 'emerging properties' arise out of unpredictable encounters between multiple kinds of actants (to use Bruno Latour's term), and the agency for any particular act is distributed across a variety of kinds of bodies.

Agency thereby becomes a social phenomenon, where the limits of sociality are expanded to include all material bodies participating in the relevant assemblage.

For example, an ecological public is a group of bodies, some human, most not, that are subjected to harm, defined as a diminished capacity for action. The ethical implication of such a stance is that we should recognize our entanglement within larger assemblages: we should become more sensitive to the demands of these publics and the reformulated sense of self-interest that calls upon us to respond to their plight. Materiality, usually conceived as inert substance, should be rethought as a plethora of things that form assemblages of human and non-human actors—humans are but one force in a potentially unbounded network of forces.

What vibrates in vibrant matter is its immanent life force or its soul (in the precise Aristotelian sense of the active principle immanent to matter), not subjectivity. New Materialism thus refuses the radical divide matter/life and life/thought—selves or multiple agents are everywhere in different guises. A basic ambiguity nonetheless persists here: are these vital qualities of material bodies the result of our (the human observer's) 'benign anthropomorphism', so that the vitality of matter means that 'everything is, in a sense, alive', or are we effectively dealing with a strong ontological claim asserting a kind of spiritualism without gods, with a way of restoring sacredness to worldliness? If 'a careful course of anthropomorphism' can help reveal the vitality of material bodies, it is not clear whether that vitality is a result of our perception being animistic or of an actual asubjective vital power—an ambiguity which is deeply Kantian.

New Materialism takes the step back into (what can only appear to us moderns as) premodern naivety, covering up the gap that defines modernity and reasserting the purposeful vitality of nature: 'a careful course of anthropomorphization can help reveal that vitality, even though it resists full translation and exceeds my comprehensive grasp'. Note the uncertainty of this statement: Bennett is not simply filling in the gap, she remains modern enough to register the naivety of her gesture, admitting that the notion of the vitality of nature is beyond our comprehension, that we are moving into an obscure area.

The move that defines New Materialism should be opposed to the properly Hegelian dialectical-materialist overcoming of the transcendental dimension or the gap that separates subject from object: New Materialism covers up this gap, reinscribing subjective agency into natural reality as its immanent agential principle, while dialectical materialism transposes back into nature not subjectivity as such but the very gap that separates subjectivity from objective reality.

If, then, New Materialism can still be considered a variant of materialism, it is materialist in the sense in which Tolkien's

Middle-earth is materialist: as an enchanted world full of magical forces, good and evil spirits etc., but strangely without gods—there are no transcendent divine entities in Tolkien's universe, all magic is immanent to matter, as a spiritual power that dwells in our terrestrial world. However, we should strictly distinguish the New Age topic of a deeper spiritual interconnection and unity of the universe from the materialist topic of a possible encounter with an inhuman Other with whom some kind of communication could be possible. Such an encounter would be extremely traumatic, since we would have to confront a subjectivized Other with whom no subjective identification is possible, it having no common measure with 'being human.' Such an encounter is not an encounter with a deficient mode of an Other Subject, but an encounter with an Other at its purest, with the abyss of Otherness not covered up or facilitated by imaginary identifications which make the Other someone 'like us,' someone we can emphatically 'understand.'

It's 1987. A hurricane and stock market crash bring the world of finance capital, corrupt cops, cocaine and a single mum in collision.

Futures

Futures

In retrospect it seems absurd to have been angry enough at the beginning of the 1970s to have wound up doing a 10-year jail term: ruling class vengeance for the working class self-consciousness and confidence of the 1960s is now more vindictive than ever, on a scale unimaginable back then, and makes any sensible person angrier than ever. In defence of my younger self I would say that the vengeance was foreseen back then, if not the scale. Worker organisation was under rhetorical attack—a mix of lame satire and a narrative of uncompetitiveness—which then became a legal and police attack; comrades were being killed by the police in Italy; the British state showed that constitutional rights were conditional; and one of the building blocks of 'neoliberal globalisation' was put in place: the suspension of the dollar-gold link and the introduction of floating exchange rates. The latter two happened during the month of my arrest; what floating rates did was to make the value of a currency directly dependent on the level of labour discipline.

Vengeance? A real political economy involves both the psychic and the economic—social discipline and the rate of profit. Years ago, when education and cultural opportunity opened up to make for a mass creative audacity as reward to our mums and dads for fighting a war, people like myself were seen by the elite as taking the piss. Since then, lessons have been learned by the ruling-class. Taking the piss is now exclusive to lame satirists, and the space for mass creativity is squashed when there are no cheap places to live, and education is expensive and strictly functional. In the present English climate this vengeance has developed a whole structure of punishment, whether managerial, policing or media finger-pointing.

The poor, and most of all the 'ungrateful poor', are subject to psychologising and individualised failure, with the 'welfare' system made a snakes-and-ladders of stingy rewards and sanctions. The constant individualising of blame helps to divert blame away from the 'economic' world at a time when the neoliberal model and narrative of capitalism had to be rescued by public money. It can only make a sensible person very angry to see how, in the name of competitiveness or 'balancing the books', the crisis was 'flipped' to make it a more shameless monologue than ever. There is a debate still ongoing about worldwide aggregate rate of profit. One side suggests that it is and has been falling steadily over a long period, the other that the capitalist offensive, recognisable as such by 1975, has reversed this decline. Either way, the crisis itself was caused by an excess of claims on future profits that assumed unrealistic flows of income when the incomes for those without capital was under attack by the same offensive.

The new economic model and its endless economic boom fantasy was built on personal debt. This far outweighs 'national' debts but the 'flip' proclaimed the opposite. It was suddenly discovered that Greek national debt was excessive, though it had been public knowledge that they were 'cooking the books' for many years, and suddenly it was 'sovereign' debt that was the problem. Sovereign debt then became a 'crisis' of particular government spending: that of any spending on the poor, while unaddressed tax avoidance on profits meant the debt itself would continue. Capitalism's solution to its own crisis, with the help of its many useful idiots, has been to create more asset bubbles and carry the war on the poor to new levels.

Some of the building blocks that have made all this possible took place in 1987, the period in which my recently published novel *Futures* is set. It was the year of the so-called 'Big Bang', a set of 'deregulations' of finance capital, or rather its political empowerment as the main source of capitalist social discipline and lever of accumulation. The perceived advantage was that this acted as a remote source of discipline appearing merely to interpret economic 'reality', while in fact creating such 'reality'. What was not immediately apparent was that it would create claims on worldwide aggregate profits that exceeded those profits.

One of the things the novel tries to do is talk the talk of this capitalism without what Malcolm X called the flim-flam, all that slimy phrase-making that began with 'trickle-down'. The dialogue of financial analysts Phil Stone and Jack Sharp shows their underlying class contempt—they talk about 'overalls' having it too easy—but what it also involves is the evaluation of the future price of things. In this all 'factors' are equal, a rise in interest rates in one place, no different to the death of miners and its effect on the South African Rand. It is in this spirit that they pursue the fantasy of a cocaine futures market, for in 'free-market' ideology, cocaine is just another commodity. What they are also able to do in their coke-fuelled riffs is to nail the identifiable chains of cause and effect in a world of globalized exploitation. These are usually hidden in real production chains with their sub-contracted sub-contractors across continents: hidden by the power of financial decisions made not just thousands of miles away but in social worlds completely different from those where people feel the effects; by the lack of recognition for all the human acts that make such a world possible, especially the unpaid labour of mothers; by capital's useful idiots and even by avant-garde philosophers, who by use of dodgy analogy consign cause-and-effect to a reductionist or Newtonian dustbin.

To work at undermining the flim-flam is important work for writers who do not believe that 'There Is No Alternative'. There are different ways this is being done, like the sharp and angry 'anti-dictionaries' of the Wealth of Negations collective, for example. What fiction can do, which is special, is to pull together the different 'worlds' that the dominant monologue keeps apart. I did not choose the heroine of the novel as a single mother/low-level cocaine dealer as an anti-stereotype. She is not a cipher or a symbol (though anyone who thinks being a single mum is a cushy number can only live in a world of nannies and servants) but a fully realized person, a good and responsible mum trying to survive and not be stuck in that real poverty of people who can't afford to go out or eat out. She is someone who would be in line for blame and punishment, but it is only as such a realised person that she makes the link from the analysts to the very unromanticized 'gangster' at the top of the cocaine supply chain. Unromanticized because he is also a strategic police informer and, more than that, a bore who mimics the language of neoliberalism and managerialism. He uses its dodgy analogies, metaphors and homilies, which I think acts as a mirror image to that of the analysts.

The novel appeared many years ago in French where there is less marketing obsession with genre, and reviews pointed to how well and subtly it was plotted. Plot is a contentious business when it comes to fiction, but I think the debate is crude. Of course there is such a thing as crude plotting full of cardboard characters, and many of the novels I most admire, whether by James or Joyce or James Kelman, do not—and do not have to—work much with plot as such. But in the case of *Futures* the plot is a series of ironies, and come naturally from both character and situation, as in Phil's reaction to his loss of authority as a result of the Big Bang itself. I hope the attempt to do that, to allow the ironies to unfold hidden causes and effects without banging the reader over the head, has worked.

I'm currently doing some readings around the country. I enjoy reading from the novel but hope that such occasions will open up into a discussion of the political possibilities of writing with an emphasis on craft and style. Because language does matter. In recent years, phrases and headlines have returned as tools of the psychic and economic reaction of a mean and stingy capitalism, and have become at least as important as visual imagery, something that didn't seem likely not so long ago. In a standard ruling-class pincer, phrase-laden pieces from professional opinionists proclaim the decline of reading as an inevitable trend, while their class is doing its damndest to make their claim a reality by closing libraries and cutting down on the books in those that remain. It's not that anti-capitalists should also become slick phrase-makers, but that they should write with verve and fresh confidence.

An Idiot's Guide To...
Fly Posting

A: What's the point of your poster?

If it's art go to C. If it's a political or music/event promotion then you've got to consider the traceability of your content—go to B.

B: Be cute

If a quick online search can lead to an address then you've got to be a bit cute about where you're sticking. Some councils or corporations will want to fine you. You'll fall foul of the Town & Country planning act, which will lead to potentially £100 per poster. The good news is you'll get 48 hours from the date of the notice to remove the poster. Get yourself a before and after photo to cover your arse.

C: What are you sticking with?

Paste comes in a variety of forms, generally speaking you don't need it to stick for months so decorators paste will do. Wheat paste sticks like shit to a blanket but is a hassle to make. Permanent spray mount is quite expensive but aerosol flooring adhesive can work well for small runs.

D: Caught by the fuzz?

You're either looking at a civil offence and court appearance for fly posting and a fine of £100 to £500 and no criminal record. Or, the wrong copper on the wrong day will hit you with criminal damage and a similar fine but with the pain of going back to the cells for a few hours. If you're going over a billboard or similar surface that was 'built to be posted on' then you have a slim chance of getting off on these grounds. If not you get a criminal record for criminal damage, which makes you sound like a bit of a twat if you're going for the sort of job where they check on these sort of things. If you're not then who cares.

E: What's it made of?

Don't use anything too thin or it'll rip as soon as it gets wet and you'll waste time dicking about with it—80gm to 150gm paper is good enough. Don't bother with inkjet printed posters, the ink will run either when you post it or when it gets rained on. Toner or other permanent inks are the way to go (as with Lithographic printing). Your newsagents photocopier will most likely print with toner, some screen printing processes will be ok too.

If you're taking out a whole billboard you'll need twelve 60" by 40" (that's inches) sections (known as 4 sheet posters) printed in portrait. You can find printers online that use the blue-backed paper that helps no end when you're working at large scale. You pre-soak (for seconds) the poster in water and roll each piece from bottom to top. The advantage of this blue-backed paper is it remains strong when wet and you can move it around without tearing it, which is vital when lining up large images made up of sections.

F: Don't be an arsehole

Going through the middle of someone else's posters (especially other people's fly posting) or going over the windows of a shop that's in business or getting a refurb is a quick way to make people hate you and spend all their time ripping you down. Derelict shops or boarded up sites are probably your best bet. One poster in the corner of a billboard will probably last longer than twenty through the middle of it. Remember, nothing will make the council or police check their CCTV more than some-one who posted every junction box and street sign in town: choose the best two out of ten and don't overcook the beans.

G: Tools

Paste squirted out of a washing up liquid bottle is one of the best guerilla ways to carry it that I have seen. A fat paintbrush or a soft-bristled broom (for height) is the way you apply your paste to the area you're posting. Stick your poster on, line up then run your brush over the top easing out air bubbles from the middle outwards. Some small steps or a milk crate will help you get your poster above hand-height and elude the ripping hands of passers by. If you're working from a ladder carry your paste in a bucket that hangs from the ladder with an 'S' hook.

H: Look the part

Wear the internationally acclaimed cloak of invisibility, more commonly known as the Hi Vis. Everyone will want to ask you directions to random streets and landmarks, but no one ever thinks: who's that sly dog? Look kosher and you disappear in plain sight—the more Hi Vis items of clothing the better.

I: Related slang

'Buttering up' = putting your paste on to the site to be posted. 'Victory roll' = driving back past a site you've hit afterwards to see what it looks like from a moving vehicle. 'Hero' = the local that's going to report you to the police and rip down all your posters. 'As filthy as a bill poster's bucket' = insert body parts or other places before this phrase at your discretion. 'Sovereignty' = You posted the site before any one else and regard it as yours over and above other people who follow in your wake.

Show a little respect, don't cover up artists or musicians or other small-scale businesses. Try not to post historical buildings or beautiful places or you'll just be regarded as a wanker. Offensive language or images will get a council team cleaning you down within hours, be clever with your use of language and elude to absolute filth with subtlety and people will get your message.

Be funny, use your head. If in doubt, don't do it—there'll be another day. Or just ignore everything you've just read: I'm still making it up as I go along.

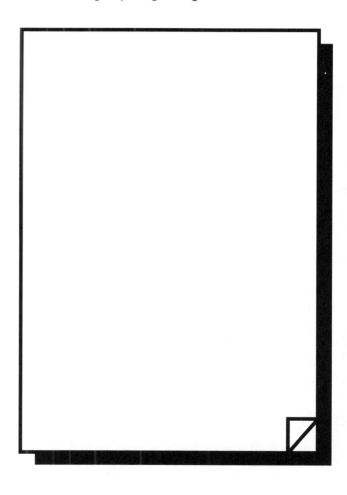

Over the Rainbow

Queer Assimilation, Queer Citizenship, State Violence

I used to live in a house with someone who thought that it was really obvious that capitalism works for almost everyone. One day she came home and she was super excited and she said look at this image on the Downing Street website, it's an image of two men in suits (both white) holding a rose between their hands. She says isn't this just amazing, isn't this progress.

David Cameron said at the time,

I run an institution, the Conservative Party—which for many many years got itself on the wrong side of this [gay marriage] argument, it locked people out who were naturally Conservative from supporting it [...]

What is and was always clear is that the current government's reason for supporting gay marriage is to incorporate gay men and women (but not trans* people, for example) into the Conservative Party and its paradigms; of free enterprise, private ownership, and socially conservative ideas. Much of the rhetoric around the gay marriage debate framed itself in exactly these terms, that gay citizens should have the same rights and opportunities as everybody else, without any hint towards explaining which gay people are included here or whose bodies exactly comprise 'everybody else'.

Many queer people will empathise with the frustration of the question posed to the UK earlier this year: 'do you support gay marriage?' The question is designed to a) only allow one answer from queer folk and allies and b) entirely hide a deeper question: do you support marriage—the acknowledgement by the state of the legitimacy of a sexual relationship—at all? And thus, the 'gay marriage question', as with any question of queer inclusions, produces a discursive bind, intended to foreclose critique of the institution into which queers (apparently) seek entry.

In positioning queers as if we are inside of and supported by the state, the outside is collapsed and with it the possibility for real critique of the state and its various manifestations (marriage, the police, capitalist economies etc.). This reproduction of state power by queers newly included in its official mechanisms also necessarily reproduces state violence. Entering a union specifically sanctioned by the state helps to cement the institution of marriage; so that as an institution it is stronger, less penetrable, with higher walls to scale. Thus, those who are still not appropriate sexual citizens may be further discriminated against, further excluded and further abused. For example, a marriage where one partner is a non-citizen is so heavily scrutinised, expensive and difficult (the UKBA arrive to break up your marriage of 'convenience') because marriage gains power and legitimisation the more proper subjects it includes. It is precisely this inclusion of some gay relationships, then, that excludes in this case, non-monogamous relationships, trans* and non-binary subjects, queer people of colour and migrant queer people in a way that is bolstered by normative queer assimilation.

The production of an acceptable sexual subject—a proper queer citizen—like the production of any subject, necessarily produces an abject unacceptable other. More than neutralising dissent, the production of proper queer citizens by the state also produces the social and corporeal deaths of (other) others.

Downing Street's neatly dressed workers may now be afforded more freedoms despite their sexual preference (and because of their subscription to proper sexual and romantic codes), but these supposed freedoms in the workplace, for example, also strengthen the institution of capitalist labour production and more specifically of institutions that are explicitly involved in the production of state violence. In an article titled Queer Necropolitics and the Expanding Carceral State: Interrogating Sexual Investments in Punishment (2013), Sarah Lamble describes how in January 2011, UK L(esbian)G(ay)B(i) and possibly and divisively soon to be T(rans*) charity Stonewall—an organisation named after the New York anti-police riots by members of the gay community in 1969—listed the UK home office, responsible for immigration, policing and security as its number one employer in a roll of 'LGBT-friendly' places to work. Home secretary Theresa May basked in the slick rainbow sheen of a 'diverse' and 'tolerant' workplace, forming a protective queer mask over the actual work—of deportation, racism, police violence etc.—performed by this place.

Since 2010 the site of the home office has become the space in which acceptable sexual citizenship and queer personhood is most visibly and violently produced. LGBT asylum seekers in the UK are increasingly forced to prove they are queer, as opposed to, necessarily, that they face danger in their countries of origin. This proof inevitably takes the form of often graphic sexual 'evidence'—that victims of extreme domestic and sexual violence, for example, may be forced to present photographic or video evidence of their sex life and be cruelly interrogated on their intimate sexual practices. This is the price of queer citizenship, the sharpened edges of acceptable identities.

Analysing dozens of cases, the report exposed officials' frequently crass approach. Sample questions included: 'Was it loving sex or rough?'; 'So you had intercourse with him not just blow jobs'; and 'What have you found is the most successful way of pulling men?'

'Did you put your penis into x's backside?' and 'When x was penetrating you, did you have an erection? Did x ejaculate inside you? Why did you use a condom?' Even as 'human rights injustices' are expanded to include abuse of

LGBT non-citizens, so as to instrumentalise the suffering of others in conflicts abroad, real live bodies escaping geographical sites where homosexuality is illegal are met with derision, abuse and disbelief by the state, which cannot imagine a queer subject who is also an outsider, who is abused, incomplete, other.

This same state, however, is still positioned by many queer and LGBT people and organisations as a body that has the power to protect the individual from an other—as opposed to one who allows and perpetuates violence. Lamb highlights this shift in LGBT and queer organisations from one that naturally positioned itself against the police and the prison industrial system, to one which increasingly relies on these carceral mechanisms for protection of individual subjects and the legitimacy of queer struggles. On 18th July 2014 *Pink News* (Europe's largest gay news service) reported that the Manchester police had just unveiled a new Pride-themed patrol car. This car has the predictable rainbow decal on the side and bears the statement 'Police with Pride' as well as 'LET'S END HATE CRIME' in giant rainbow letters, and 'REPORT IT' in black text below.

In 2011 anti-gay posters started appearing around Tower Hamlets. The posters featured the text 'GAY FREE ZONE' and decontextualized quotations from the Qur'an, feeding neatly into the same Islamaphobic and racist stereotypes connecting Islam to homophobia and misogyny that have repeatedly been activated as justifications for war in Iran and Iraq. Local Muslim groups, including the British Association of Muslims and the East London Mosque, and the gay Muslim group Imaan, publicly condemned the posters and when a teenage Asian Muslim boy was found to be responsible he was charged and sentenced to a fine of £100. However, local LGBT groups, particularly Rainbow Hamlets, issued a press statement calling for greater punishment, in particular demanding jail time—state violence as proof that the state take seriously the threat of violence (in the form of posters, here) against queer individuals.

On September 7th 2013 I had my first outing working as a Legal Observer for Legal Defence and Monitoring Group (LDMG). The EDL (English Defence League), a far-right, racist and particularly Islamaphobic anti-immigration organization, marched through Tower Hamlets. A group of anti-fascists and members of the largely Muslim local community gathered to try to block the streets to prevent them from marching. 282 anti-fascists were arrested after having been contained for six hours under section 12 of the Public Order Act. Their police bail conditions stated that they did not have permission to participate in anti-fascist action for three months. All charges were dropped. 5 legal observers were arrested, and I only just managed to get out of the containment. While in the kettle three young Muslim boys asked if they could have some space to pray. The policewoman said no.

It should be noted that the EDL has its own active LGBT division, which has almost 4,000 'likes' on Facebook. Their description reads: 'This Division of EDL is for us queers and those straight people who think we have the right to live'. Following this, the page continues 'We call for the banning of the Burkha [sic] and the instant cessation of mosque-construction, based on the fact that the government has no idea who is living here'—a chillingly succinct image of who is included in having the right to live (here). The LGBT division of the EDL, a far right street organisation prone to making Nazi salutes at demonstrations, also mentions the 2011 posters, stating 'Gay Free Zone posters were copied from the Nazis, who put Juden Heraus (jews get out) posters up in Germany.'

On September 12, 2014 Leicester Police's Firearms and Dogs unit tweeted an image @Stonewall with the caption: 'We believe it's our differences that unite us. The more diverse, the more effective we are.' The image shows seven white men in a triangular offense pattern. Each is wearing full riot gear, a gas mask (which totally hides their features) and each carries a semi-automatic weapon. Each man wears rainbow shoelaces.

This is the image of men who will shoot and teargas and stamp on you; this is the image of the men who will hold you down; smash your head in; watch you bleed; kick you; this is an image of the men who are invisible behind their dystopian sadist masculinity; these are the men promoting diversity and their human side and their dripping fucking rainbow laces falling across your broken face.

This is the image of effective diversity.

This is the image of progress.

PRICE 45p

WOMEN
BEHIND
THE
WIRE

BULLETIN OF THE ARMAGH CO-ORDINATING
GROUP LONDON.

Radical Print Revolution?
Objects Under Capitalism

A 'radical print' revival of posters, newspapers and pamphlets has been taking place over the last few years. STRIKE!, of course, is part of it. Artists and designers, often citing inspiration from the explosion of print that ensued from the radical and social movements of the 1960s and 70s, seem to be in the vanguard and perhaps fittingly their efforts are as much disseminated in galleries as at political gatherings or in radical or independent bookshops.

Institutions are taking notice in other ways too. Ciara Phillips, who cites Sister Corita the radical poster-making nun as her prime influence, has been nominated for the Turner Prize for a gallery residency that involved making posters with local activists and a talk by members of the 1970s feminist poster collective, See Red Women's Workshop. This week students from art schools in Manchester, Salford and Liverpool participated in a 'poster procession' to the People's History Museum (PHM) carrying placards made for a one-day Art of Protest project set by the V&A and PHM1. The 'winners' efforts were then acquired for the PHM collection.

For their poster workshop at the Anarchist Bookfair STRIKE! invoke the 'order' by the Mai '68 Atelier Populaire that their posters are purely for use in sites of revolutionary conflict and not to be commodified as works of art for sale or 'bourgeois' display. (Is the People's History Museum a site of bourgeois display?). The Ateliers specified the appropriate sites of conflict, 'the street' and 'the factory'. Although the factory motif of 'zig-zag roof plus chimney' appear in the posters of the 'radical print' revival (sometimes recycled from those of the Ateliers), STRIKE! have thankfully let us off the hook: public display is all they ask.

What accounts for these reenactments and revivals—if that is what they are? Are they akin to 1970s tribute bands? Are they just the cutting edge of 'vintage', a self-announced radical fringe of retro-style? The inky wing of so-called 'craftivism'? A desperate bid by designers to create products of distinction? How are the motivations different to those cranking out independent radical print media in the late twentieth century? And what is it all for? I'm not entirely sure but these are a few thoughts and a bit of history. My remarks refer to the UK context.

The most obvious point is that privileging print to communicate political ideas in the contemporary technological moment seems perverse. Why choose a medium that in comparison to digitally networked technologies is costly, laborious and difficult to widely distribute? Isn't the point of 'radical media' to try and communicate political ideas and information to as wide an audience as possible? The reason why there was an eruption of radical and social-movement print media in the 1970s is because a) there were hundreds of political groups and campaigns and b) because print was the main, if not sole, means of technology available to communicate. Screen-printing and small offset litho, had become newly accessible technologies and were taken up with gusto, becoming the bedrock of this proliferation. Duplicators such as the infamous Gestetner should not be left out either. Thousands of pamphlets were cranked out on these devices and their use persisted despite the so-called 'offset revolution'. By accessible I mean available, affordable and relatively easy to learn.

Screen-printing had been partly popularized in British art schools through its adoption by pop artists, Warhol most famously. Pop artists liked screen-printing because of its semi-industrial, manufacturing and commercial associations—packaging and billboards. Screen-printing was not at this time associated with 'craft', either for pop artists or the radical poster-makers that adopted it. Craft was retrograde, about escaping from the world; DIY, or self-help as it was often called, was another matter. It was about getting round 'the system', the electricity board, the housing problem, the communications problem. It was about taking matters, and in the case of printing, the means of communicative production, into our own hands by what means were available.

Neither did many radical printers in the UK refer to what they were doing as 'printmaking', or to themselves as 'artists' or even designers. The turn to political poster-making by artists for example was mostly an explicit rejection of the world of galleries, of the attendant 'fine art' associations of 'printmaking' and its precious 'limited editions'. It was about cultural production in the service of politics, not politics in the service of art or an artists' 'practice' or designer's portfolio. Radical print groups did not have 'studios' either: they had printshops or print workshops. Many of those involved in printing weren't interested in print for its own sake—it was a means to an end, instrumental to the communication of politics. Bashing out 500 posters or 10,000 leaflets or 200 pamphlets wasn't for art, for craft, for appreciation of the affective qualities of a 'handmade' artifact or especially for love of an often frustrating, dirty and fume-saturated process, it was mostly about making propaganda, sharing information and creating discussion about issues and politics that felt really important, urgent even.

People banded together to set up radical printing presses because it was difficult to get political material printed. And of course there was the money problem. The cheaply produced and graphically unremarkable pamphlets shown here give a partial flavour. A 1974 Squatters Handbook (32pp A5, offset litho), packed with legal and practical information and contacts for over forty squatting groups across the country; a 1977 pamphlet-newsletter of PROMPT (32pp A5, offset litho) providing arguments for the autonomous mental-health movement along with vital information gleaned on medication; 'Women Behind the Wire' (43pp, A4, duplicated) was the 1981 bulletin of London's Armagh Co-ordinating Group, set up in response to a call for women's movement solidarity from female Irish republican prisoners in Armagh Jail; 'Breaching the Peace' (36pp, A5, offset litho) was a contentious 1983 radical feminist critique of the burgeoning women's peace movement, produced to generate movement debate (36pp, A5, offset litho). War Report (4pp, A4 offset litho) was put together by independent journalists during the first Iraq war in response to the grossly biased and censored coverage in the mainstream press.

Squatters, psychiatric patients, IRA sympathizers, radical lesbians, unpatriotic journalists, all would have had difficulty getting it printed 'commercially', unpopular (and mostly skint) as they were. This is why radical and community printshops were set up. The problems were those that continue to beset social and radical movements and their communicative attempts: preaching to the converted, actual distribution, the struggle to find a resonant language, paying the bills. In many ways, the web would have been perfectly suited for much of the material produced and as we all know it has indeed provided a home for a myriad of marginal, oppositional and unpopular ideas. But also, despite the hassle (which even with sympathetic printers, it still often was), all this print, its spaces of production and dissemination—meetings, events, radical bookshops and centres, comrades' and sisters' houses—was more than just 'information and propaganda'. It was a vital part of the material culture and the structure of feeling of radical and oppositional movements. It was not just about the struggle but also of it. It was both its evidence and affirmation, part of making it tangible and sustaining 'illusio'.

Tangibility seems to be part of what informs the resurrection, but possibly of a different sort. I think designers in particular got fed up with the 'digital everything', they wanted to be involved in palpable, immutable and keep-able objects, and with visibly 'slow' production. It came along with, and is to some extent (at least the turn to hand-printing) part of the craft revival, itself a similar reaction. However the re-turn to print can also be seen as sign of design distinction, not for 'the commons' but against the 'common web' and the tools and platforms that keep moving the rope between the trained and untrained, the cognoscenti and the rest. So it's partly about access and specialist knowledge again, and money and time; stumbling blocks that restrict the uptake of other forms of 'slow' production/consumption. And the objects themselves, the print stuff, what kind of thing or commodity are they—or might they be? This is partly what STRIKE! are trying to get at.

I have thought about the 'radical print' surge of the 1970s, particularly the posters, as a sort attempt to create socialist objects akin to those proposed by the Russian Constructivists of the 1920s, particularly Boris Arvatov. Sure some were for placards, pickets and flyposting, but many went up in workplaces and homes too. The concept of the socialist object, unlike the utilitarian view, embraced the affective properties of things. It proposed that in contrast to the enslaved, sedating and 'finished' thing-possessions of bourgeois commodity culture, the socialist object would be a co-worker, an active and equal comrade that, like its new mode of production, enriched the bodies of the social-ist project. This would require them not to be exploited by being treated in the same way as objects under capitalism. Is this possible?

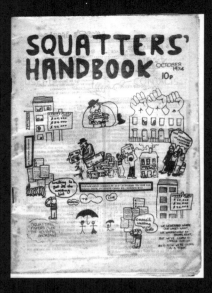

SQUATTERS' HANDBOOK

OCTOBER 1974 10p

WAR REPORT

NO 1 SATURDAY FEBRUARY 2 1990 50P

Iraqi forces face Napalm threat

MILITANT napalm on both sides of the Atlantic suspect that the US plans to use Napalm against Iraqi forces in the Gulf.

Food shortages hit Palestine

HUMAN rights workers in Jerusalem have charged that the 23-hour curfew imposed in the occupied territories since January 17 'endangers the lives and livelihood of 1.5 million Palestinians'.

Iraqi deaths

OVER 200,000 Iraqis were killed in the first week of the Gulf War, Manfred Opel, a retired airforce general who is now a Social Democrat MP, claimed last week.

CIA ignored

PRESIDENT Bush's initial justification for the allied presence in the Gulf had no basis in fact, a White House official told the New York daily Newsday.

Off the air

IN the run-up to war, the three major US television networks devoted less than half per cent of their airtime to popular opposition to the Bush administration's Gulf policy.

Africa famine

MILLIONS more people could starve in Africa if the West continues to concentrate resources on the Gulf war, according to Oxfam director Frank Judd. He said the cut in already exacerbated acute fuel shortages for relief trucks in Ethiopia, where food supplies are inadequate.

"PROMPT"

Promotion of the Rights of
'Mental Patients' (in 'Therapy'?)

A "SUPPORT
PROMPT"
EDITION

No. 8/9

CONTROVERSIAL ISSUES:

"THE CASE AGAINST
THE USE OF E.C.T."

25p
DONATION

JOHN FRIEDBERG. M.D.

A NEUROLOGIST CHALLENGES
THE PSYCHIATRIC MYTH
(WITH REFERENCES)

AND

"ANTI- PSYCHIATRY"

DRUGS DIRECTORY.

SIDE-EFFECTS OF OVER 90 DRUGS
IN COMMON USE TODAY.

DOUBLE ISSUE
EDITION

**Breaching
the Peace**

a collection of radical feminist papers

An Anarchist Guide to...
Christmas

It's no surprise to discover that Kropotkin was interested in Christmas. In Russian culture, St. Nicholas was revered as a defender of the oppressed, the weak and the disadvantaged. Kropotkin shared the sentiments. But there was also a family link. As everyone knows, Kropotkin could trace his ancestry to the ancient Rurik dynasty that ruled Russia before the upstart Romanovs and which, from the first century CE, controlled the trade routes between Moscow and the Byzantine Empire. Nicholas' branch of the family had been sent out to patrol the Black Sea. But Nicholas was a spiritual man and sought an escape from the piracy and brigandage for which his Russian Viking family was famed. So he settled under a new name in the southern lands of the Empire, now Greece, and decided to use the wealth that he had amassed from his life of crime to alleviate the sufferings of the poor.

Unpublished archival sources recently discovered in Moscow reveal that Kropotkin was fascinated by this family tie and the striking physical similarity between himself and the figure of Father Christmas, popularised by the publication of *A Visit from St. Nicholas* (better known as *The Night Before Christmas*) in 1823. Kropotkin was not quite so portly as Klaus, but with a cushion stuffed up his tunic, he felt he could pass. His friend Elisée Reclus advised him to drop the fur trim on the outfit. That was a good idea as it would also allow him to wear a bit more black with the red. He'd decided to follow Elisée's advice on the reindeer, too, and used a hand-driven sleigh. Kropotkin wasn't normally given to dressing up. But exploiting the resemblance to spread the anarchist message was excellent propaganda by the deed. Anticipating *V*, Kropotkin thought that we could all pose as Santa Claus. On the edge of one page Kropotkin writes: 'Infiltrate the stores, give away the toys!' Faint remnants on the back of a postcard read:

On the night before Christmas, we'll all be about
While the people are sleeping, we'll realise our clout
We'll expropriate goods from the stores, 'cos that's fair
And distribute them widely, to those who need care.

His project notes also reveal some valuable insights into his ideas about the anarchistic features of Christmas and his thinking about the ways in which Victorian Christmas rituals might be adapted. He wrote,

We all know that the big stores—John Lewis, Harrods and Selfridges—are beginning to exploit the sales potential of Christmas, establishing magic caves, grottos and fantastic fairylands to lure our children and pressurise us to buy gifts that we do not want and cannot afford. If you are one of us you will realise that the magic of Christmas depends on Father Christmas' system of production, not the stores' attempts to seduce you to consume useless luxuries.

Kropotkin described the sprawling workshops at the North Pole, where elves worked all year, happily because they knew that they were producing for other people's pleasure. Noting that these workshops were strictly not-for profit, craft-based and run on communal lines, Kropotkin treated them as prototypes for the factories of the future (outlined in Fields, Factories and Workshops). Some people, he felt, thought that Father Christmas's dream to see that everyone received gifts on Christmas day, was quixotic. But it could be realised. Indeed, the extension of the workshops—which were quite expensive to run in the Arctic—would facilitate generalised production for need and the transformation of occasional gift-giving into regular sharing. 'We need to tell the people,' Kropotkin wrote, 'that community workshops can be set up anywhere and that we can pool our resources to make sure that everybody has their needs met!'

One of the issues that most bothered Kropotkin about Christmas was the way in which the inspirational role that Nicholas had played in conjuring Christmas myths had confused the ethics of Christmas. Nicholas was wrongly represented as a charitable, benevolent man: saintly because he was beneficent. Absorbed in the figure of Father Christmas, Nicholas' motivations for giving had become further skewed by the Victorians' fixation with children. Kropotkin didn't really understand the links, but felt that it reflected an attempt to moralise childhood through a concept of purity that was symbolised in the birth of Jesus. Naturally he couldn't imagine the creation of the Big Brother Santa Claus who knows when children are asleep and awake and comes to town apparently knowing which have dared to cry or pout. But sooner or later, he warned, this idea of purity would be used to distinguish naughty from nice children and only those in the latter group would be rewarded with presents. Whatever the case, it was important both to recover the principle of Nicholas' compassion from this confusing mumbo-jumbo and the folkloric origins of Santa Claus. Nicholas gave because he was pained by his awareness of other people's hardship. Though he wasn't an assassin (as far as Kropotkin knew), he shared the same ethics as Sofia Petrovskaya. And while it was obviously important to worry about the wellbeing of children, the anarchist principle was to take account of everyone's suffering. Similarly, the practice of giving was mistakenly thought to require the implementation of a centrally-directed plan, overseen by an omniscient administrator. This was quite wrong: Father Christmas came from the imagination of the people (just consider the range of local names that Nicholas had accrued— Sinterklaas, Tomte, de Kerstman). And the spreading of good cheer—through festivity—was organised from the bottom up.

Buried in Christmas, Kropotkin argued, was the solidaristic principle of mutual aid.

Kropotkin appreciated the significance of the ritual and the real value that individuals and communities attached to carnivals, acts of remembrance and commemoration. He no more wanted to abolish Christmas than he wished to see it republicanised through some wrong-headed bureaucratic re-ordering of the calendar. It was important, nonetheless, to detach the ethic that Christmas supported from the singularity of its celebration. Having a party was just that: extending the principle of mutual aid and compassion into everyday life was something else. In capitalist society, Christmas provided a space for special good behaviours. While it might be possible to be a Christian once a year, anarchism was for life.

Kropotkin realised his propaganda would have the best chance of success if he could show how the anarchist message was also embedded in mainstream culture. His notes reveal that he looked particularly to Dickens' *A Christmas Carol* to find a vehicle for his ideas. The book was widely credited with cementing ideas of love, merriment and goodwill in Christmas. Kropotkin found the genius of the book in its structure. What else was the story of Scrooge's encounter with the ghosts of Christmas past, present and future than a prefigurative account of change? By seeing his present through his past, Scrooge was given the chance to alter his miserly ways and re-shape both his future and the future of the Cratchit family. Even if it was only remembered once a year, Kropotkin thought, Dickens' book lent anarchists a perfect vehicle to teach this lesson: by altering what we do today, by modelling our behaviours on Nicholas, we can help construct a future which is Christmas!

#CopsOffCampus

CC appears in court charged with two counts of assault PC after mass-arrest at Cops Off Campus demo 5th Dec 2013. CC is acquitted on both counts. The case against his co-defendant, RB, also charged with assault PC, is thrown out at half-time for lack of evidence.

'Victim' No. 1: PC Smythe
I felt his knee sweep across my thigh and groin. I have absolutely no doubt that he was trying to knee me in the testicles.

Under cross-examination:
Shown this photo: (headlock)

Smythe:
I think that was completely justified. They were coming into my personal space.

'Victim' No. 2: Inspector Harman
Our intention was to clear a sterile area, to clear the protesters out of the area. I saw a male officer grabbed by a protester (CB) causing the officer to fall forward to the floor. I ran through and pushed protesters away and picked the officer up. Someone grabbed my hat. Various hats had been lost or stolen that day, so I put my hand onto my hat, to grab onto my hat. Then I felt someone strike my throat. I couldn't go after them because of the other protesters.

Under cross-examination:
Defence barrister Dan from HJA: (shows this footage)
That officer (you ran to assist) has now gone back to CB and

is delivering punches to CB. It looks like that officer is using excessive force on a protester lying prone on the ground.

Harman:
I can't comment.

CC speaks his own defence:
The protest was about police violence on campus. I covered my face partly because it was a cold day but also because I believe in our civil liberty to protest anonymously. The atmosphere to begin with was carnivalesque—there were people with musical instruments, people in costumes, people chanting. Then somebody said there were police inside the university building, which was ironic since the protest was 'cops off campus' and students were locked out of the building. The police were behind the gates of Senate House using overhead baton strikes against protesters, and when they couldn't reach them that way, they'd jab protesters with the ends of the batons. The crowd started chanting 'Shame on you!'

Another serial of officers waded into the crowd, pushing people, trying to form a line across the gates. I put my placard in front of Inspector Brockway's face. As he said in his evidence, it was only 'quite near' his face, and he put his hand between it and his face and pushed it away. I was getting a message across, not using the placard as a weapon. The placard was commissioned for STRIKE! Magazine from artist Peter Willis and it was a play on the Metropolitan Police slogan 'Total Policing'. As well as saying 'Total c*nts'—I put an asterisk to make sure it was only offensive to police—it also had other words on it describing the Metropolitan police: violent, racist, petty, barbaric, London's biggest gang.

At this point PC Smythe grabs me by the wrist. I think he's trying to take my placard away from me. He's pulling me and the placard and trying to grab me. I think losing my placard would infringe my right to protest, which is exactly what this protest is about. I want to get away to continue to protest peacefully. I say 'get your fucking hands off me,' and I say this because he has his fuckings hands on me.

Then Smythe smashes me down into a headlock. There's no advance warning and I didn't believe I was under arrest. I put my hands up and my knee up to try to leverage myself out of his grip. Two others in the crowd saw the assault by PC Smythe and helped to pull his arms so I could get away.

At the other cordon in Russell Square police also had their batons drawn, which was provocative at a protest against police violence. I was angry because I'd just been assaulted by an enormous man. There was a lot of adrenaline. I was not just shouting 'fuck the police,' I was shouting 'no justice, no peace, fuck the police.' I thought it was pretty ironic that the police were being violent at a protest against police violence. There's the chant 'Who killed Mark Duggan' and I'm saying 'YOU killed Mark Duggan', which is true because the Metropolitan Police did kill Mark Duggan. So I was standing there showing my placard to the police, getting my message across. Then it started raining, and I went to get a tea at Costa Coffee.

Later I find the remainder of the protest up on Euston Road. It's a cat-and-mouse situation with the protest being chased by police down Euston Road towards the top of Gower Street. There are several lines of police there stopping people from going south.

Outside Euston Square station, I see a police officer assaulting a man I now know to be CB. The man has a bicycle and long red hair. CB says something to the officer as he walks past, and gesticulates. The officer catches what he says and grabs CB. CB is 19 or 20 and very skinny. The officer is a massive guy. He probably has a stone for every year of CB's age. CB would not have been able to pull him to the floor, as alleged. The officer pushes him to the ground.

I've been to many protests and this was easily the most violence I've seen at a protest. I've seen much more hostile crowds provoke less of a reaction from the police. But we've heard the reason for this violence already from the officers' evidence. The police believed there to be 'anarchist elements' at the protest. Remember how the City of London police had a campaign telling people to shop their 'anarchist neighbours' as terrorists?

I was shocked by the violence. I wanted to stop CB being beaten up. I saw something illegal and I wanted to stop it. I grabbed the arm of the officer on CB, but lost my grip.

Then other officers rushed in, rucking and mauling like a rugby game. One of the officers runs in from about 5 feet away with his fist and arm up like this, and jumps on CB. If Inspector Harman had been trying to pull the officers off CB, I would never have touched him. But he was going in to assist the assault. I had already been the victim of an assault that day. Just as I would on the street if I saw a little kid being beaten up by a massive guy—doesn't matter if that massive guy is wearing a uniform—I would intervene. I was attempting to remove Harman from the area, essentially, because he seemed to be piling in to the assault on CB. There were lots of people there, because all those people thought there was an assault going on. The police have portrayed them as a mob but I would call them concerned and brave citizens.

At this point I was in a state of fear and panic. I flipped off Inspector Harman's hat. Flicking his cap was a non-violent act which was intended to distract him from participating in the attack on CB. Then I was running away. I saw him coming at me with his fists raised. It's absolute nonsense to say that I struck him in the throat. It's possible that someone else did, but I was running away. It was like a war-zone, people screaming and crying. You just want to get out of there.

Then I am grabbed from behind by two officers—I am grabbed in the face and they smash my head into a plate glass window. At no stage do any of these people say I am under arrest. I say, 'What the actual fuck are you doing?' The response is a punch in the face by a third officer. They damage my nose so that I can't breathe properly for 3–4 weeks. As if that isn't enough, as they drag me into a containment,

I am pushed again to the ground by a fourth officer and he stands over me, stamping on my legs. It was like a bar fight. That level of violence was completely unnecessary. I was pulled into a containment and later arrested to prevent breach of the peace. That containment was not already in place as Harman said. When that incident happened, it was just a of bunch of riot cops running around. I was angry that I had been assaulted violently by several members of the Metropolitan Police and yet I was the one in custody.

(The prosecutor attempted to stop footage of this assault on CC being shown because he thought it was 'not relevant', but he was overruled by the judge.)

We've pointlessly targeted cannabis users in Lewisham, while other people legally drink their drugs.

Enforcing Westminster's crime concerns in Lewisham
#ACAB

 **METROPOLITAN POLICE** TOTALLY POINTLESS

We cause the 2011 by shoot an unarm civilian a lying abc And we with it.

How can it be a lawful k
#Duggan

 METROPOLITAN POLICE TOTALLY UNLA

ts
dead

:hen
t.
away

idn't have a gun?

You're 28 times more likely to be stopped and searched in London if you don't have white skin, because we're still *really* racist.

The only workplace still tolerating racism in 2014
#ACAB

METROPOLITAN POLICE **TOTALLY RACIST**

Housing Boom Boom

'New apartments launching. Register your interest today' gloats a colourful banner in Hoxton station, East London. While once houses were built or renovated for, y'know, living in, now they are launched like snazzy products. Areas have become marketable, homes accessories and entire communities repackaged with all the not-so-pretty bits pushed out of sight and out of mind.

This is a symptom of a market that is run not for the majority of people but for the profit of few, during a housing crisis that continues to deepen across London and the UK (A.K.A. a property boom). Currently landlords, developers and politicians have the power to play with cities in the same way pre-teens play The Sims, pushing the boundaries as far as possible until eventually the powerless little pixel people disappear into oblivion.

While hundreds of thousands of spare properties (read: investments) of the rich lie empty and it remains illegal to occupy them, the 'spare' bedrooms of some of the worst-off people in England and Wales are being taxed in what's called an 'under occupancy charge'. This bedroom tax has left two thirds of households affected in rent arrears while one in seven face eviction. It will no doubt contribute to a further rise in the 1.8million households in Britain who are on waiting lists for social housing.

In the mean time, many former social housing blocks are being demolished and redeveloped to make way for more expensive luxury flats, while most people can't afford to pay rent on their expensive but un-luxurious flats. So-called solutions to rocketing rent prices include 'affordable homes', stuck on the back end of the luxury 'developments'. Sadly these remain unaffordable for most, still costing 80% of the extortionate market rate, even on the few occasions the requisite ratios are actually built.

These are just a few of the issues in a crisis that is being deepened by Tory cuts on council budgets, where housing budgets are hardest hit. However, unlike the *The Sims*, who have no choice but to suffer on the computer screen while their child rulers go back to their toast and soldiers, local people have the power to come beyond the screens of politicians and developers to be heard. While the beneficiaries of the property boom count their cash, a boom in housing activism is beginning to counter the current political agenda.

In October, activists including those from The Radical Housing network, a collective of local English groups, organised the successful blockade of the world's largest property fair, despite police violence. The fair facilitates the selling off of public land to developers for 'regeneration' with massive profit margins. The protest and blockade sent a strong message that people want alternative investment with social profit for everyone, not more cash for a few.

Then there are the likes of the women of Focus E15 Mothers who, after being evicted from a hostel for homeless mothers (closed to make way for, you guessed it, luxury flats), have been campaigning against the displacement and social cleansing taking place in their area and across London.

Their occupation of empty, boarded up council homes gained huge media attention, forcing councillors to consider their call for an end to the out of control free-market in housing. At the last Focus E15 event a banner read 'This is the beginning of the end of the housing crisis', and if people continue to take innovative direct action and support the work of local and national housing campaigners, it can be.

TXT: NIALL MCDEVITT

The Human Elephant
(In the Inhuman Room)

I was in his soul as if inside a palace that had been deliberately emptied so that no one as ignoble as myself could be seen in it.

Rimbaud

For the socially cleansed

1.

it is come, the time of our decanting. goodbye to the interconnecting, anti-gravity walkways with their strips of frosted glass, hello to regular paths and irregular paving-stones. goodbye to our streets in the air, hello to pound shops and charismatic chapels. we had mystical mansions, we had 1,000 keys, so they jealously took it away, who cannot understand our tribal croaks, our medicine men, our ghetto aromas, our pirate smiles. six castles of communism loomed worryingly large for them. six ships we sailed into bureaucratic, pea-soup seas. six rectangles of Hel

2.

only Glasspool is left, his one white car, an unnamable on the 10th floor, and the decanted old woman who comes back to walk her decanted dog. our houses, our shops were illumined by the original planners who had based everything on light, on sunlight, and we could buy anything, the spices of earth, from neighbours who lived in the same lighting, whose living-rooms were also chemists, launderettes, hairdressers, shebeens. 'environmental determinism' says Glasspool. verily, the overclass envies the underclass, covets what the other doesn't have

3.

when the communal heating system stopped, we resorted to small convector heaters. they trash any commune, any communing. the big dystopia kills off little utopias. when the communal heating system stopped, we felt the Cold War creeping back under our psychedelic snake draught-excluders. did you know the anti-pyramidal city had been built by gypsies, riding on Indian elephants? Ganesh was our foreman, trunk stuffed with bhang-lassi. the river Saddhus were out-of-it, Kali was disarmed. no slum dogs, no millionaires could touch us then

4.

nor were we decanted politely. no pinkies were extended to us. the war on brutalism was brutalist. savagely they gentrify (never once suspecting how nice we are). the streets in the air are an empty estate, a flotation jerusalem. our fathers and mothers were buried here in a 60s tab of orange sunshine and a free love climax, even as the big-fellow chief dubbed us 'the forgotten'. we fondly remember the vomit running up our oesophagi, his tigrish chrism. but as his hug was the beginning of the end for Gaddaffi, his eulogy was a kick in the balls of Cockaigne

5.

here the human elephant (inhuman castle) in a graffiti-rich greyness, a welcoming Hel, empty rooms in the endangered species, showroom trials, rigged judges, juries, developers, developers, the developments in the detail (so the thesis goes). national salvation, sociopolitical failure, the 40-year day, an affordable toilet, a criminal idyll, more robinhood than neighbourhood (so the thesis went). the elephant—child of the mammoth is invisible to those who only see tusks, see ivory, and aim their sights. 'darling, how can you miss?' a giant graffito: SAVE OUR ESTATE

6.

we've been decanted and pepperpotted—in spite of because of our iconic status—from our gridded elevations, from our streets in the air, having refused to hand in identities, or give DNA samples. oh the flushed ova! 'shooting an elephant' wrote Orwell, a guilty authority. we have been dispersed, all he go one one, we shan't see ourselves for miles, for years. we'll live. they are only killing our living-rooms, amazing as they were. let the ill-affordable houses come, clad in trespa, and let those who can ill afford them piss into ladyporterloos. let the regrouping be unforeseen

IT'S A TYPE OF MOLE FOUND IN INFANTS AT BIRTH, IT'S QUITE RARE, IN AN EVEN RARER FORM KNOWN AS 'WEREWOLF SYNDROME' THEY CAN COVER MOST OF THE BODY.

APART FROM THE NEVUS MY OWNER'S MUM ALWAYS THOUGHT THERE WAS SOME—THING DIFFERENT ABOUT HER

maybe that's just how girls are?

SO SHE WENT TO MANY DOCTORS FOR HELP AND ADVICE.....

KATE BUSH WAS HER FAVOURITE

you watch my record player!

"IT'S ME IT'S KATHY!"

(AND EDITH PIAF) →

NON RIEN DE RIEN NON JE NE REG RET TE RI EN

IT HELPS YOU UNDERSTAND - YOU SEE - WHERE WE ARE NOW, KNOWING WHERE WE'VE COME FROM.

TILLEY AND DEL THE PIGGIE

Fly-Print Workshop

Inspired by the Mai '68 Atelier Populaire, *STRIKE! Magazine* curated a room for counter-propaganda production at the London Anarchist Bookfair 2014. Comrades came armed with ideas and slogans, created their designs, and participated in actual printing of risograph posters.

Two riso-printers were firing all day, and all material was produced strictly for public display. Nobody could have predicted the rampant creativity that was unleashed, nor the joy it produced. Over 50 different designs were turned out and taken back to home-towns all over the land.

Some of the images from the day are below, and you can order the actual posters from our website. Remember: strictly for public display...

The posters produced by the ATELIER POPULAIRE are weapons in the service of the struggle and are an inseparable part of it. Their rightful place is in the centers of conflict, that is to say, in the streets and on the walls of the factories. To use them for decorative purposes, to display them in bourgeois places of culture or to consider them as objects of aesthetic interest is to impair both their function and their effect.

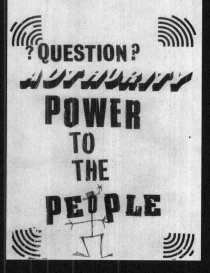

WE DUN WANNA
MARRY WE JUST
WE JUST WANNA
LUV & FUCK

? QUESTION ?
AUTHORITY
POWER
TO
THE
PEOPLE

OPEN DIALOGUE:
David Ziggy Greene, Paul Ashley Brown, Dimitri Pieri & Alternative Press spent an afternoon at Speakers' Corner.

Hyde Park's infamous Speakers' Corner is often considered the last beacon of free speech. Each Sunday dozens of members of the public give in to their urges to stand upon their soapboxes (more likely a step-ladder these days) to let it all out in what appears to remain an unregulated arena.

Regulars include Tony Allen whose first speech was in 1978.

As well as the old schoolers, notable names that have graced the corner include Karl Marx, William Morris, Vladimir Lenin, George Orwell, Marcus Garvey & Lord Soper.

(Shouting hot air may be free but sitting comfortably isn't.)

Located near the affluent area of Park Lane, Speakers' Corner has roots dating back to 1855 after Sunday trading bill riots broke out in the area.

Later, the Chartists held mass protests against the suppression of the rights of working people, the Reform League organized huge rallies & then the Parks Regulation Act of 1872 has allowed people to make a public address ever since.

In recent times, this ranting hotbed has faced certain threats from the Royal Parks. After restoration works' the area in early 2014 the area was significantly reduced, the nearest toilet facilities were closed & the nearest cycle path runs directly through the standing area. But it's still an amazing & refreshing place to spend an afternoon.

Further reading - speakerscorner.net
soundsfromthepark.org.uk - newagenda.org

P. A. Brown

D. Pieri

Dimitri Pieri - twitter.com/dimitripieri
Alt Press - alternativepress.org.uk

David Ziggy Greene - samu.co.uk
Paul Ashley Brown - paulashleybrown.co.uk

S.O.S

PLANET EARTH

CONTRIBUTORS

María María Acha-Kutscher
Jon Active
Dr. Nafeez Mosaddeq Ahmed
Fahim Alam
Pavan Amara
Iphgenia Baal
Jess Baines
Siana Bangura
John Barker
Mark Beechill
Lucca Benn
Natalie Bennett
Sam Berkson
Marco Bevilacqua
Luther Blisset
Hannah Blows
Robbie Blundell
Fran Boait
Ian Bone
Leah Borromeo
Brandalism
Cat Brogan
Vitalik Buterin
Federico Campagna
Carl Cederström
Emma Charleston
We Are Cognitive
London Anarchist Bookfair
Collective
Rhi Colvin
Tom Cordell
Venus Cumara
Dr. D
Alain de Botton
Tilly & Dell
Stanley Donwood
Danny Dorling

Edgarrr
Feminist Fightback
Kasia Fijalkowska
Matt Fish
Mark Fisher
Peter Fleming
Catherine Flood
Laura Oldfield Ford
Doug Fraser
Anthony Freda
Spike Gascoigne
Lindsey German
Nick Gibb
Guerrilla Girls
David Graeber
Andy Green
Gavin Grindon
The Debacle Reading Group
Clifford Harper
David Harvey
Thomas Heaphy
Rebecca Hendin
John Hoppy Hopkins
Richard Houguez
The Indignados
Ewa Jasiewicz
Rhian E. Jones
Marwan Kaabour
Suzi Kemp
Peter Kennard
Ruth Kinna
Marie le Conte
Spelling Mistakes Cost Lives
Ivar Martinsson
Emily May
Catherine McConnell
Niall McDevitt

Lucy McKay
Hannah Meese
Theo Middleton
Natasha T Miller
Queen Mob
Robert Montgomery
John McDonell MP
Decca Muldowney
Adrian Nettleship
Chris Nineham
Lucy Nurnberg
Trenton Oldfield
David Orrell
Sam Pash
Pierce Penniless
Dead Philosophers
Srđja Popović
Bill Posters
Michael Powell
Nina Power
Jai Preece
Dean Puckett
Jyotsna Ram
Adam Ramsay
Max Reeves
John Riordan
Greg Ruggiero
David Runciman
Climate Rush
Matt Russell
William Saroyan
Aardvark On Sea
Richard Seymour
Martin Shakeshaft
David Shillinglaw
Daniel Simpson
Marina Sitrin

Ralph Steadman
Linda Stupart
JD Taylor
Jade They
Hunter S Thompson
The Occupied Times
Selina Todd
Ed Tolkien
Anna Trench
Micah White
Jason Wiley
Heathcote Williams
Peter Willis
Cei Willis
Grace Wilson
See Red Woman's Workshop
Robby Wrongfoot
Slavoj Žižek

IMPRINT

STRIKE!
Anthology 1—8

Design
Robbie Blundell & Hannah Blows

Print
Calverts, London

Published by
STRIKE! 2015

ISBN: 978-0-9934734-0-1

Special thanks to
Craig, Rowan, Maia, Lucy, Alexis, Peter
and May Day Rooms.